THE ∞ INFINITY ENTITY

THANOS ANNUAL #1

WRITER: **JIM STARLIN**

PENCILER: **RON LIM**

INKER: **ANDY SMITH**

COLORIST: **VAL STAPLES**

LETTERER: **VC's JOE CARAMAGNA**

COVER ARTISTS: **DALE KEOWN** & **IVE SVORCINA**

ASSISTANT EDITOR: **JON MOISON**

EDITOR: **WIL MOSS**

INFINITY ENTITY

WRITER: **JIM STARLIN**

PENCILER: **ALAN DAVIS**

INKER: **MARK FARMER**

COLORIST: **WIL QUINTANA** WITH **JORDAN BOYD** (#1)

LETTERER: **VC's JOE SABINO**

COVER ARTISTS: **ALAN DAVIS, MARK FARMER** & **JORDAN BOYD**

ASSISTANT EDITOR: **ALANNA SMITH**

EDITORS: **TOM BREVOORT** WITH **WIL MOSS**

COLLECTION EDITOR: **MARK D. BEAZLEY**

ASSOCIATE EDITOR: **SARAH BRUNSTAD**

ASSOCIATE MANAGING EDITOR: **ALEX STARBUCK**

EDITOR, SPECIAL PROJECTS: **JENNIFER GRÜNWALD**

SENIOR EDITOR, SPECIAL PROJECTS: **JEFF YOUNGQUIST**

SVP PRINT, SALES & MARKETING: **DAVID GABRIEL**

BOOK DESIGNER: **ADAM DEL RE**

EDITOR IN CHIEF: **AXEL ALONSO**

CHIEF CREATIVE OFFICER: **JOE QUESADA**

PUBLISHER: **DAN BUCKLEY**

EXECUTIVE PRODUCER: **ALAN FINE**

The Mad Titan known as **THANOS** is obsessed with two things: power and death, the former of which he uses to bring about the latter.

In pursuit of these obsessions, Thanos gained control of the **INFINITY GAUNTLET** — a weapon of unimaginable power — which briefly made him the equivalent of a god. Ever since, his life has often been intertwined with the Gauntlet and its Gems in one way or another.

Currently Thanos is imprisoned on Earth, trapped in a "living death" by the very person he came there to kill: his son Thane. But it is only a matter of time before the Mad Titan is free once more!

The following details a key moment in Thanos' life when he was faced with a future that may lead beyond death itself...

THE INFINITY ENTITY. Contains material originally published in magazine form as THE INFINITY ENTITY #1-4 and THANOS ANNUAL #1. First printing 2016. ISBN# 978-0-7851-9421-7. Published by MARVEL WORLDWIDE, INC., a subsidiary of MARVEL ENTERTAINMENT, LLC. OFFICE OF PUBLICATION: 135 West 50th Street, New York, NY 10020. Copyright © 2016 MARVEL. No similarity between any of the names, characters, persons, and/or institutions in this magazine with those of any living or dead person or institution is intended, and any such similarity which may exist is purely coincidental. Printed in Canada. ALAN FINE, President, Marvel Entertainment; DAN BUCKLEY, President, TV Publishing & Brand Management; JOE QUESADA, Chief Creative Officer; TOM BREVOORT, SVP of Publishing; DAVID BOGART, SVP of Business Affairs & Operations, Publishing & Partnership; C.B. CEBULSKI, VP of Brand Management & Development, Asia; DAVID GABRIEL, SVP of Sales & Marketing, Publishing; JEFF YOUNGQUIST, VP of Production & Special Projects; DAN CARR, Executive Director of Publishing Technology; ALEX MORALES, Director of Publishing Operations; SUSAN CRESPI, Production Manager; STAN LEE, Chairman Emeritus. For information regarding advertising in Marvel Comics or on Marvel.com, please contact Vit DeBellis, Integrated Sales Manager, at vdebellis@marvel.com. For Marvel subscription inquiries, please call 888-511-5480. Manufactured between 5/6/2016 and 6/13/2016 by SOLISCO PRINTERS, SCOTT, QC, CANADA.

9 8 7 6 5 4 3 2 1

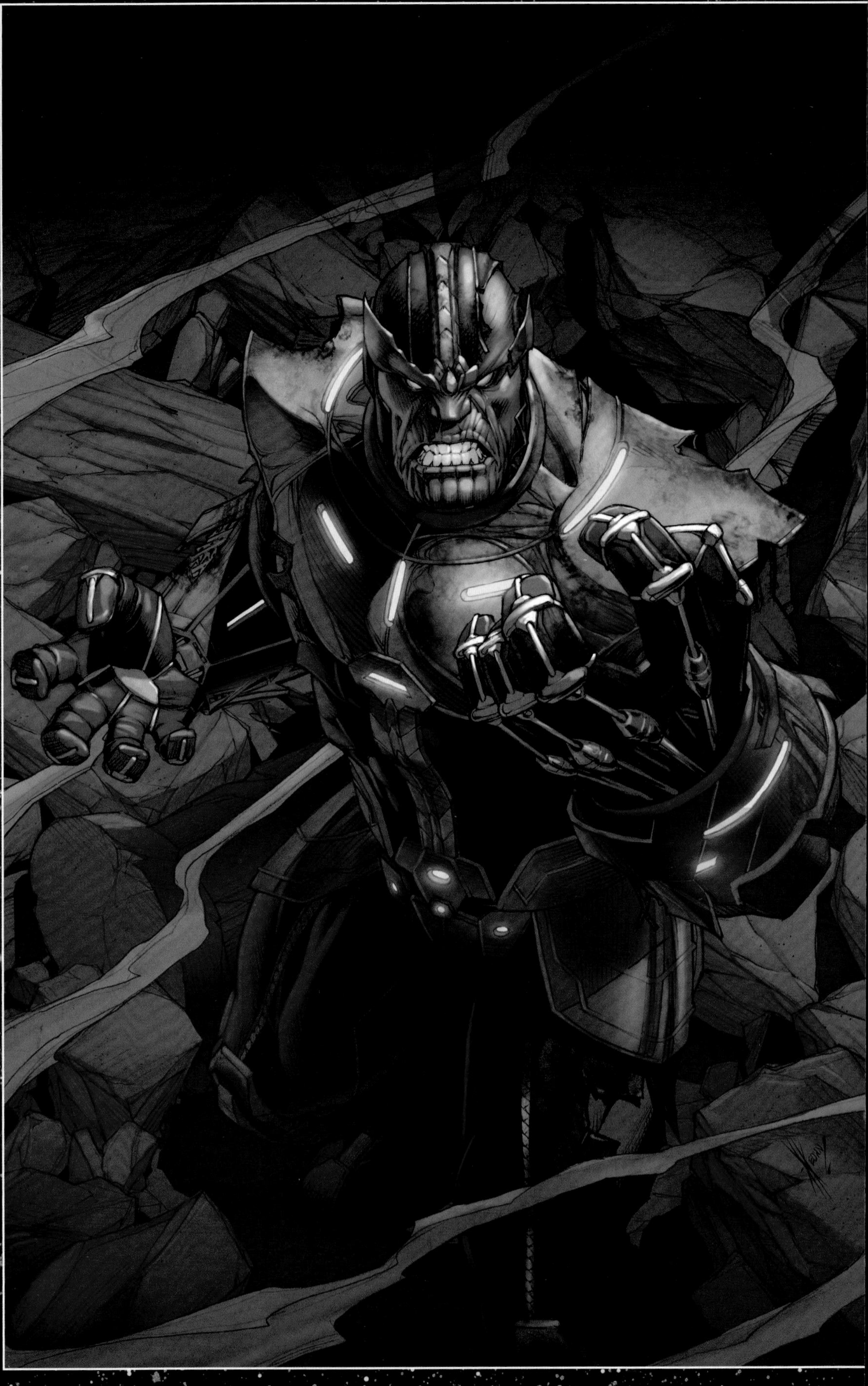

THANOS ANNUAL 1

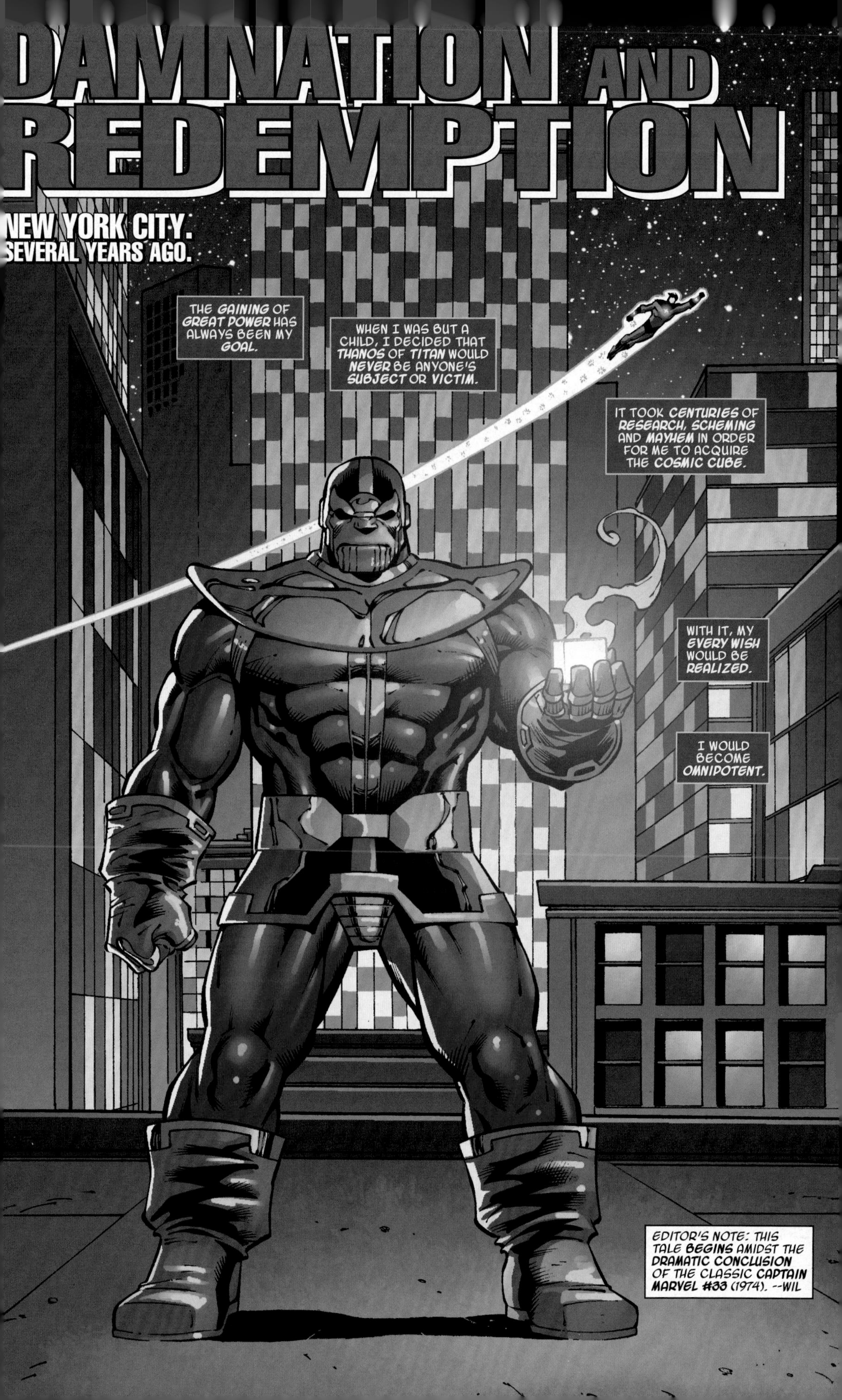
DAMNATION AND REDEMPTION
NEW YORK CITY. SEVERAL YEARS AGO.
THE GAINING OF GREAT POWER HAS ALWAYS BEEN MY GOAL.
WHEN I WAS BUT A CHILD, I DECIDED THAT THANOS OF TITAN WOULD NEVER BE ANYONE'S SUBJECT OR VICTIM.
IT TOOK CENTURIES OF RESEARCH, SCHEMING AND MAYHEM IN ORDER FOR ME TO ACQUIRE THE COSMIC CUBE.
WITH IT, MY EVERY WISH WOULD BE REALIZED.
I WOULD BECOME OMNIPOTENT.
EDITOR'S NOTE: THIS TALE BEGINS AMIDST THE DRAMATIC CONCLUSION OF THE CLASSIC CAPTAIN MARVEL #33 (1974). --WIL

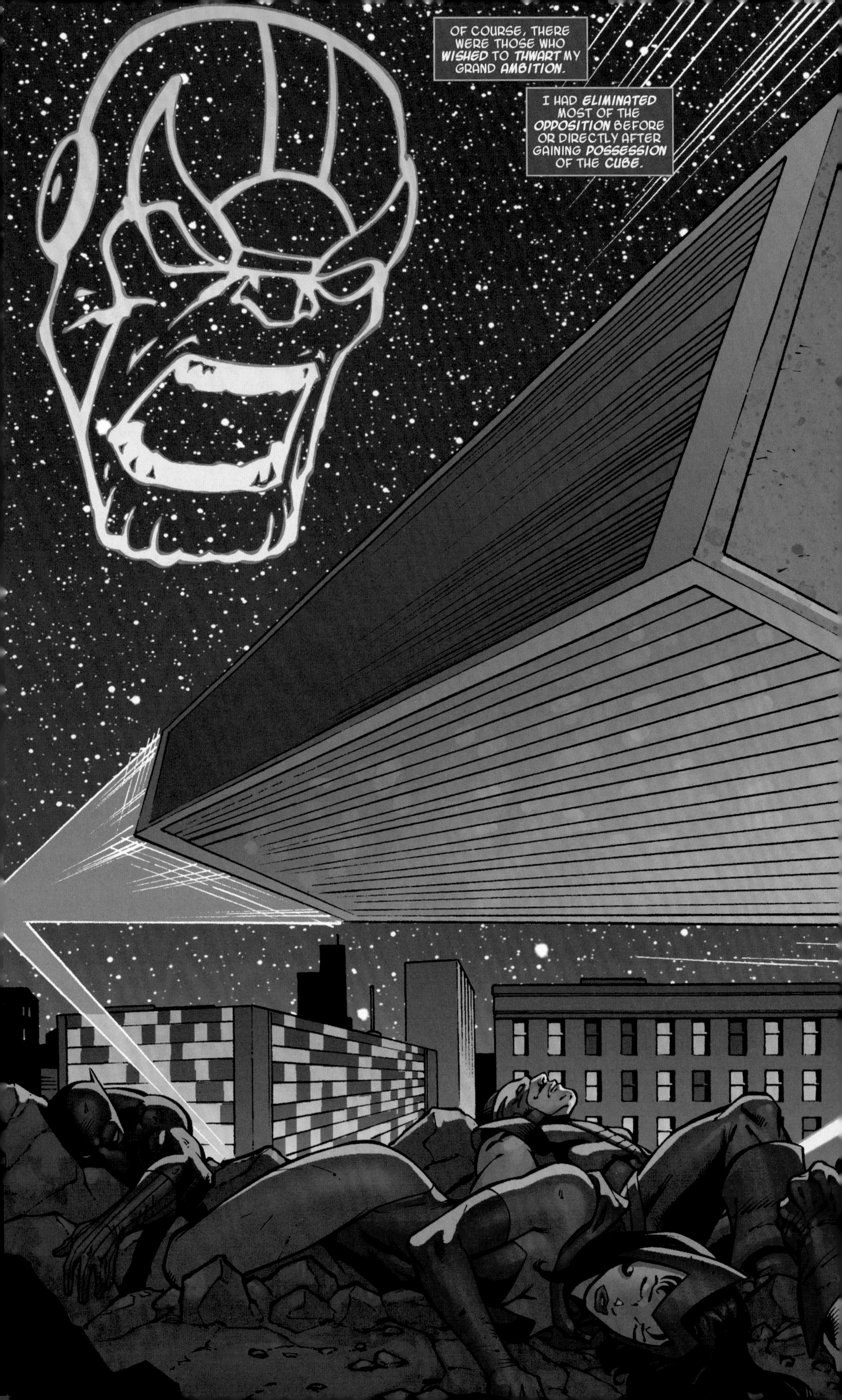
OF COURSE, THERE WERE THOSE WHO WISHED TO THWART MY GRAND AMBITION.
I HAD ELIMINATED MOST OF THE OPPOSITION BEFORE OR DIRECTLY AFTER GAINING POSSESSION OF THE CUBE.

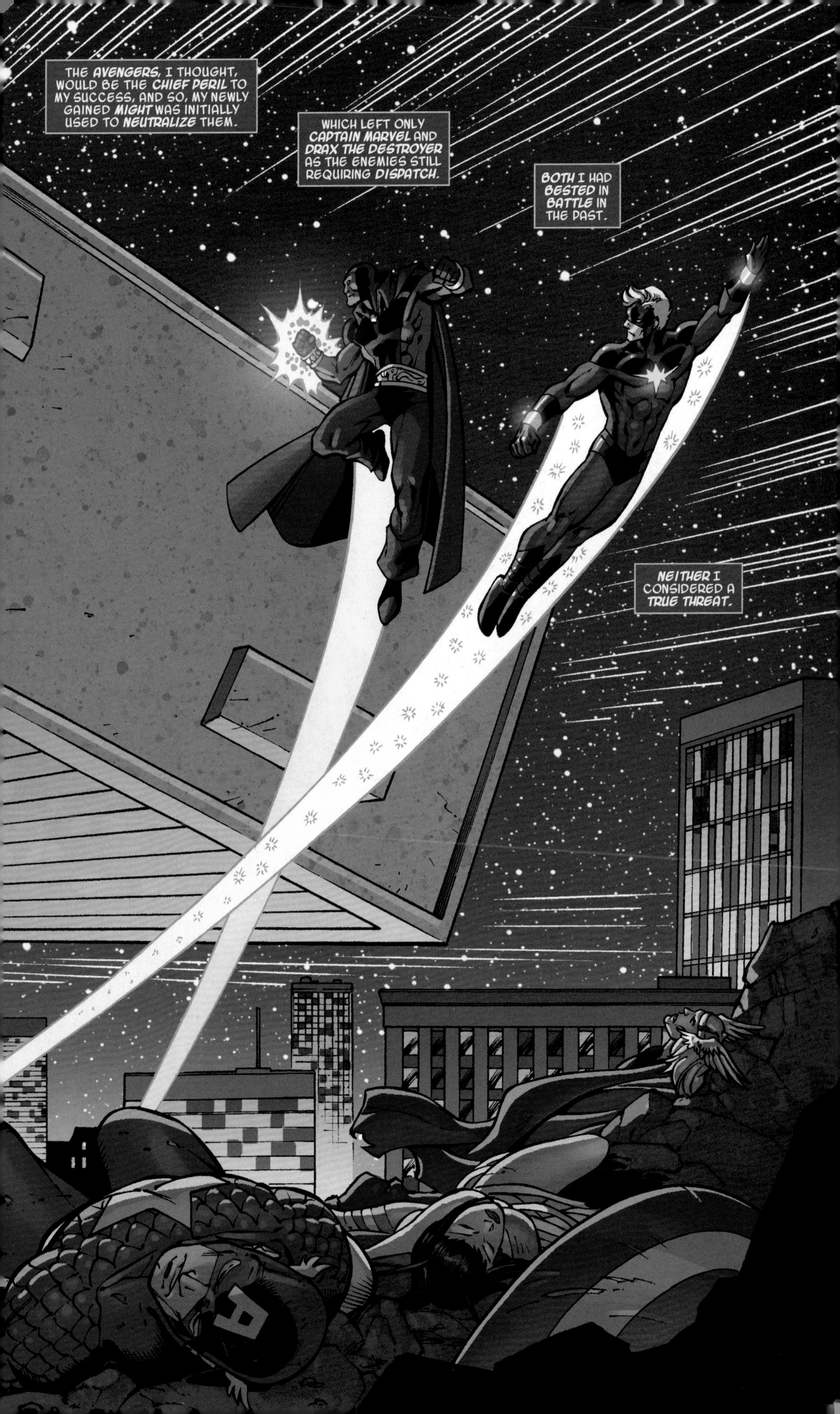
THE AVENGERS, I THOUGHT, WOULD BE THE CHIEF PERIL TO MY SUCCESS, AND SO, MY NEWLY GAINED MIGHT WAS INITIALLY USED TO NEUTRALIZE THEM.
WHICH LEFT ONLY CAPTAIN MARVEL AND DRAX THE DESTROYER AS THE ENEMIES STILL REQUIRING DISPATCH.
BOTH I HAD BESTED IN BATTLE IN THE PAST.
NEITHER I CONSIDERED A TRUE THREAT.

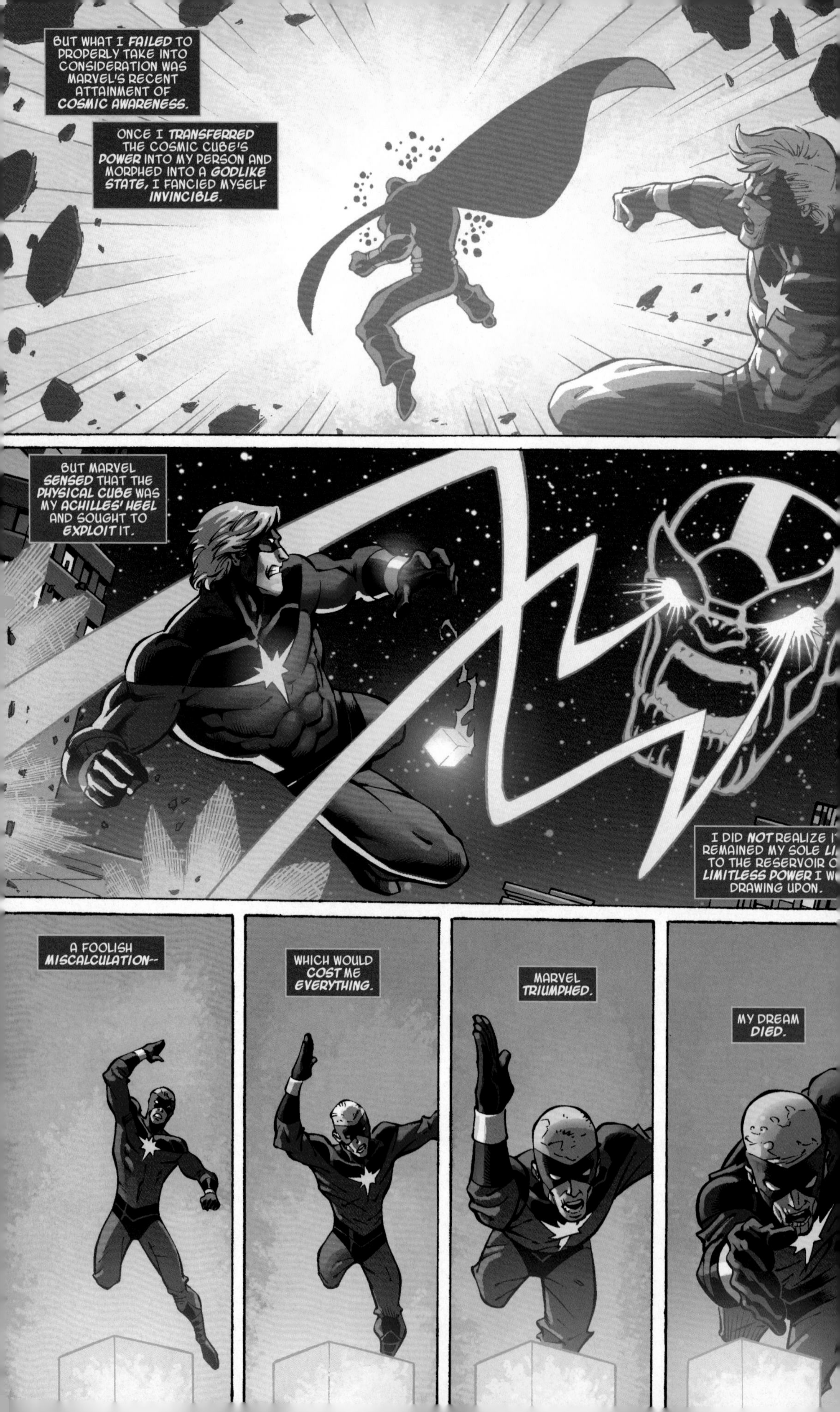
BUT WHAT I FAILED TO PROPERLY TAKE INTO CONSIDERATION WAS MARVEL'S RECENT ATTAINMENT OF COSMIC AWARENESS.
ONCE I TRANSFERRED THE COSMIC CUBE'S POWER INTO MY PERSON AND MORPHED INTO A GODLIKE STATE, I FANCIED MYSELF INVINCIBLE.
BUT MARVEL SENSED THAT THE PHYSICAL CUBE WAS MY ACHILLES' HEEL AND SOUGHT TO EXPLOIT IT.
I DID NOT REALIZE I REMAINED MY SOLE LI TO THE RESERVOIR O LIMITLESS POWER I W DRAWING UPON.
A FOOLISH MISCALCULATION--
WHICH WOULD COST ME EVERYTHING.
MARVEL TRIUMPHED.
MY DREAM DIED.

THE *GREAT POWER*, WHICH I HAD SACRIFICED *EVERYTHING* FOR, WAS STRIPPED FROM ME WITH ONE *WELL PLACED BLOW.*

IT NEARLY COST MARVEL HIS LIFE, BUT HE WOULD QUICKLY RECOVER.

WHEREAS *EVERYTHING* I HAD BECOME ENDED.

AN INSTANT LATER I FOUND MYSELF *REINCORPORATED* TO THE *FLESH* AND *HELPLESSLY BOBBING* ABOUT, *IN ORBIT* ABOVE EARTH'S ATMOSPHERE.

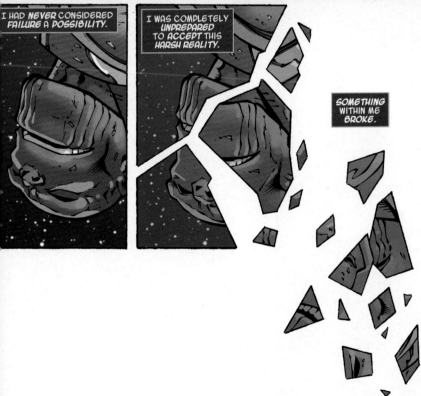

I HAD *NEVER* CONSIDERED FAILURE A *POSSIBILITY.*

I WAS COMPLETELY *UNPREPARED* TO *ACCEPT* THIS *HARSH REALITY.*

SOMETHING WITHIN ME BROKE.

I HAD COME TO *THE END* OF MY STORY.

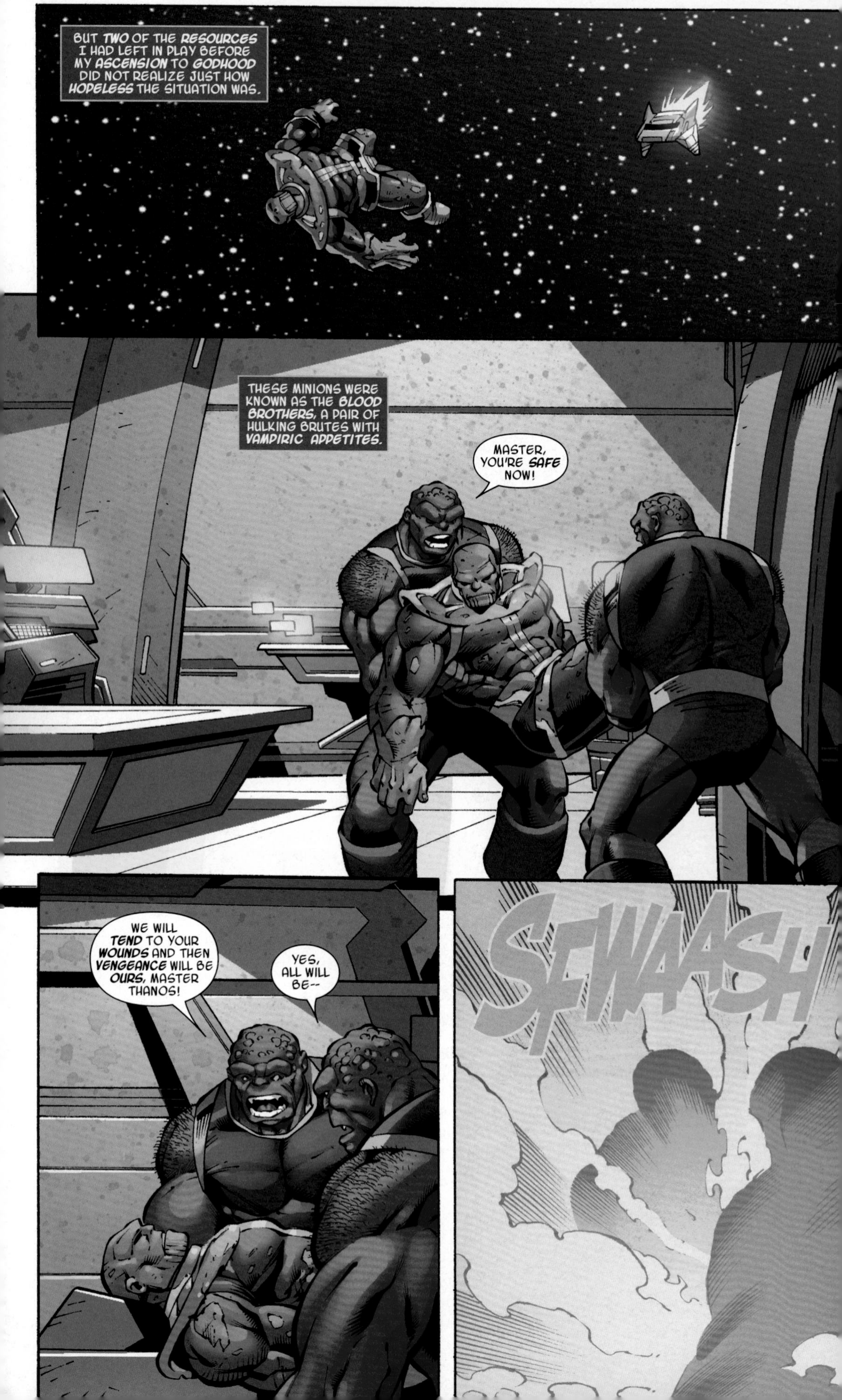

BUT TWO OF THE RESOURCES I HAD LEFT IN PLAY BEFORE MY ASCENSION TO GODHOOD DID NOT REALIZE JUST HOW HOPELESS THE SITUATION WAS.
THESE MINIONS WERE KNOWN AS THE BLOOD BROTHERS, A PAIR OF HULKING BRUTES WITH VAMPIRIC APPETITES.
MASTER, YOU'RE SAFE NOW!
WE WILL TEND TO YOUR WOUNDS AND THEN VENGEANCE WILL BE OURS, MASTER THANOS!
YES, ALL WILL BE--
SFWAASH

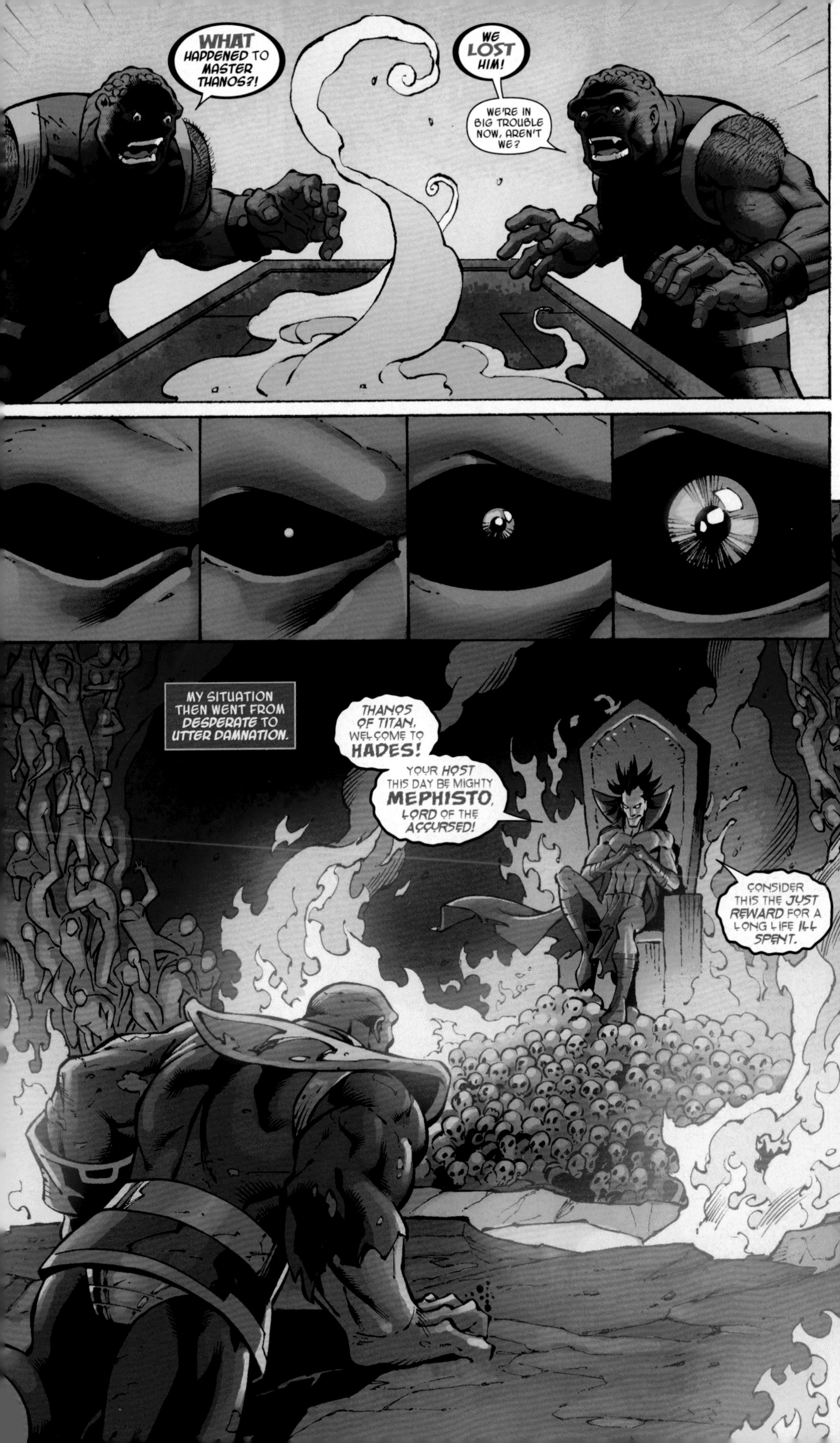
WHAT HAPPENED TO MASTER THANOS?!
WE LOST HIM!
WE'RE IN BIG TROUBLE NOW, AREN'T WE?
MY SITUATION THEN WENT FROM DESPERATE TO UTTER DAMNATION.
THANOS OF TITAN, WELCOME TO HADES!
YOUR HOST THIS DAY BE MIGHTY MEPHISTO, LORD OF THE ACCURSED!
CONSIDER THIS THE JUST REWARD FOR A LONG LIFE ILL SPENT.

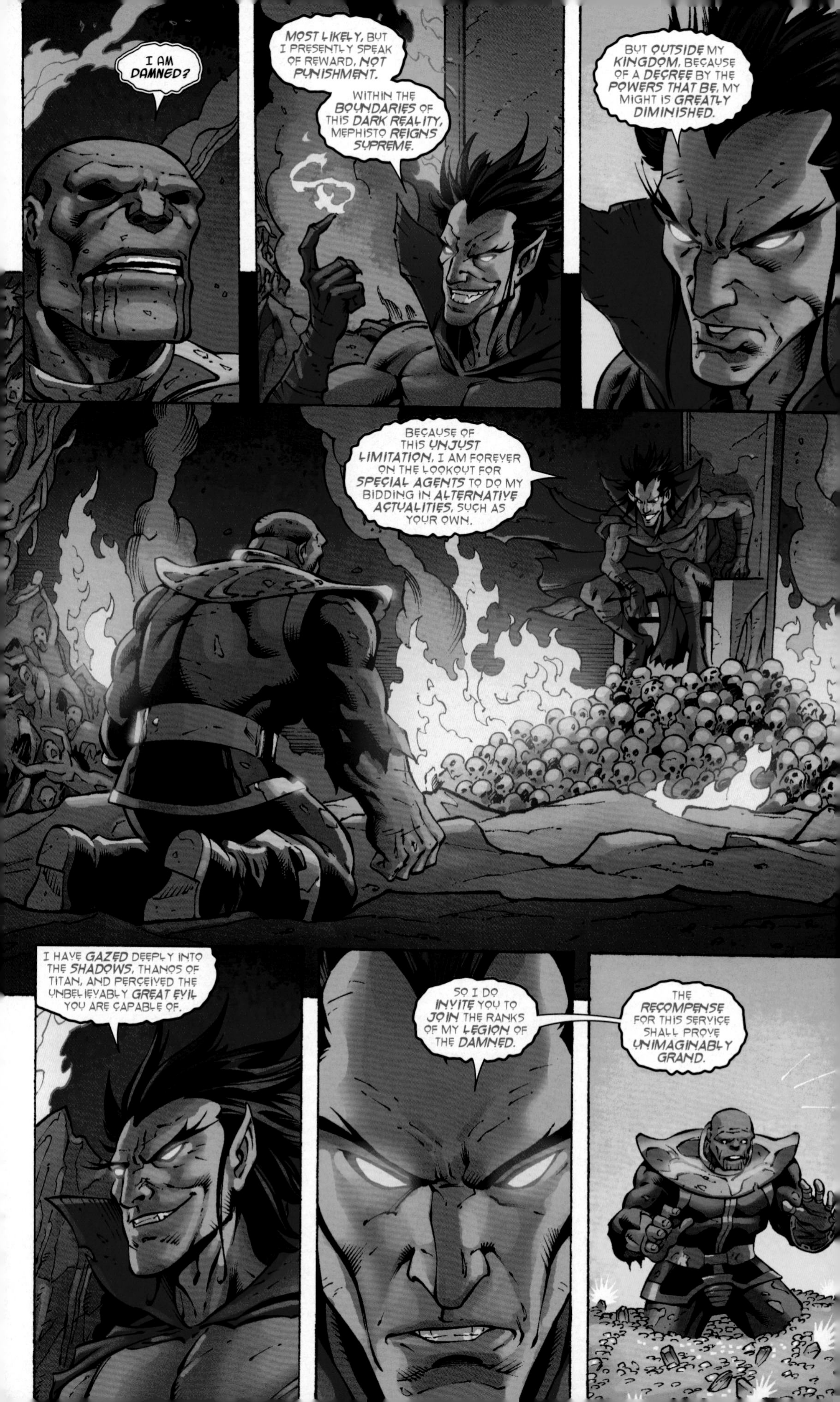
I AM DAMNED?
MOST LIKELY, BUT I PRESENTLY SPEAK OF REWARD, NOT PUNISHMENT.
WITHIN THE BOUNDARIES OF THIS DARK REALITY, MEPHISTO REIGNS SUPREME.
BUT OUTSIDE MY KINGDOM, BECAUSE OF A DECREE BY THE POWERS THAT BE, MY MIGHT IS GREATLY DIMINISHED.
BECAUSE OF THIS UNJUST LIMITATION, I AM FOREVER ON THE LOOKOUT FOR SPECIAL AGENTS TO DO MY BIDDING IN ALTERNATIVE ACTUALITIES, SUCH AS YOUR OWN.
I HAVE GAZED DEEPLY INTO THE SHADOWS, THANOS OF TITAN, AND PERCEIVED THE UNBELIEVABLY GREAT EVIL YOU ARE CAPABLE OF.
SO I DO INVITE YOU TO JOIN THE RANKS OF MY LEGION OF THE DAMNED.
THE RECOMPENSE FOR THIS SERVICE SHALL PROVE UNIMAGINABLY GRAND.

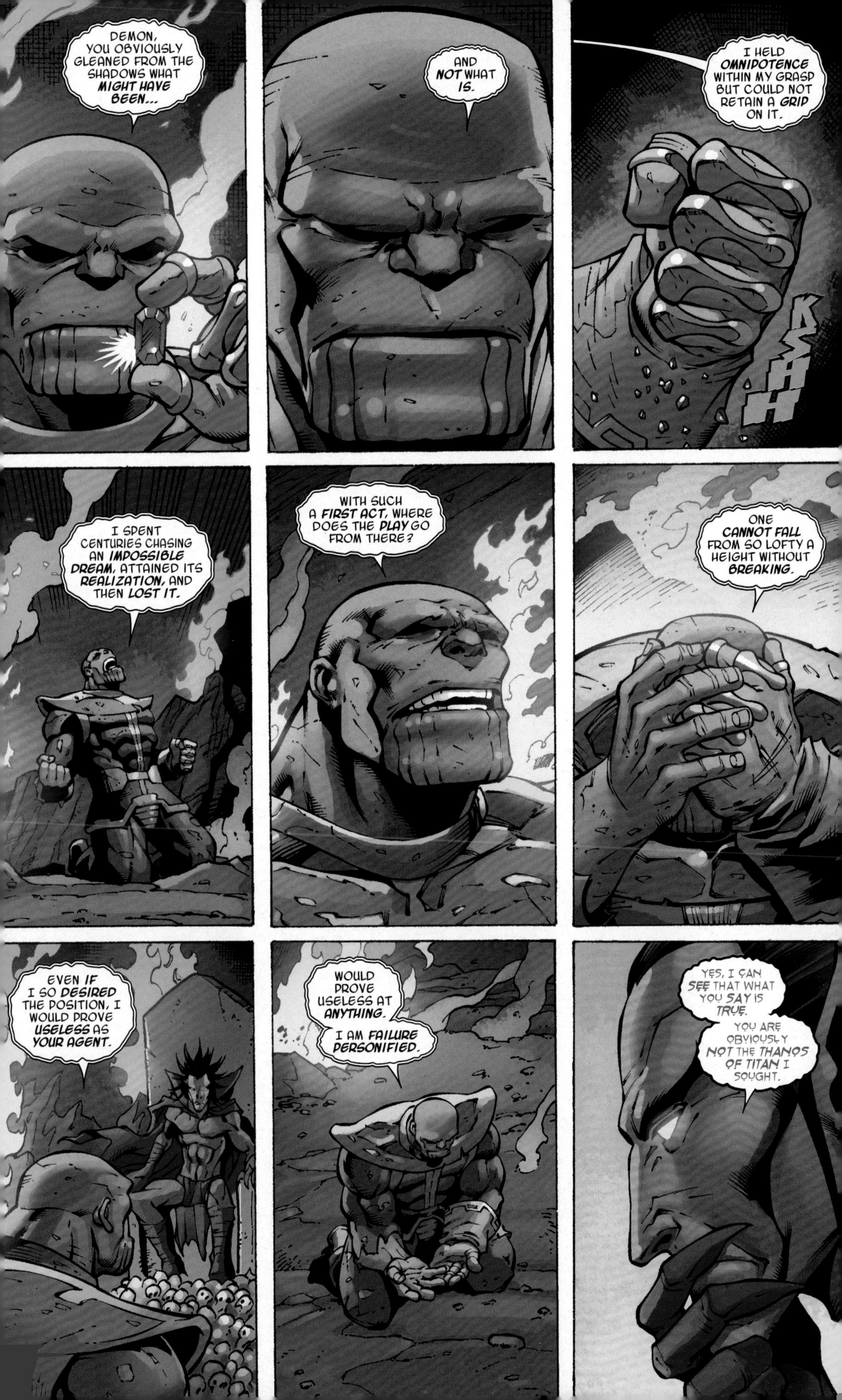
DEMON, YOU OBVIOUSLY GLEANED FROM THE SHADOWS WHAT MIGHT HAVE BEEN...
AND NOT WHAT IS.
I HELD OMNIPOTENCE WITHIN MY GRASP BUT COULD NOT RETAIN A GRIP ON IT.
KSHH
I SPENT CENTURIES CHASING AN IMPOSSIBLE DREAM, ATTAINED ITS REALIZATION, AND THEN LOST IT.
WITH SUCH A FIRST ACT, WHERE DOES THE PLAY GO FROM THERE?
ONE CANNOT FALL FROM SO LOFTY A HEIGHT WITHOUT BREAKING.
EVEN IF I SO DESIRED THE POSITION, I WOULD PROVE USELESS AS YOUR AGENT.
WOULD PROVE USELESS AT ANYTHING.
I AM FAILURE PERSONIFIED.
YES, I CAN SEE THAT WHAT YOU SAY IS TRUE.
YOU ARE OBVIOUSLY NOT THE THANOS OF TITAN I SOUGHT.

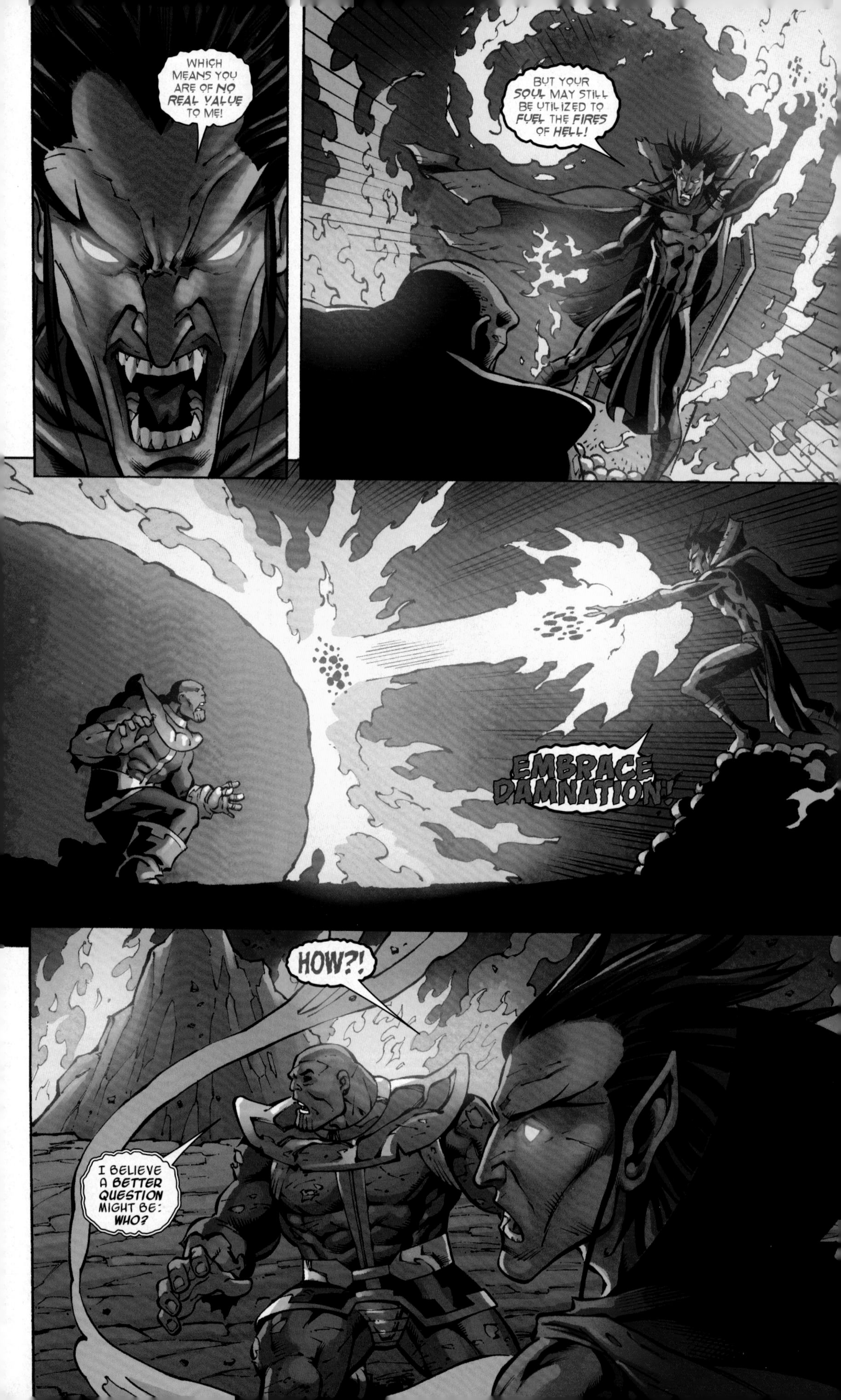
WHICH MEANS YOU ARE OF NO REAL VALUE TO ME!
BUT YOUR SOUL MAY STILL BE UTILIZED TO FUEL THE FIRES OF HELL!
EMBRACE DAMNATION!
HOW?!
I BELIEVE A BETTER QUESTION MIGHT BE: WHO?

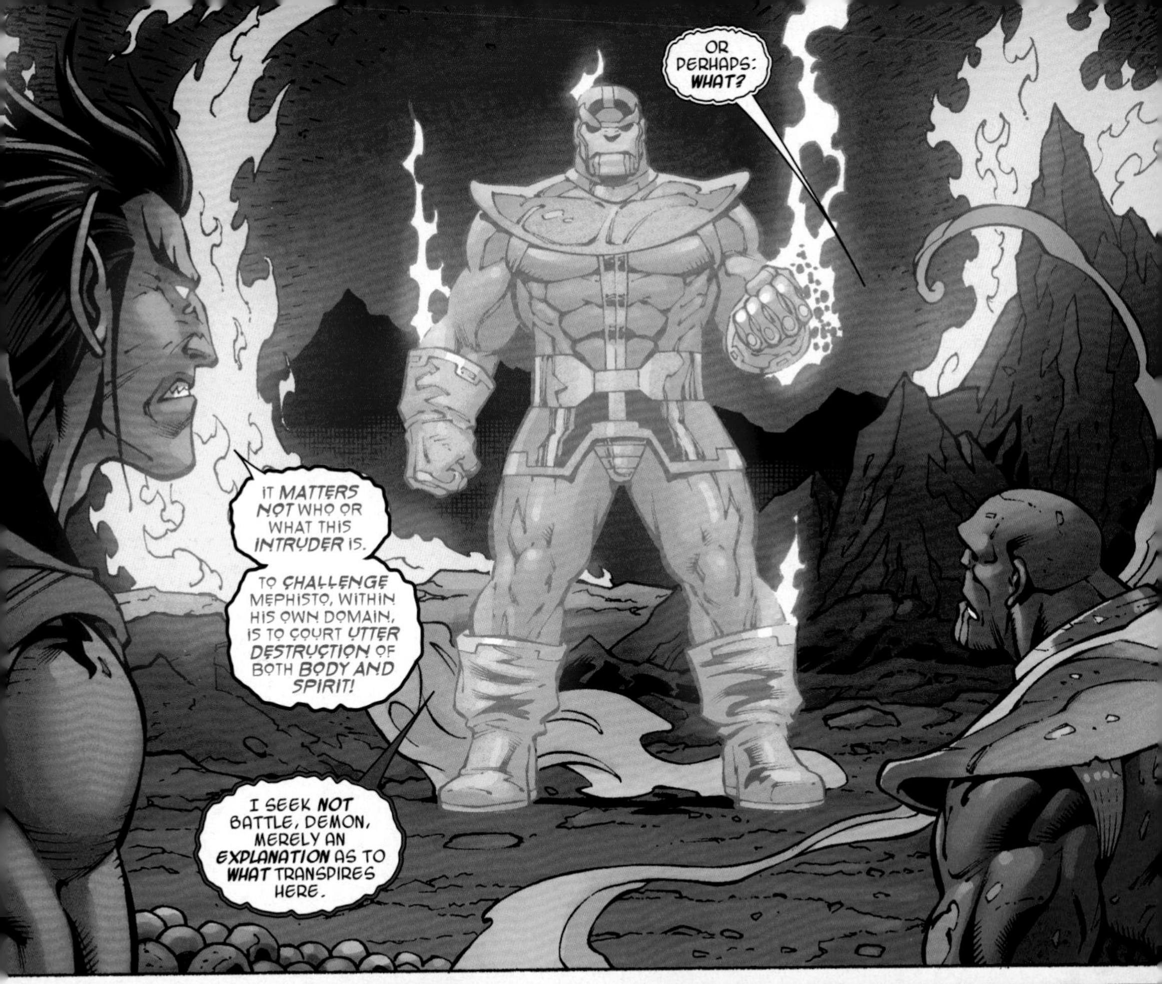
OR PERHAPS: WHAT?
IT MATTERS NOT WHO OR WHAT THIS INTRUDER IS.
TO CHALLENGE MEPHISTO, WITHIN HIS OWN DOMAIN, IS TO COURT UTTER DESTRUCTION OF BOTH BODY AND SPIRIT!
I SEEK NOT BATTLE, DEMON, MERELY AN EXPLANATION AS TO WHAT TRANSPIRES HERE.

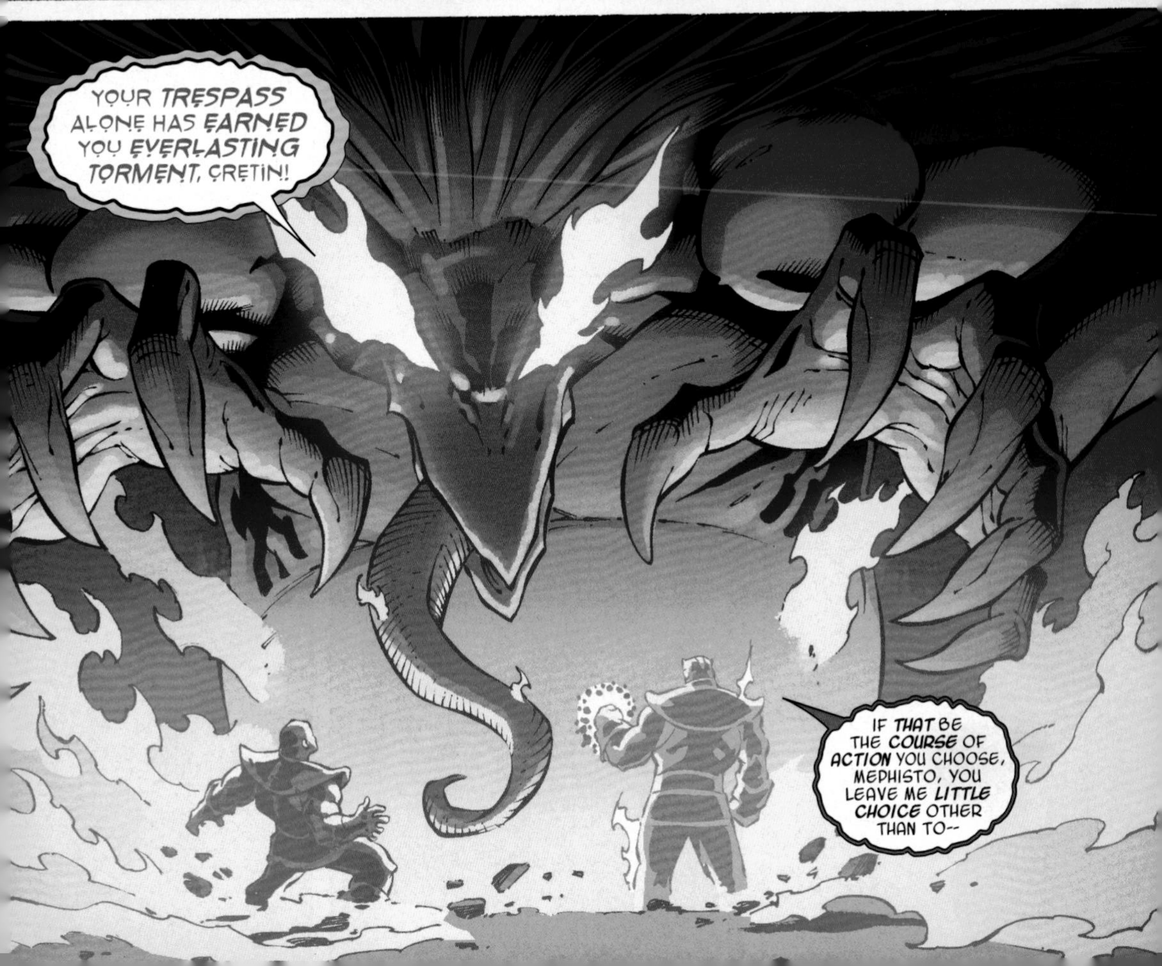
YOUR TRESPASS ALONE HAS EARNED YOU EVERLASTING TORMENT, CRETIN!
IF THAT BE THE COURSE OF ACTION YOU CHOOSE, MEPHISTO, YOU LEAVE ME LITTLE CHOICE OTHER THAN TO--

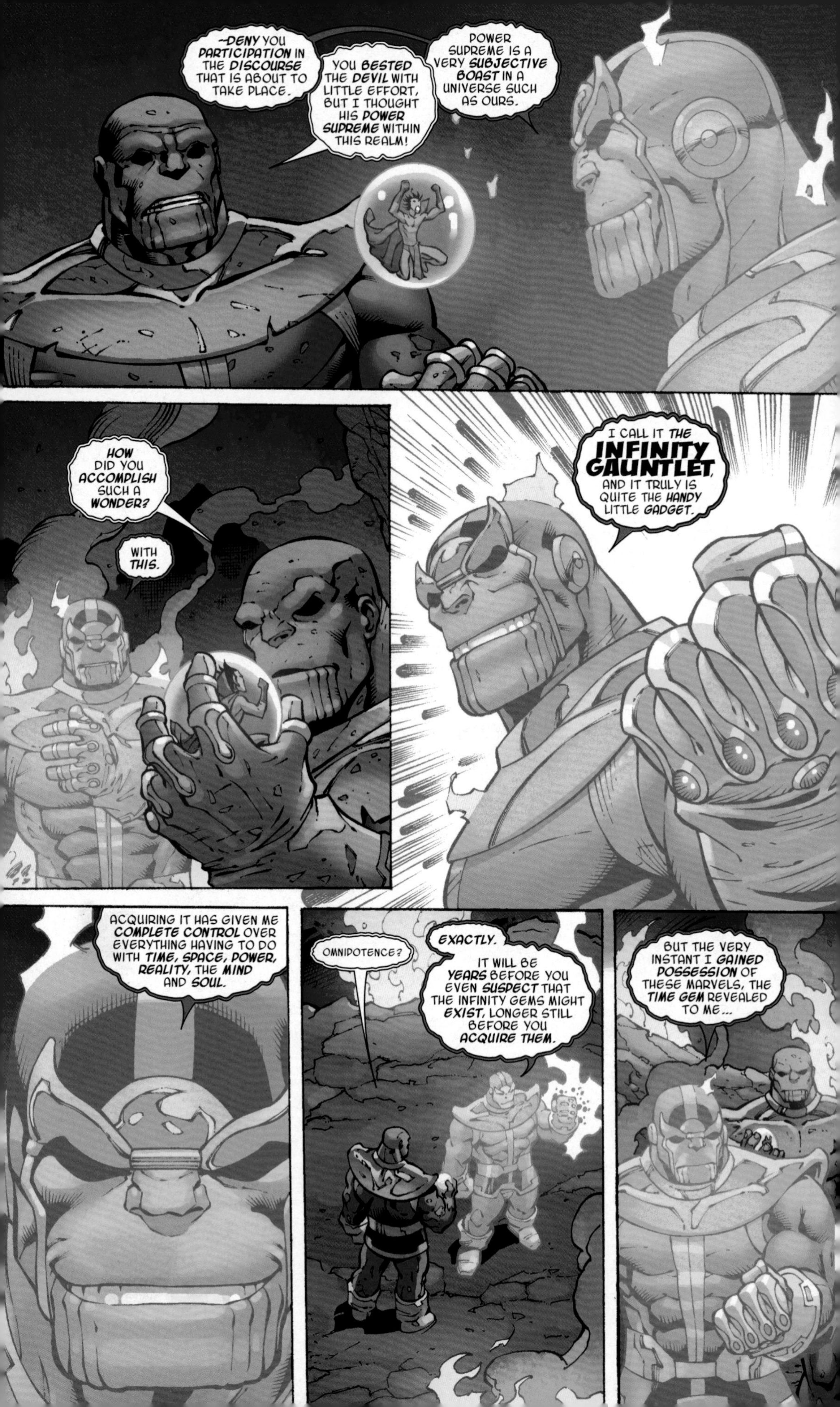

--DENY YOU PARTICIPATION IN THE DISCOURSE THAT IS ABOUT TO TAKE PLACE.
YOU BESTED THE DEVIL WITH LITTLE EFFORT, BUT I THOUGHT HIS POWER SUPREME WITHIN THIS REALM!
POWER SUPREME IS A VERY SUBJECTIVE BOAST IN A UNIVERSE SUCH AS OURS.
HOW DID YOU ACCOMPLISH SUCH A WONDER?
WITH THIS.
I CALL IT THE INFINITY GAUNTLET, AND IT TRULY IS QUITE THE HANDY LITTLE GADGET.
ACQUIRING IT HAS GIVEN ME COMPLETE CONTROL OVER EVERYTHING HAVING TO DO WITH TIME, SPACE, POWER, REALITY, THE MIND AND SOUL.
OMNIPOTENCE?
EXACTLY.
IT WILL BE YEARS BEFORE YOU EVEN SUSPECT THAT THE INFINITY GEMS MIGHT EXIST, LONGER STILL BEFORE YOU ACQUIRE THEM.
BUT THE VERY INSTANT I GAINED POSSESSION OF THESE MARVELS, THE TIME GEM REVEALED TO ME...

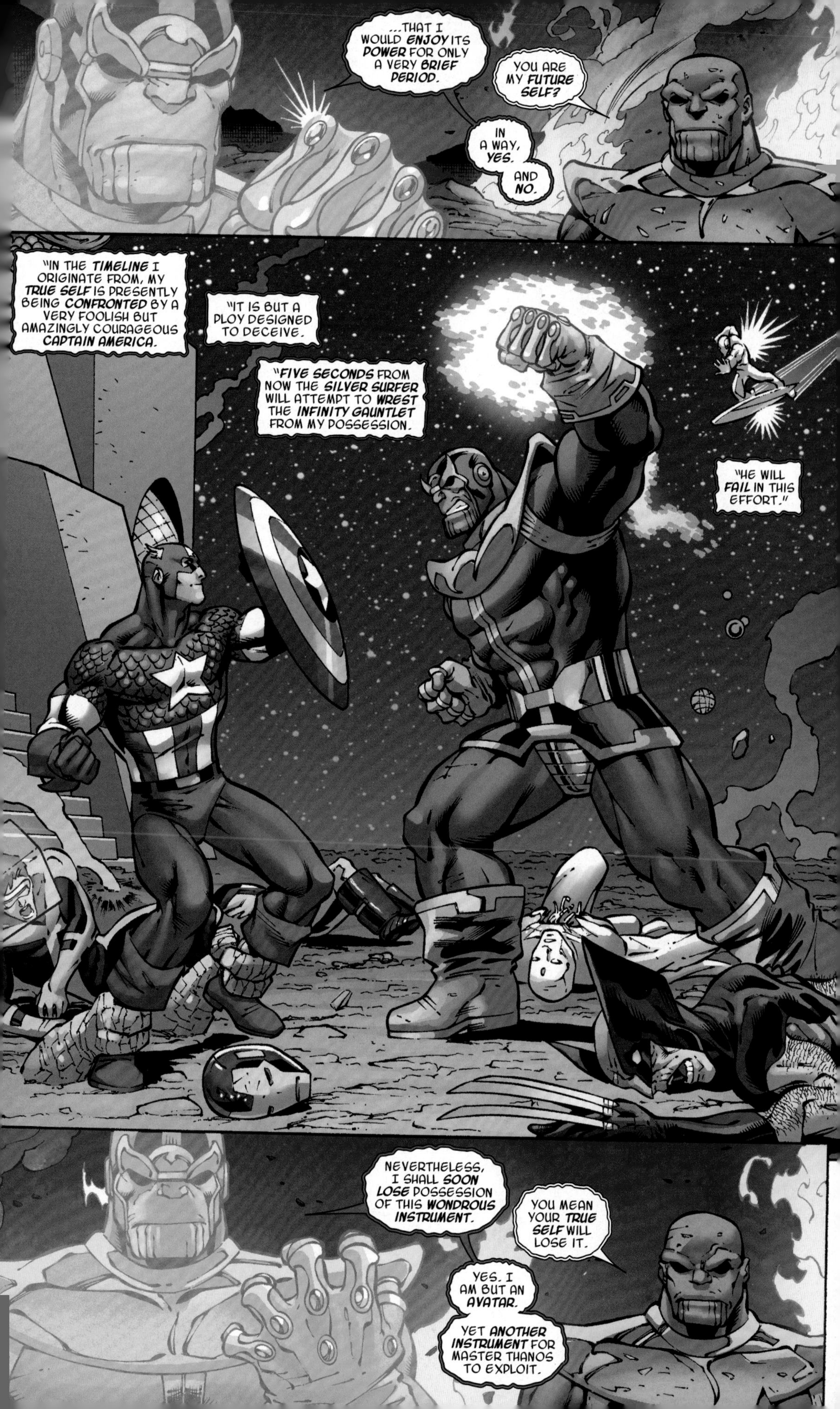

...THAT I WOULD ENJOY ITS POWER FOR ONLY A VERY BRIEF PERIOD.
YOU ARE MY FUTURE SELF?
IN A WAY, YES.
AND NO.
"IN THE TIMELINE I ORIGINATE FROM, MY TRUE SELF IS PRESENTLY BEING CONFRONTED BY A VERY FOOLISH BUT AMAZINGLY COURAGEOUS CAPTAIN AMERICA.
"IT IS BUT A PLOY DESIGNED TO DECEIVE.
"FIVE SECONDS FROM NOW THE SILVER SURFER WILL ATTEMPT TO WREST THE INFINITY GAUNTLET FROM MY POSSESSION.
"HE WILL FAIL IN THIS EFFORT."
NEVERTHELESS, I SHALL SOON LOSE POSSESSION OF THIS WONDROUS INSTRUMENT.
YOU MEAN YOUR TRUE SELF WILL LOSE IT.
YES. I AM BUT AN AVATAR.
YET ANOTHER INSTRUMENT FOR MASTER THANOS TO EXPLOIT.

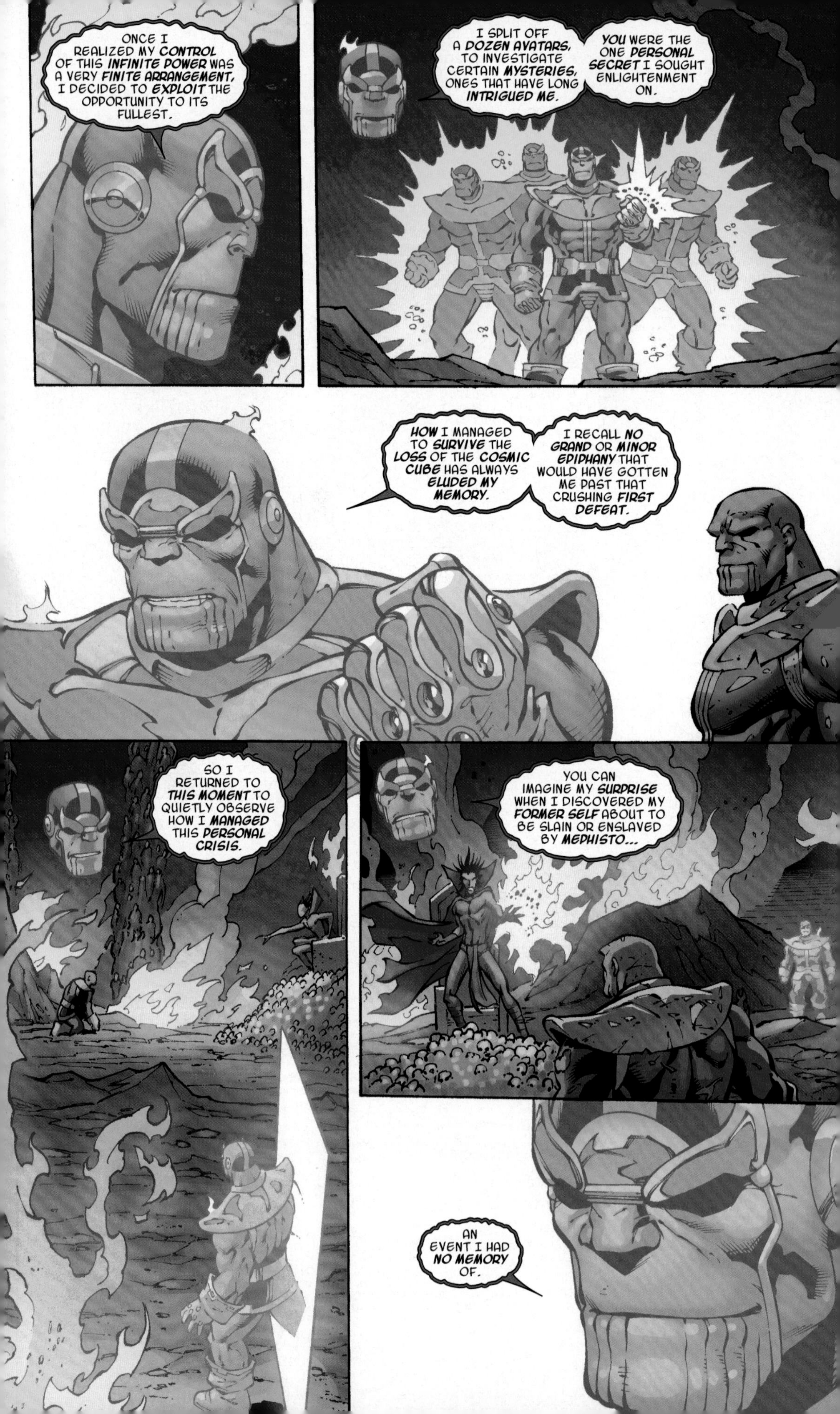
ONCE I REALIZED MY CONTROL OF THIS INFINITE POWER WAS A VERY FINITE ARRANGEMENT, I DECIDED TO EXPLOIT THE OPPORTUNITY TO ITS FULLEST.
I SPLIT OFF A DOZEN AVATARS, TO INVESTIGATE CERTAIN MYSTERIES, ONES THAT HAVE LONG INTRIGUED ME.
YOU WERE THE ONE PERSONAL SECRET I SOUGHT ENLIGHTENMENT ON.
HOW I MANAGED TO SURVIVE THE LOSS OF THE COSMIC CUBE HAS ALWAYS ELUDED MY MEMORY.
I RECALL NO GRAND OR MINOR EPIPHANY THAT WOULD HAVE GOTTEN ME PAST THAT CRUSHING FIRST DEFEAT.
SO I RETURNED TO THIS MOMENT TO QUIETLY OBSERVE HOW I MANAGED THIS PERSONAL CRISIS.
YOU CAN IMAGINE MY SURPRISE WHEN I DISCOVERED MY FORMER SELF ABOUT TO BE SLAIN OR ENSLAVED BY MEPHISTO...
AN EVENT I HAD NO MEMORY OF.

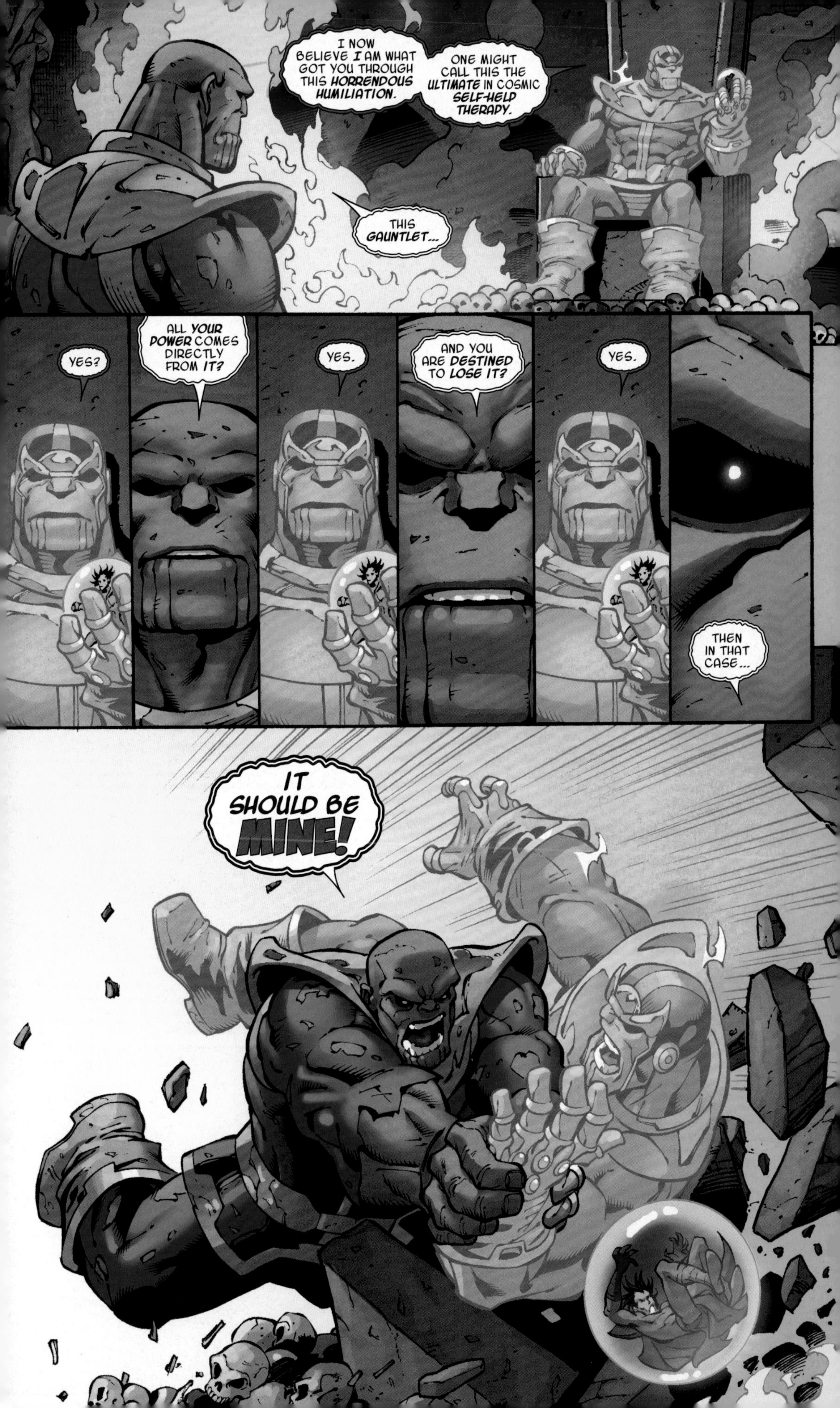

I NOW BELIEVE I AM WHAT GOT YOU THROUGH THIS HORRENDOUS HUMILIATION.
ONE MIGHT CALL THIS THE ULTIMATE IN COSMIC SELF-HELP THERAPY.
THIS GAUNTLET...
YES?
ALL YOUR POWER COMES DIRECTLY FROM IT?
YES.
AND YOU ARE DESTINED TO LOSE IT?
YES.
THEN IN THAT CASE...
IT SHOULD BE MINE!

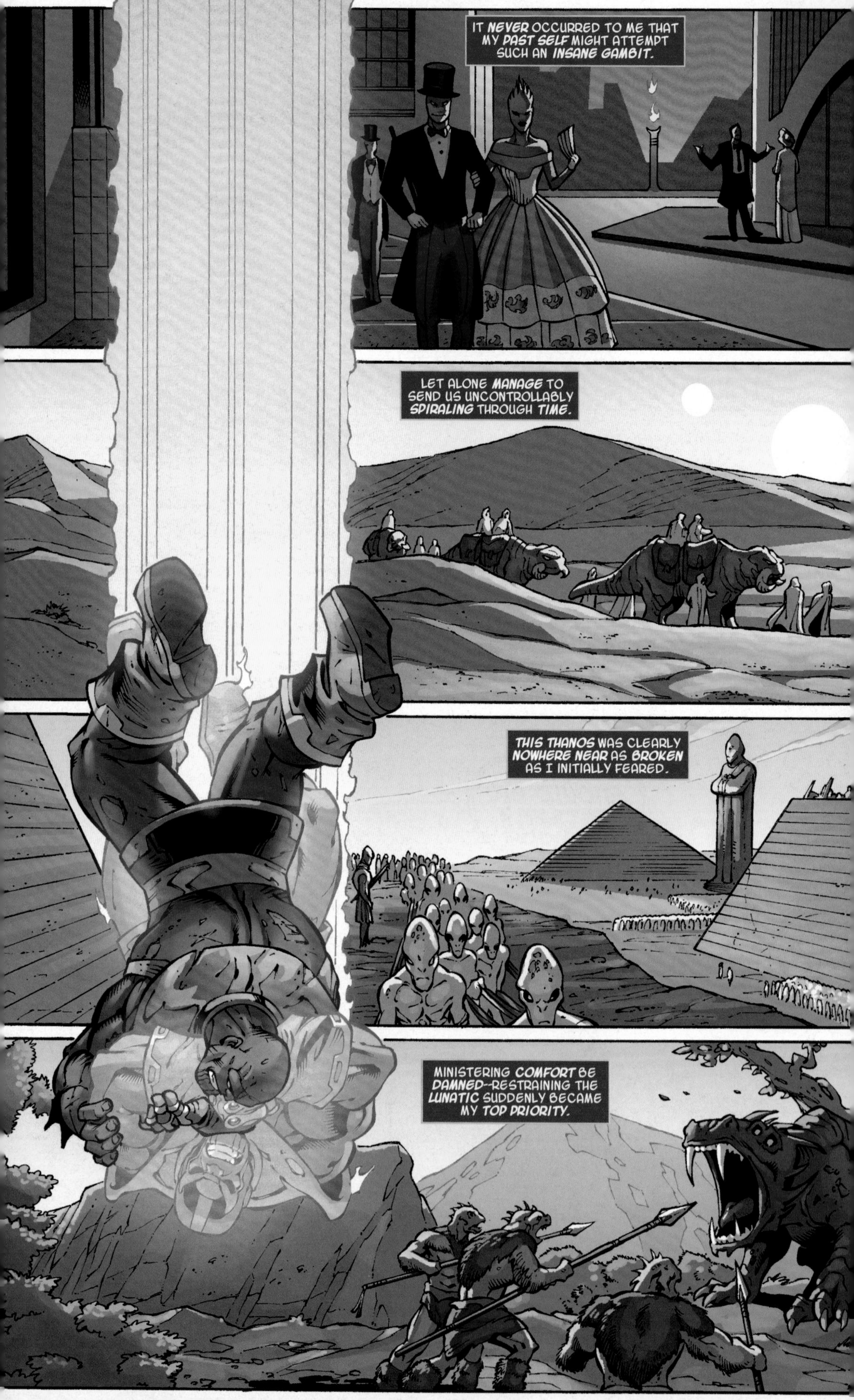
IT NEVER OCCURRED TO ME THAT MY PAST SELF MIGHT ATTEMPT SUCH AN INSANE GAMBIT.
LET ALONE MANAGE TO SEND US UNCONTROLLABLY SPIRALING THROUGH TIME.
THIS THANOS WAS CLEARLY NOWHERE NEAR AS BROKEN AS I INITIALLY FEARED.
MINISTERING COMFORT BE DAMNED--RESTRAINING THE LUNATIC SUDDENLY BECAME MY TOP PRIORITY.

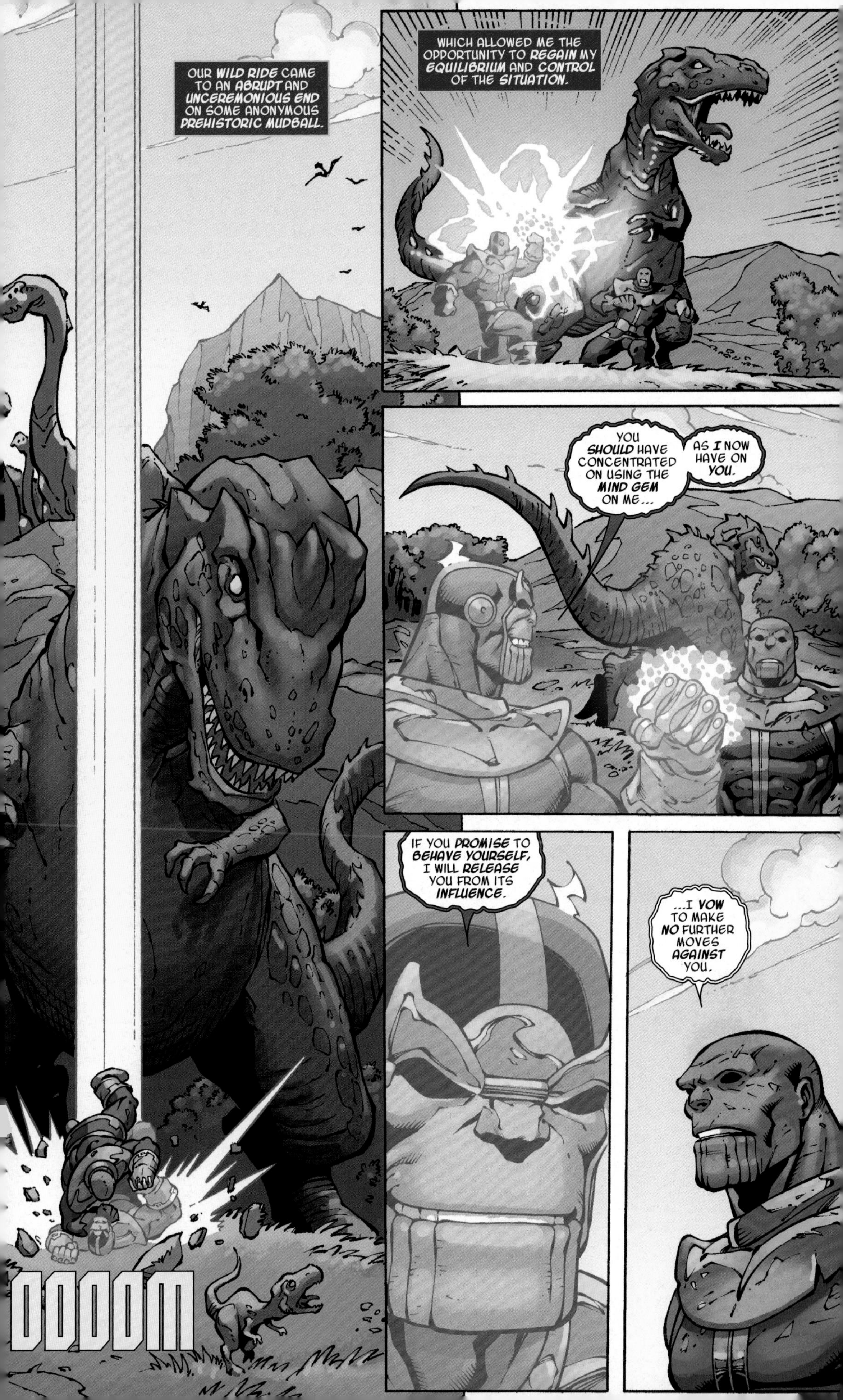
OUR WILD RIDE CAME TO AN ABRUPT AND UNCEREMONIOUS END ON SOME ANONYMOUS PREHISTORIC MUDBALL.
OOOOM
WHICH ALLOWED ME THE OPPORTUNITY TO REGAIN MY EQUILIBRIUM AND CONTROL OF THE SITUATION.
YOU SHOULD HAVE CONCENTRATED ON USING THE MIND GEM ON ME...
AS I NOW HAVE ON YOU.
IF YOU PROMISE TO BEHAVE YOURSELF, I WILL RELEASE YOU FROM ITS INFLUENCE.
...I VOW TO MAKE NO FURTHER MOVES AGAINST YOU.

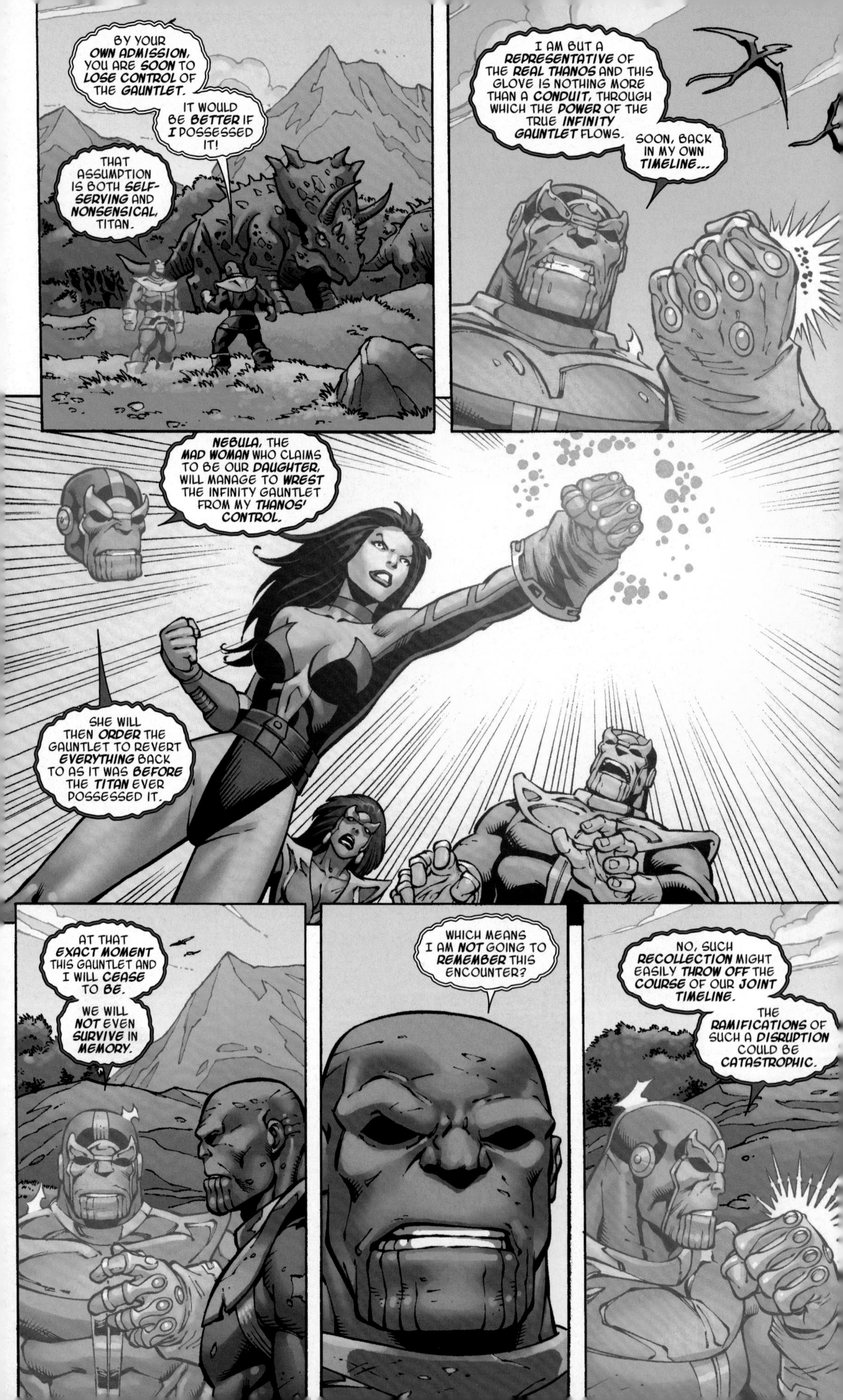
BY YOUR OWN ADMISSION, YOU ARE SOON TO LOSE CONTROL OF THE GAUNTLET.
IT WOULD BE BETTER IF I POSSESSED IT!
THAT ASSUMPTION IS BOTH SELF-SERVING AND NONSENSICAL, TITAN.
I AM BUT A REPRESENTATIVE OF THE REAL THANOS AND THIS GLOVE IS NOTHING MORE THAN A CONDUIT, THROUGH WHICH THE POWER OF THE TRUE INFINITY GAUNTLET FLOWS.
SOON, BACK IN MY OWN TIMELINE...
NEBULA, THE MAD WOMAN WHO CLAIMS TO BE OUR DAUGHTER, WILL MANAGE TO WREST THE INFINITY GAUNTLET FROM MY THANOS' CONTROL.
SHE WILL THEN ORDER THE GAUNTLET TO REVERT EVERYTHING BACK TO AS IT WAS BEFORE THE TITAN EVER POSSESSED IT.
AT THAT EXACT MOMENT THIS GAUNTLET AND I WILL CEASE TO BE.
WE WILL NOT EVEN SURVIVE IN MEMORY.
WHICH MEANS I AM NOT GOING TO REMEMBER THIS ENCOUNTER?
NO, SUCH RECOLLECTION MIGHT EASILY THROW OFF THE COURSE OF OUR JOINT TIMELINE.
THE RAMIFICATIONS OF SUCH A DISRUPTION COULD BE CATASTROPHIC.

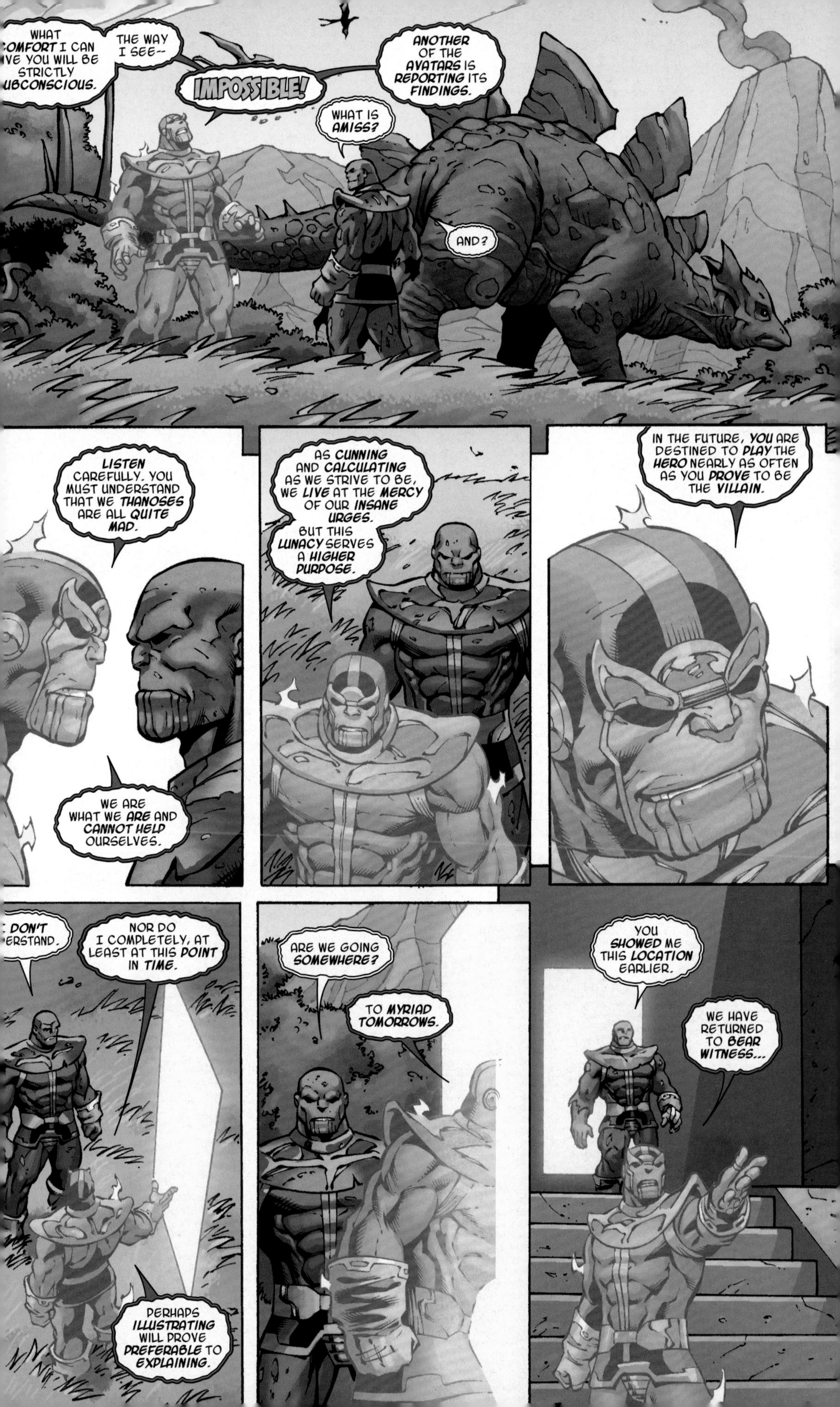
WHAT COMFORT I CAN ...VE YOU WILL BE STRICTLY ...UBCONSCIOUS.
THE WAY I SEE--
IMPOSSIBLE!
ANOTHER OF THE AVATARS IS REPORTING ITS FINDINGS.
WHAT IS AMISS?
AND?
LISTEN CAREFULLY. YOU MUST UNDERSTAND THAT WE THANOSES ARE ALL QUITE MAD.
WE ARE WHAT WE ARE AND CANNOT HELP OURSELVES.
AS CUNNING AND CALCULATING AS WE STRIVE TO BE, WE LIVE AT THE MERCY OF OUR INSANE URGES.
BUT THIS LUNACY SERVES A HIGHER PURPOSE.
IN THE FUTURE, YOU ARE DESTINED TO PLAY THE HERO NEARLY AS OFTEN AS YOU PROVE TO BE THE VILLAIN.
... DON'T ...ERSTAND.
NOR DO I COMPLETELY, AT LEAST AT THIS POINT IN TIME.
PERHAPS ILLUSTRATING WILL PROVE PREFERABLE TO EXPLAINING.
ARE WE GOING SOMEWHERE?
TO MYRIAD TOMORROWS.
YOU SHOWED ME THIS LOCATION EARLIER.
WE HAVE RETURNED TO BEAR WITNESS...

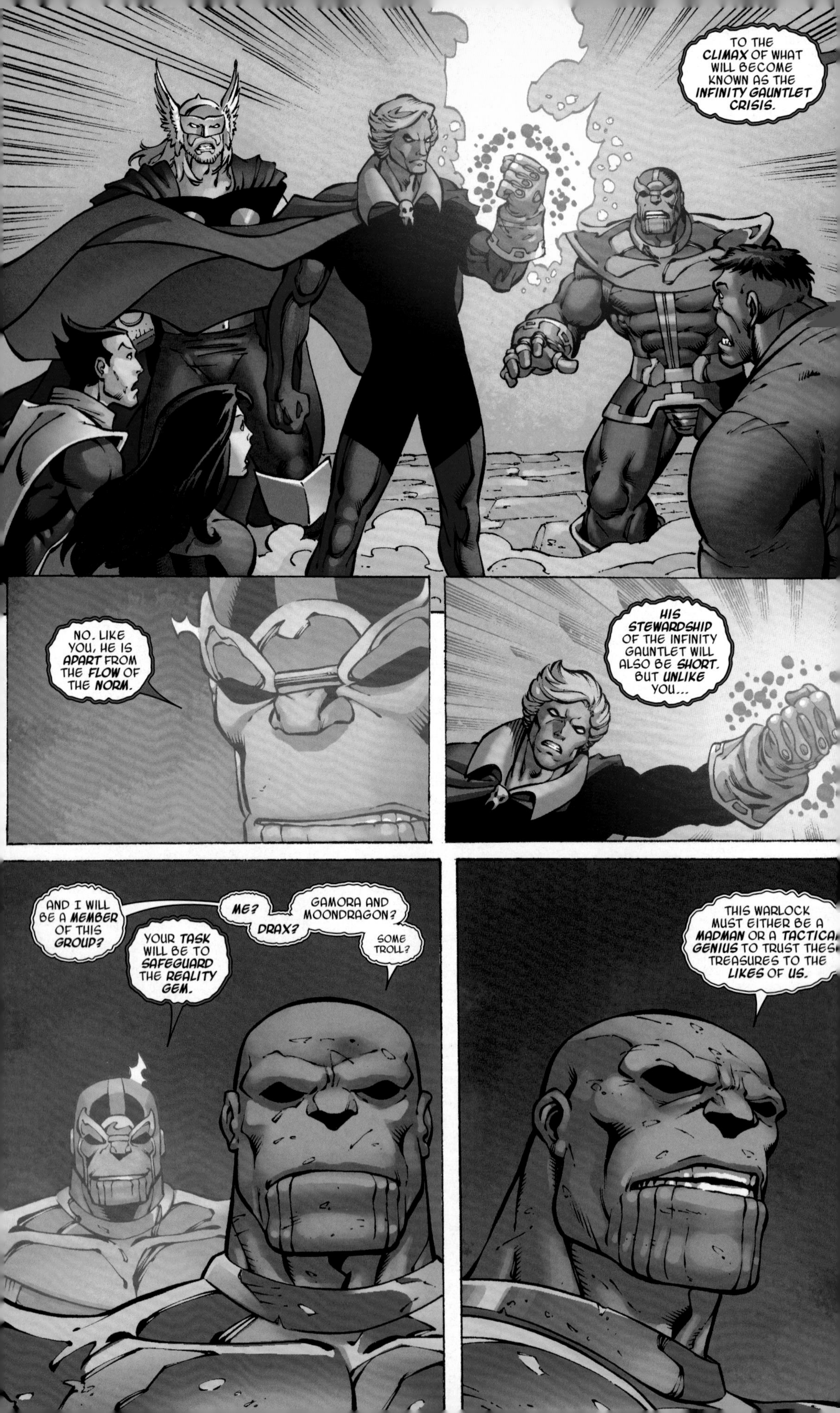
TO THE CLIMAX OF WHAT WILL BECOME KNOWN AS THE INFINITY GAUNTLET CRISIS.
NO. LIKE YOU, HE IS APART FROM THE FLOW OF THE NORM.
HIS STEWARDSHIP OF THE INFINITY GAUNTLET WILL ALSO BE SHORT. BUT UNLIKE YOU...
AND I WILL BE A MEMBER OF THIS GROUP?
ME?
DRAX?
GAMORA AND MOONDRAGON?
SOME TROLL?
YOUR TASK WILL BE TO SAFEGUARD THE REALITY GEM.
THIS WARLOCK MUST EITHER BE A MADMAN OR A TACTICA GENIUS TO TRUST THES TREASURES TO THE LIKES OF US.

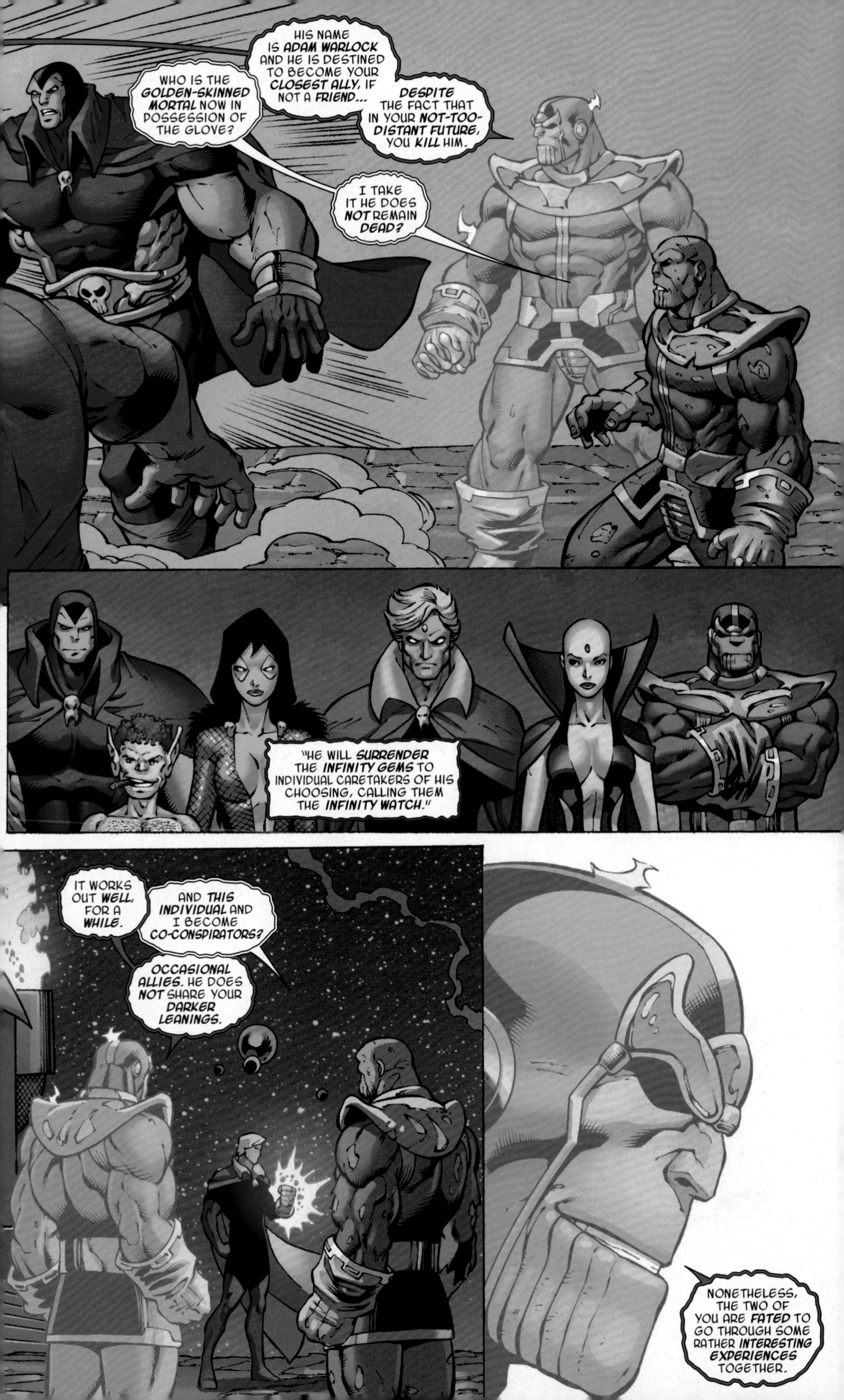
WHO IS THE GOLDEN-SKINNED MORTAL NOW IN POSSESSION OF THE GLOVE?
HIS NAME IS ADAM WARLOCK AND HE IS DESTINED TO BECOME YOUR CLOSEST ALLY, IF NOT A FRIEND...
DESPITE THE FACT THAT IN YOUR NOT-TOO-DISTANT FUTURE, YOU KILL HIM.
I TAKE IT HE DOES NOT REMAIN DEAD?
"HE WILL SURRENDER THE INFINITY GEMS TO INDIVIDUAL CARETAKERS OF HIS CHOOSING, CALLING THEM THE INFINITY WATCH."
IT WORKS OUT WELL, FOR A WHILE.
AND THIS INDIVIDUAL AND I BECOME CO-CONSPIRATORS?
OCCASIONAL ALLIES. HE DOES NOT SHARE YOUR DARKER LEANINGS.
NONETHELESS, THE TWO OF YOU ARE FATED TO GO THROUGH SOME RATHER INTERESTING EXPERIENCES TOGETHER.

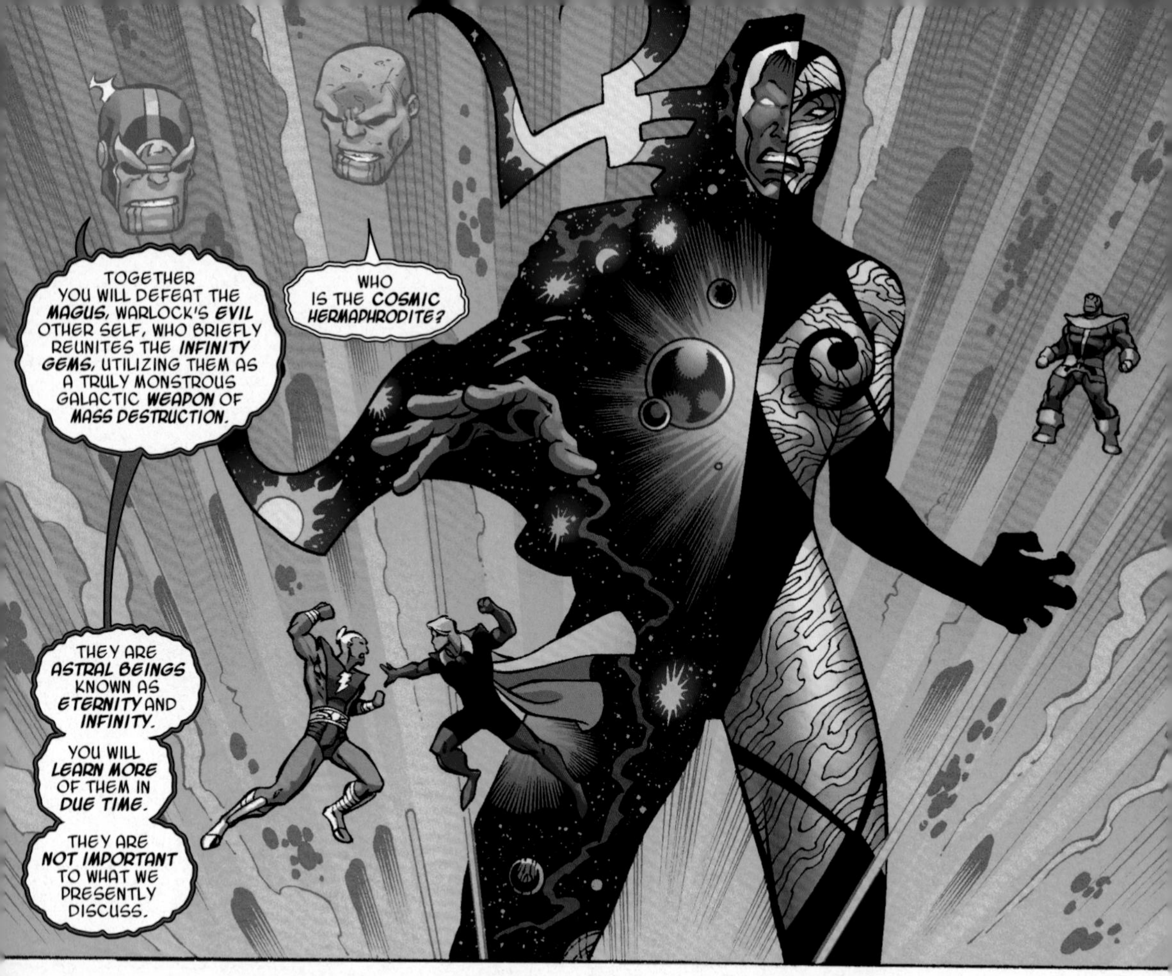
TOGETHER YOU WILL DEFEAT THE MAGUS, WARLOCK'S EVIL OTHER SELF, WHO BRIEFLY REUNITES THE INFINITY GEMS, UTILIZING THEM AS A TRULY MONSTROUS GALACTIC WEAPON OF MASS DESTRUCTION.
WHO IS THE COSMIC HERMAPHRODITE?
THEY ARE ASTRAL BEINGS KNOWN AS ETERNITY AND INFINITY.
YOU WILL LEARN MORE OF THEM IN DUE TIME.
THEY ARE NOT IMPORTANT TO WHAT WE PRESENTLY DISCUSS.

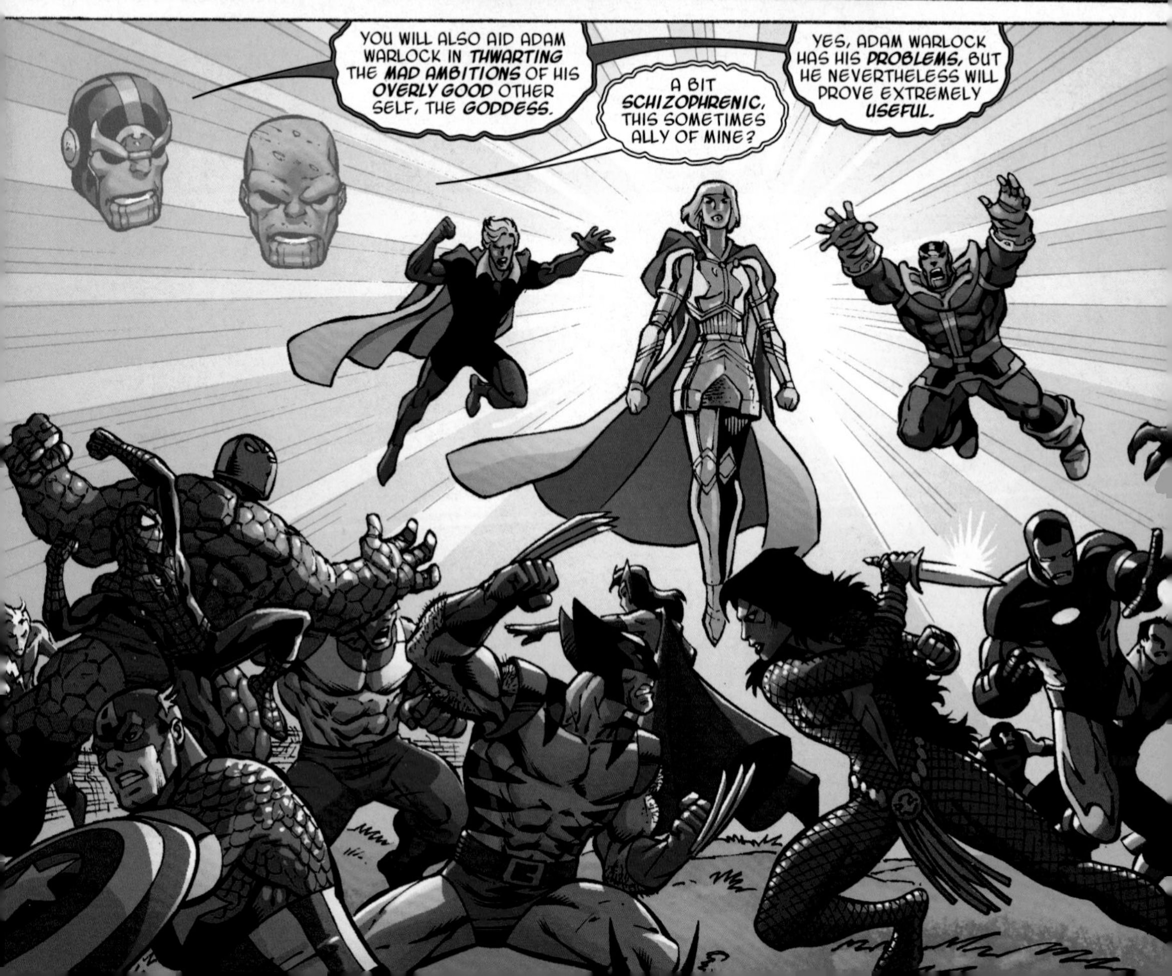
YOU WILL ALSO AID ADAM WARLOCK IN THWARTING THE MAD AMBITIONS OF HIS OVERLY GOOD OTHER SELF, THE GODDESS.
A BIT SCHIZOPHRENIC, THIS SOMETIMES ALLY OF MINE?
YES, ADAM WARLOCK HAS HIS PROBLEMS, BUT HE NEVERTHELESS WILL PROVE EXTREMELY USEFUL.

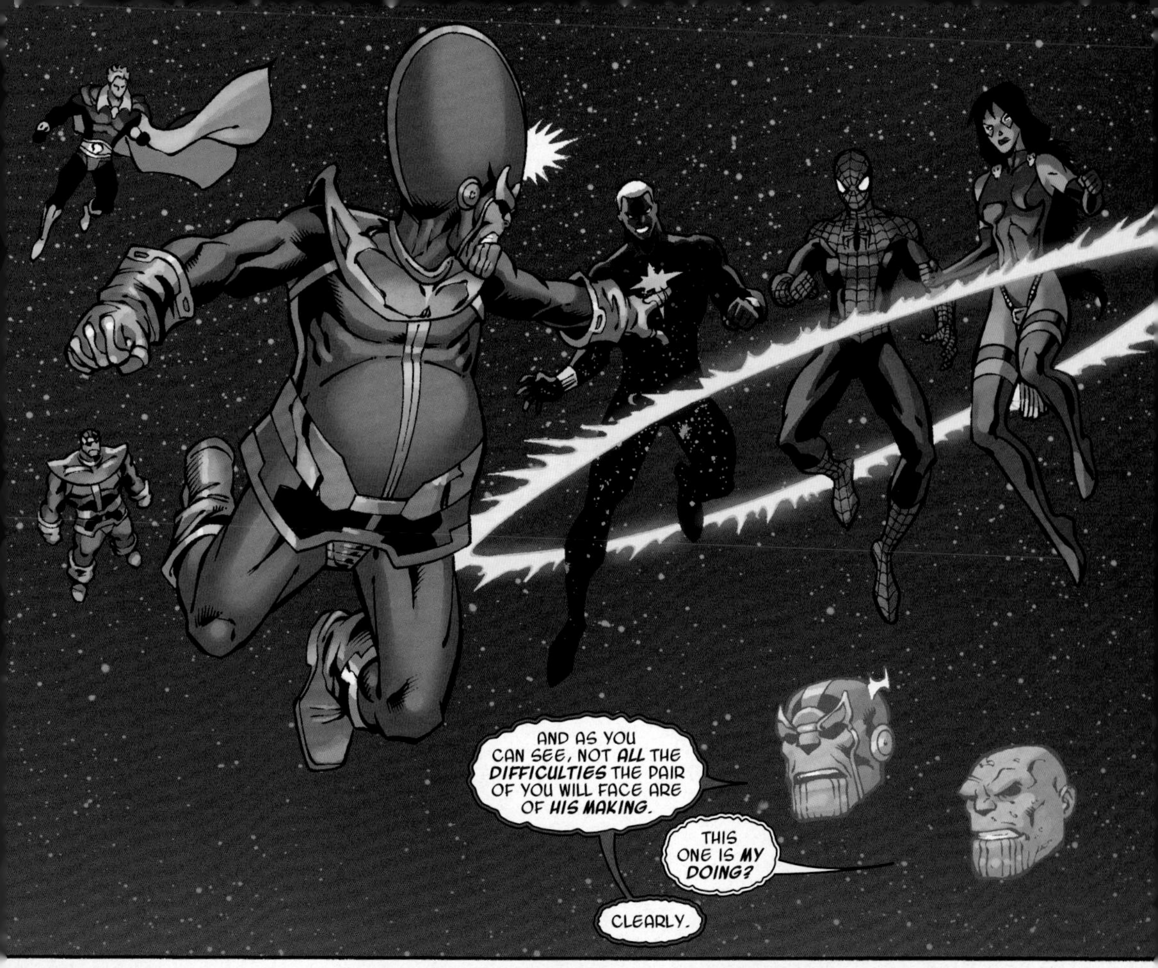
AND AS YOU CAN SEE, NOT ALL THE DIFFICULTIES THE PAIR OF YOU WILL FACE ARE OF HIS MAKING.
THIS ONE IS MY DOING?
CLEARLY.

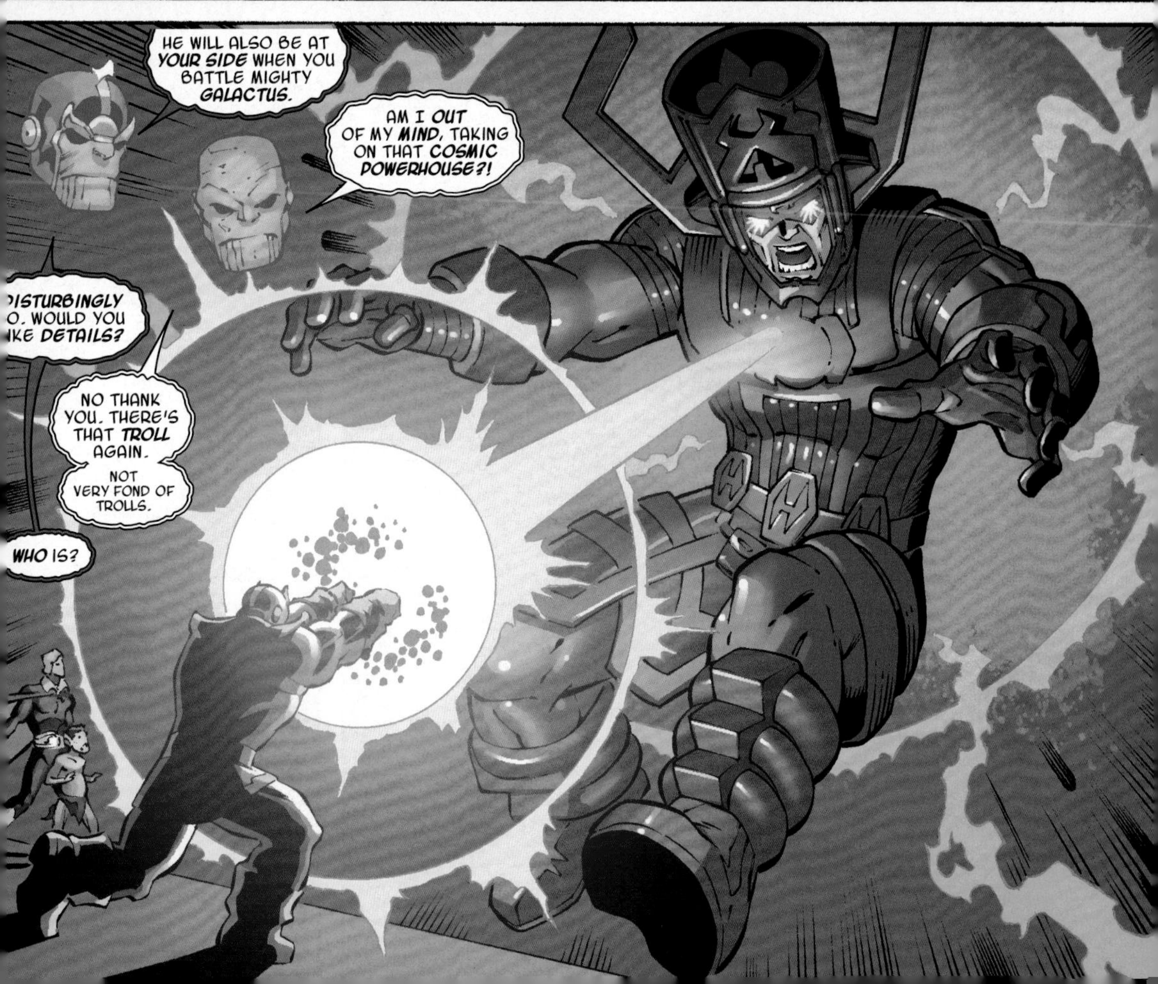
HE WILL ALSO BE AT YOUR SIDE WHEN YOU BATTLE MIGHTY GALACTUS.
AM I OUT OF MY MIND, TAKING ON THAT COSMIC POWERHOUSE?!
ISTURBINGLY O. WOULD YOU IKE DETAILS?
NO THANK YOU. THERE'S THAT TROLL AGAIN.
NOT VERY FOND OF TROLLS.
WHO IS?

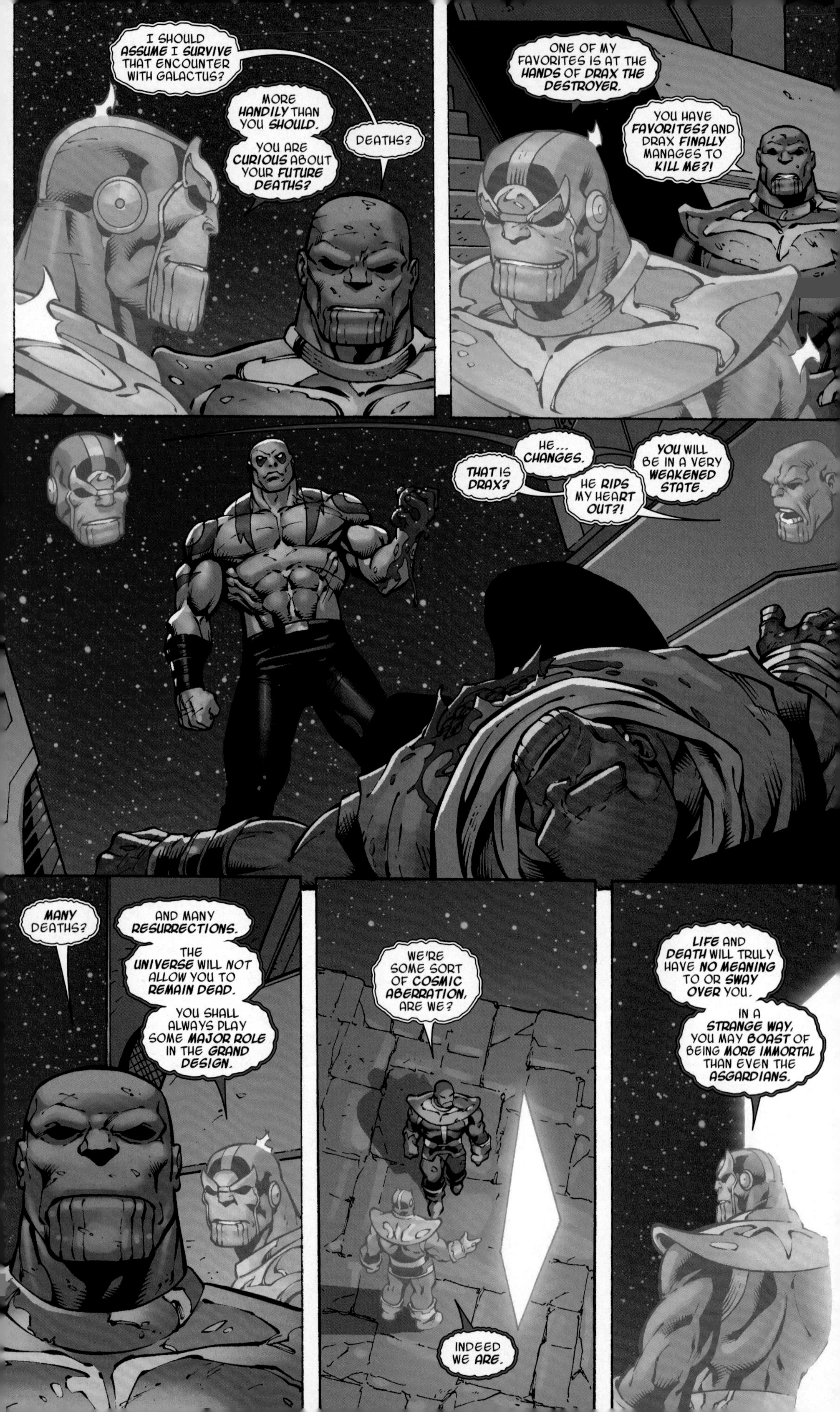
I SHOULD ASSUME I SURVIVE THAT ENCOUNTER WITH GALACTUS?
MORE HANDILY THAN YOU SHOULD.
YOU ARE CURIOUS ABOUT YOUR FUTURE DEATHS?
DEATHS?
ONE OF MY FAVORITES IS AT THE HANDS OF DRAX THE DESTROYER.
YOU HAVE FAVORITES? AND DRAX FINALLY MANAGES TO KILL ME?!
THAT IS DRAX?
HE... CHANGES.
HE RIPS MY HEART OUT?!
YOU WILL BE IN A VERY WEAKENED STATE.
MANY DEATHS?
AND MANY RESURRECTIONS.
THE UNIVERSE WILL NOT ALLOW YOU TO REMAIN DEAD.
YOU SHALL ALWAYS PLAY SOME MAJOR ROLE IN THE GRAND DESIGN.
WE'RE SOME SORT OF COSMIC ABERRATION, ARE WE?
INDEED WE ARE.
LIFE AND DEATH WILL TRULY HAVE NO MEANING TO OR SWAY OVER YOU.
IN A STRANGE WAY, YOU MAY BOAST OF BEING MORE IMMORTAL THAN EVEN THE ASGARDIANS.

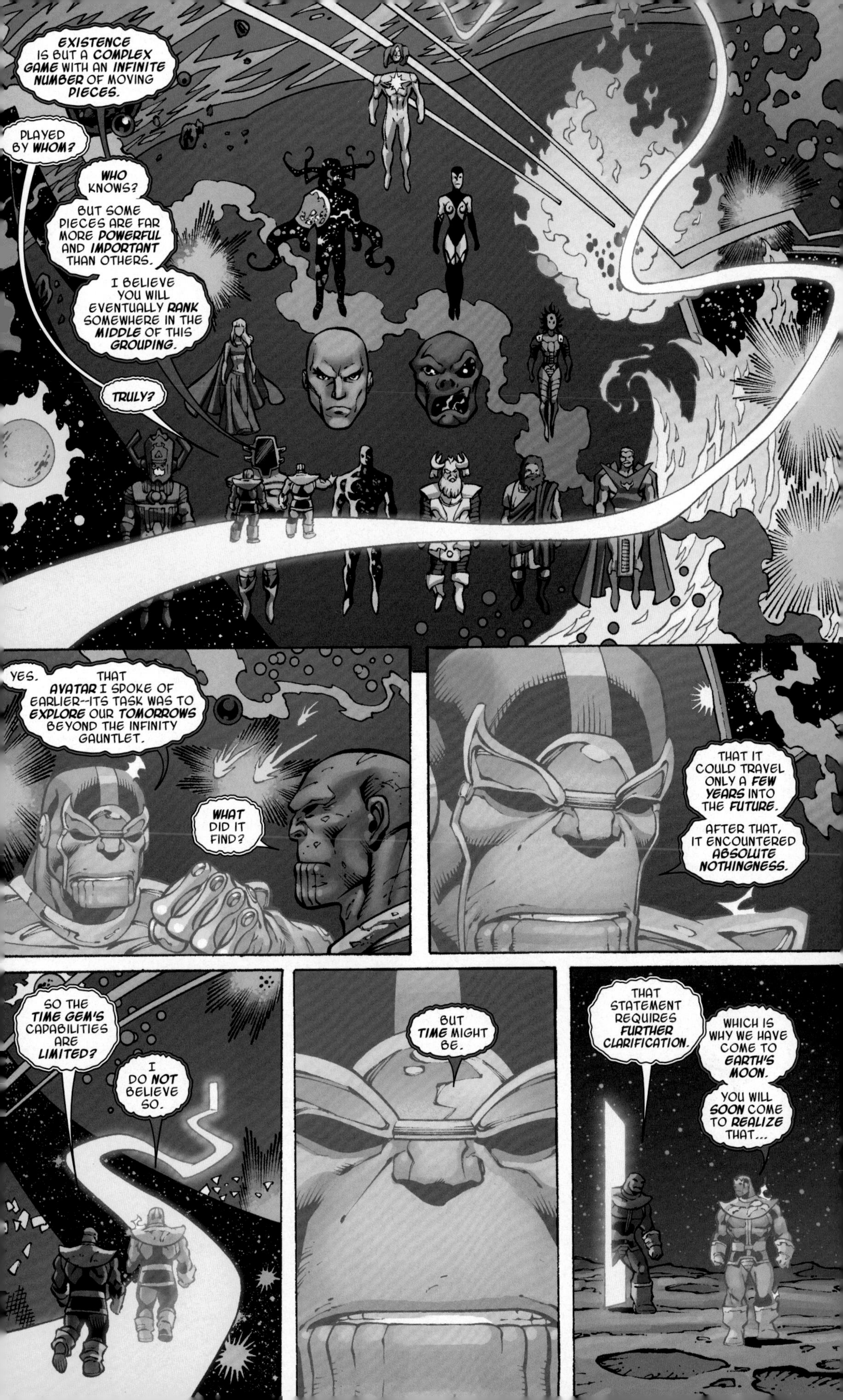
EXISTENCE IS BUT A COMPLEX GAME WITH AN INFINITE NUMBER OF MOVING PIECES.
PLAYED BY WHOM?
WHO KNOWS?
BUT SOME PIECES ARE FAR MORE POWERFUL AND IMPORTANT THAN OTHERS.
I BELIEVE YOU WILL EVENTUALLY RANK SOMEWHERE IN THE MIDDLE OF THIS GROUPING.
TRULY?
YES. THAT AVATAR I SPOKE OF EARLIER--ITS TASK WAS TO EXPLORE OUR TOMORROWS BEYOND THE INFINITY GAUNTLET.
WHAT DID IT FIND?
THAT IT COULD TRAVEL ONLY A FEW YEARS INTO THE FUTURE.
AFTER THAT, IT ENCOUNTERED ABSOLUTE NOTHINGNESS.
SO THE TIME GEM'S CAPABILITIES ARE LIMITED?
I DO NOT BELIEVE SO.
BUT TIME MIGHT BE.
THAT STATEMENT REQUIRES FURTHER CLARIFICATION.
WHICH IS WHY WE HAVE COME TO EARTH'S MOON.
YOU WILL SOON COME TO REALIZE THAT...

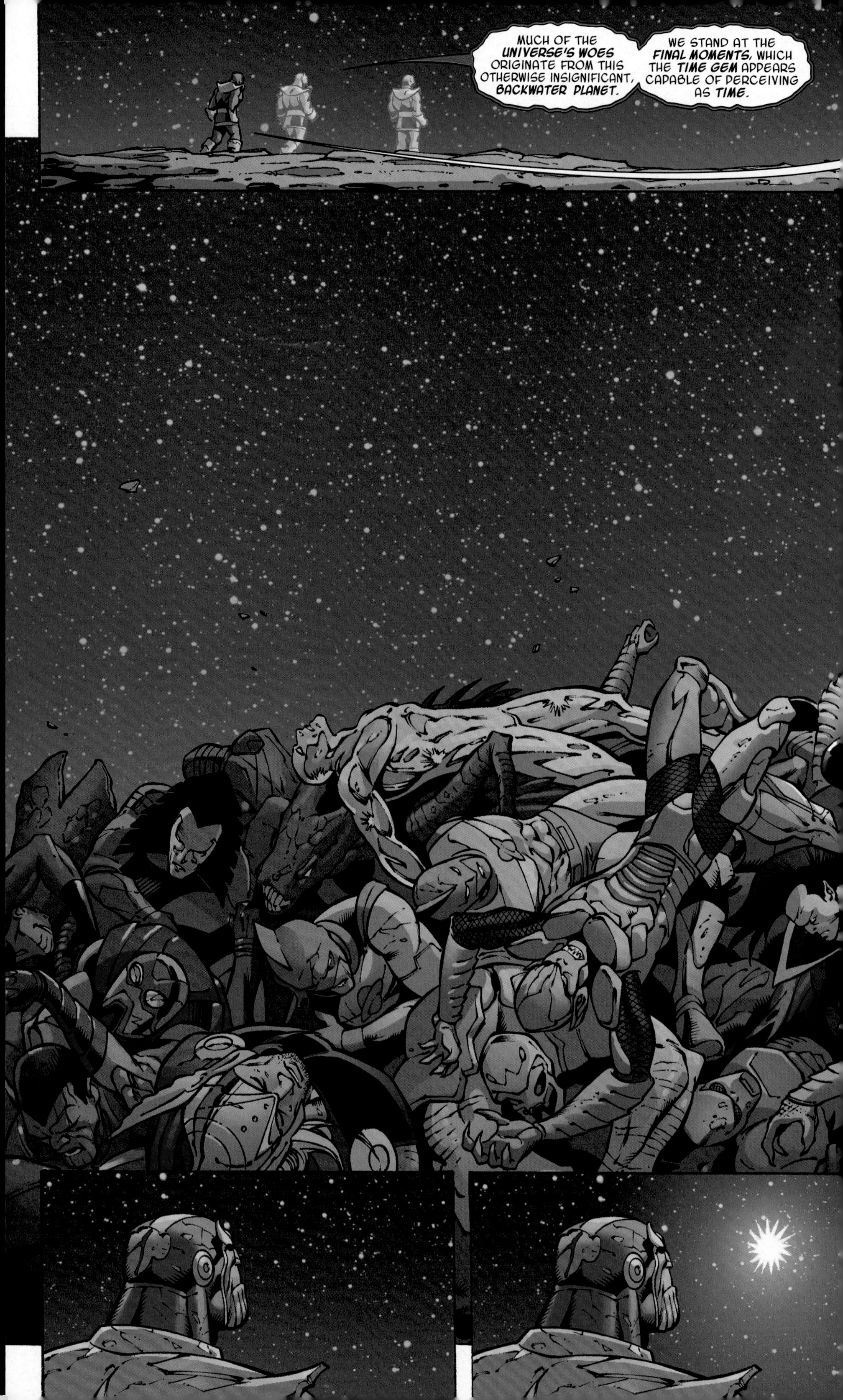
MUCH OF THE UNIVERSE'S WOES ORIGINATE FROM THIS OTHERWISE INSIGNIFICANT, BACKWATER PLANET.
WE STAND AT THE FINAL MOMENTS, WHICH THE TIME GEM APPEARS CAPABLE OF PERCEIVING AS TIME.

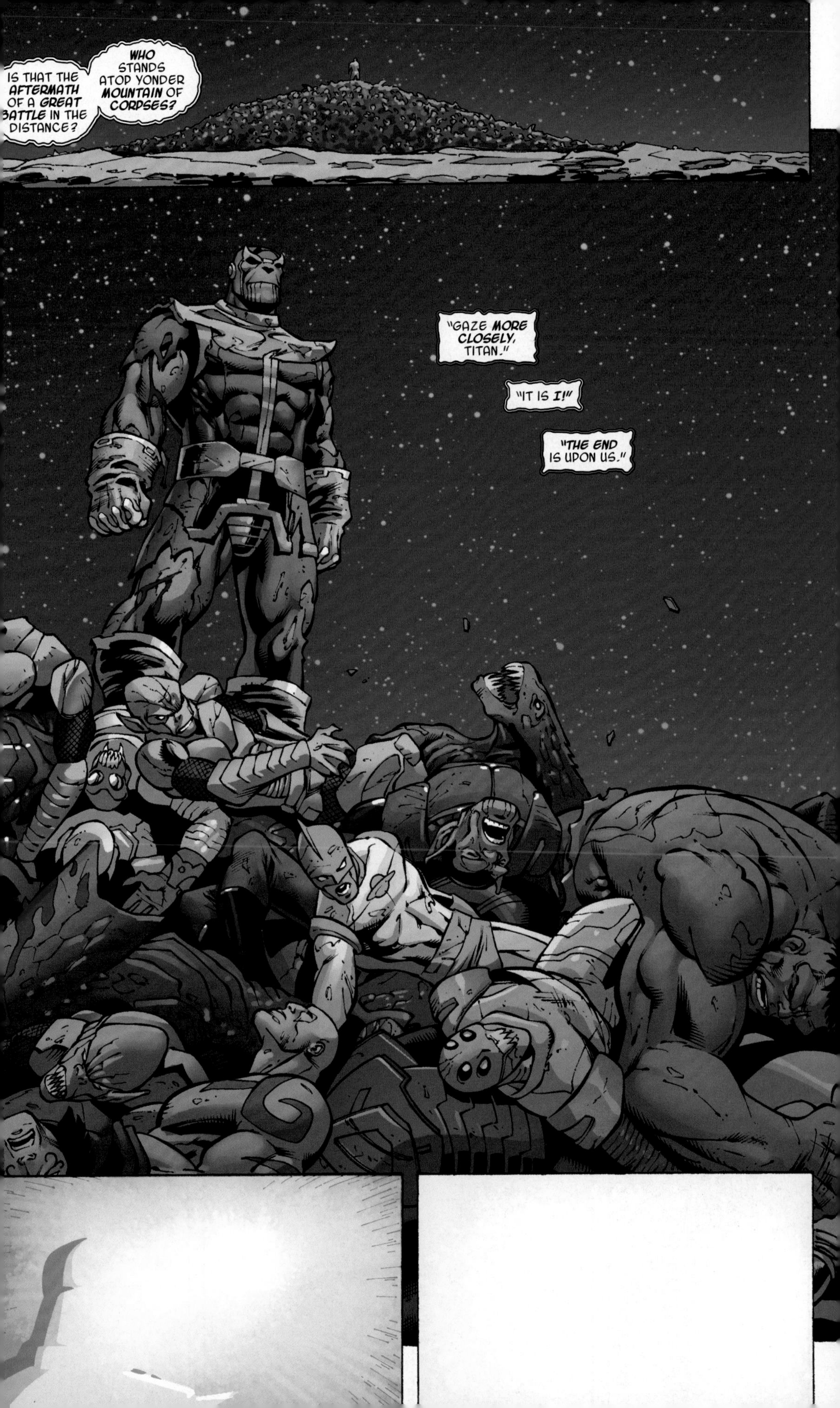
IS THAT THE AFTERMATH OF A GREAT BATTLE IN THE DISTANCE?
WHO STANDS ATOP YONDER MOUNTAIN OF CORPSES?
"GAZE MORE CLOSELY, TITAN."
"IT IS I!"
"THE END IS UPON US."

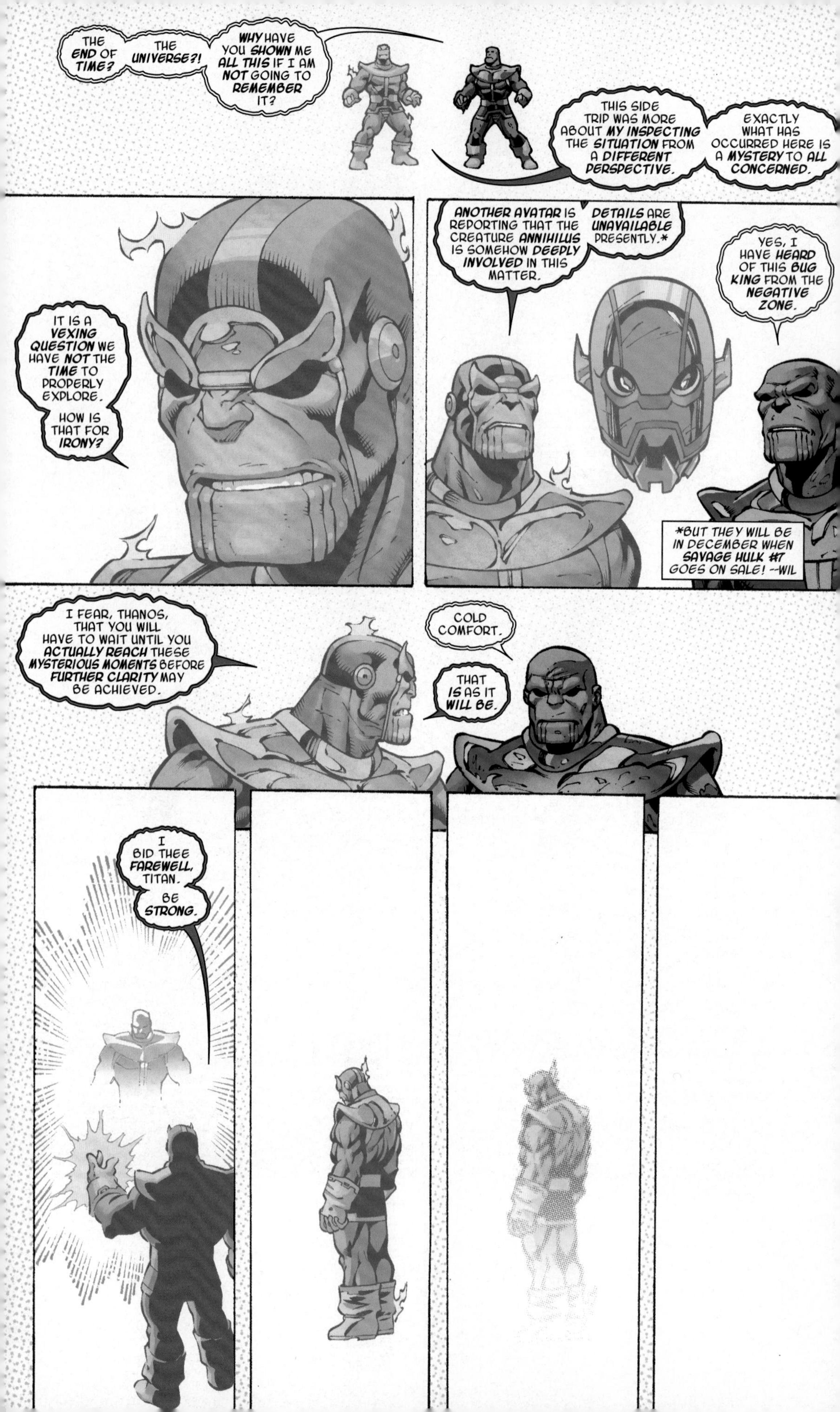

THE END OF TIME?
THE UNIVERSE?!
WHY HAVE YOU SHOWN ME ALL THIS IF I AM NOT GOING TO REMEMBER IT?
THIS SIDE TRIP WAS MORE ABOUT MY INSPECTING THE SITUATION FROM A DIFFERENT PERSPECTIVE.
EXACTLY WHAT HAS OCCURRED HERE IS A MYSTERY TO ALL CONCERNED.
IT IS A VEXING QUESTION WE HAVE NOT THE TIME TO PROPERLY EXPLORE.
HOW IS THAT FOR IRONY?
ANOTHER AVATAR IS REPORTING THAT THE CREATURE ANNIHILUS IS SOMEHOW DEEPLY INVOLVED IN THIS MATTER.
DETAILS ARE UNAVAILABLE PRESENTLY.*
YES, I HAVE HEARD OF THIS BUG KING FROM THE NEGATIVE ZONE.
*BUT THEY WILL BE IN DECEMBER WHEN SAVAGE HULK #7 GOES ON SALE! --WIL
I FEAR, THANOS, THAT YOU WILL HAVE TO WAIT UNTIL YOU ACTUALLY REACH THESE MYSTERIOUS MOMENTS BEFORE FURTHER CLARITY MAY BE ACHIEVED.
COLD COMFORT.
THAT IS AS IT WILL BE.
I BID THEE FAREWELL, TITAN.
BE STRONG.

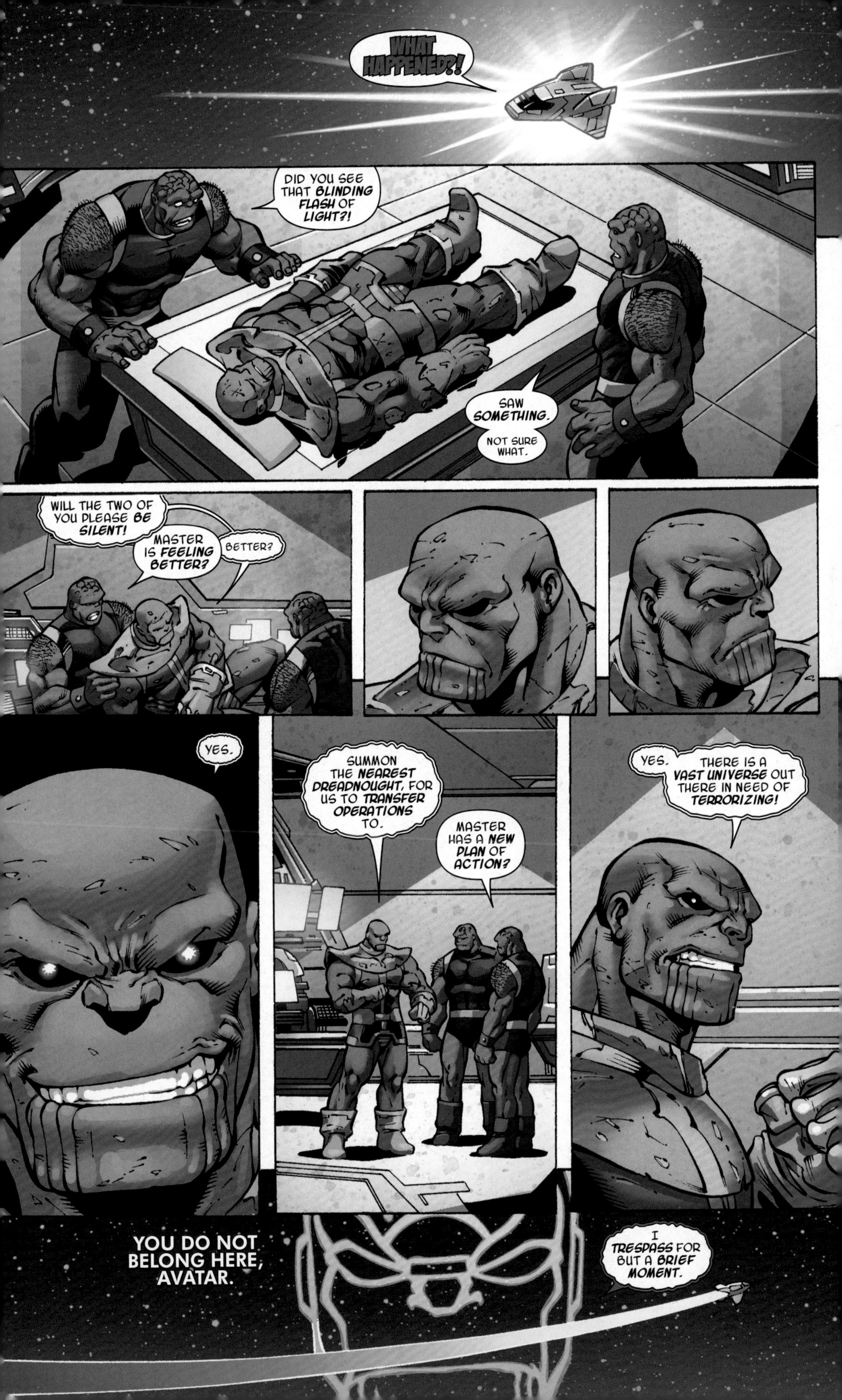

WHAT HAPPENED?!
DID YOU SEE THAT BLINDING FLASH OF LIGHT?!
SAW SOMETHING.
NOT SURE WHAT.
WILL THE TWO OF YOU PLEASE BE SILENT!
MASTER IS FEELING BETTER?
BETTER?
YES.
SUMMON THE NEAREST DREADNOUGHT, FOR US TO TRANSFER OPERATIONS TO.
MASTER HAS A NEW PLAN OF ACTION?
YES.
THERE IS A VAST UNIVERSE OUT THERE IN NEED OF TERRORIZING!
YOU DO NOT BELONG HERE, AVATAR.
I TRESPASS FOR BUT A BRIEF MOMENT.

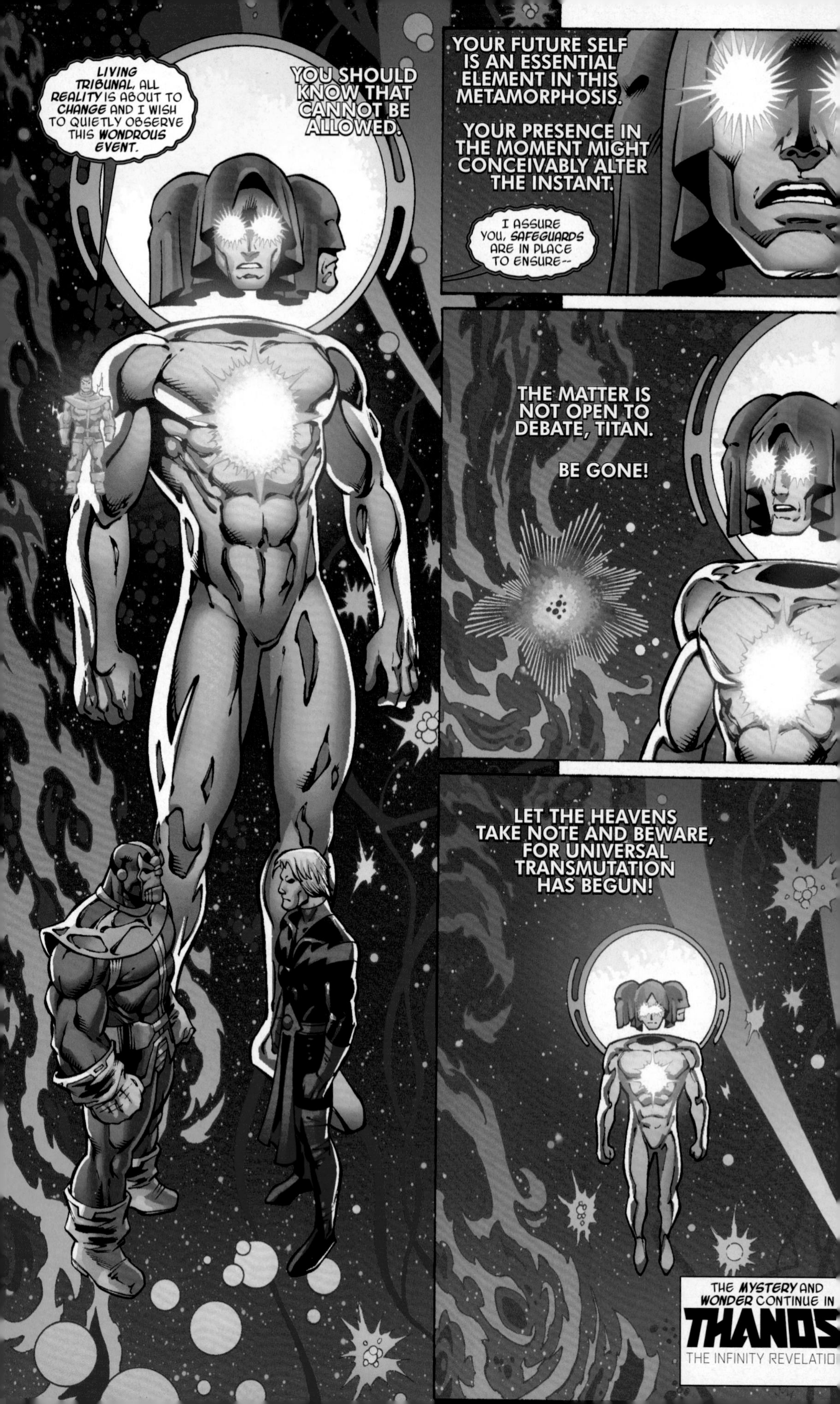

LIVING TRIBUNAL, ALL REALITY IS ABOUT TO CHANGE AND I WISH TO QUIETLY OBSERVE THIS WONDROUS EVENT.
YOU SHOULD KNOW THAT CANNOT BE ALLOWED.
YOUR FUTURE SELF IS AN ESSENTIAL ELEMENT IN THIS METAMORPHOSIS.
YOUR PRESENCE IN THE MOMENT MIGHT CONCEIVABLY ALTER THE INSTANT.
I ASSURE YOU, SAFEGUARDS ARE IN PLACE TO ENSURE--
THE MATTER IS NOT OPEN TO DEBATE, TITAN.
BE GONE!
LET THE HEAVENS TAKE NOTE AND BEWARE, FOR UNIVERSAL TRANSMUTATION HAS BEGUN!
THE MYSTERY AND WONDER CONTINUE IN
THANOS
THE INFINITY REVELATIO

THE STORY CONTINUES IN...

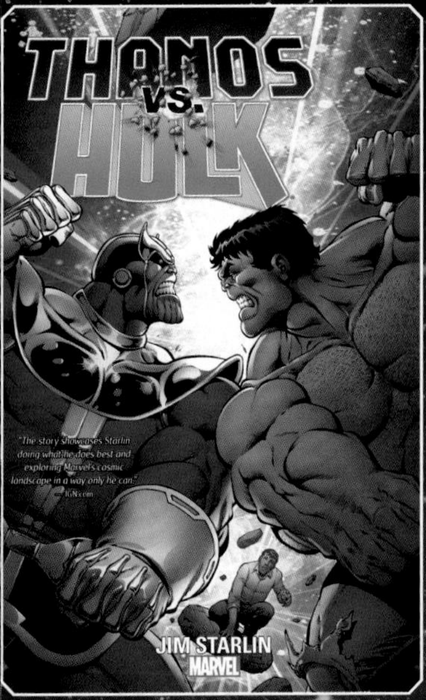
THANOS VS. HULK
"The story showcases Starlin doing what he does best and exploring Marvel's cosmic landscape in a way only he can."
—IGN.com
JIM STARLIN
MARVEL

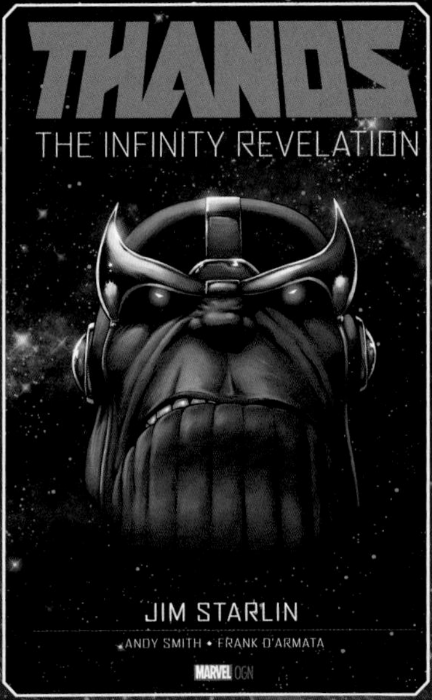
THANOS
THE INFINITY REVELATION
JIM STARLIN
ANDY SMITH • FRANK D'ARMATA
MARVEL OGN

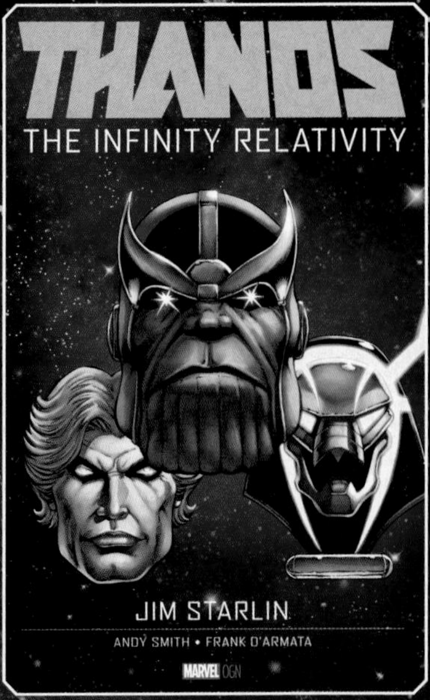
THANOS
THE INFINITY RELATIVITY
JIM STARLIN
ANDY SMITH • FRANK D'ARMATA
MARVEL OGN

ADAM WARLOCK was created by Earth scientists as an artificial, "perfect" human. For some time, he explored the cosmos, occasionally allying himself with heroes such as the Infinity Watch and the Guardians of the Galaxy. He had a dark side, however--and eventually, in order to prevent his evil self, Magus, from permanently taking over, he convinced Star-Lord to kill him.

Recently, the Adam Warlock of an alternate reality was reborn in this reality with the help of **THANOS**, who has been both an ally and an enemy to Adam over the years. This alternate reality Adam has been reborn with vast power and knowledge, as he contains the energy of his former reality within him--but he does not fully realize just how powerful he has become.

Most recently, he was helping Thanos and the Guardians of the Galaxy in their attempt to thwart Annihilus from taking over the universe. But Annihilus banished Thanos to an empty void, the severely wounded Guardians were forced to retreat, and Warlock was taken prisoner.

Or was he...?

[*THE INFINITY IDENTITY* takes place between the events of the *THANOS: THE INFINITY RELATIVITY OGN* and the forthcoming *THANOS: THE INFINITY FINALE OGN*.]

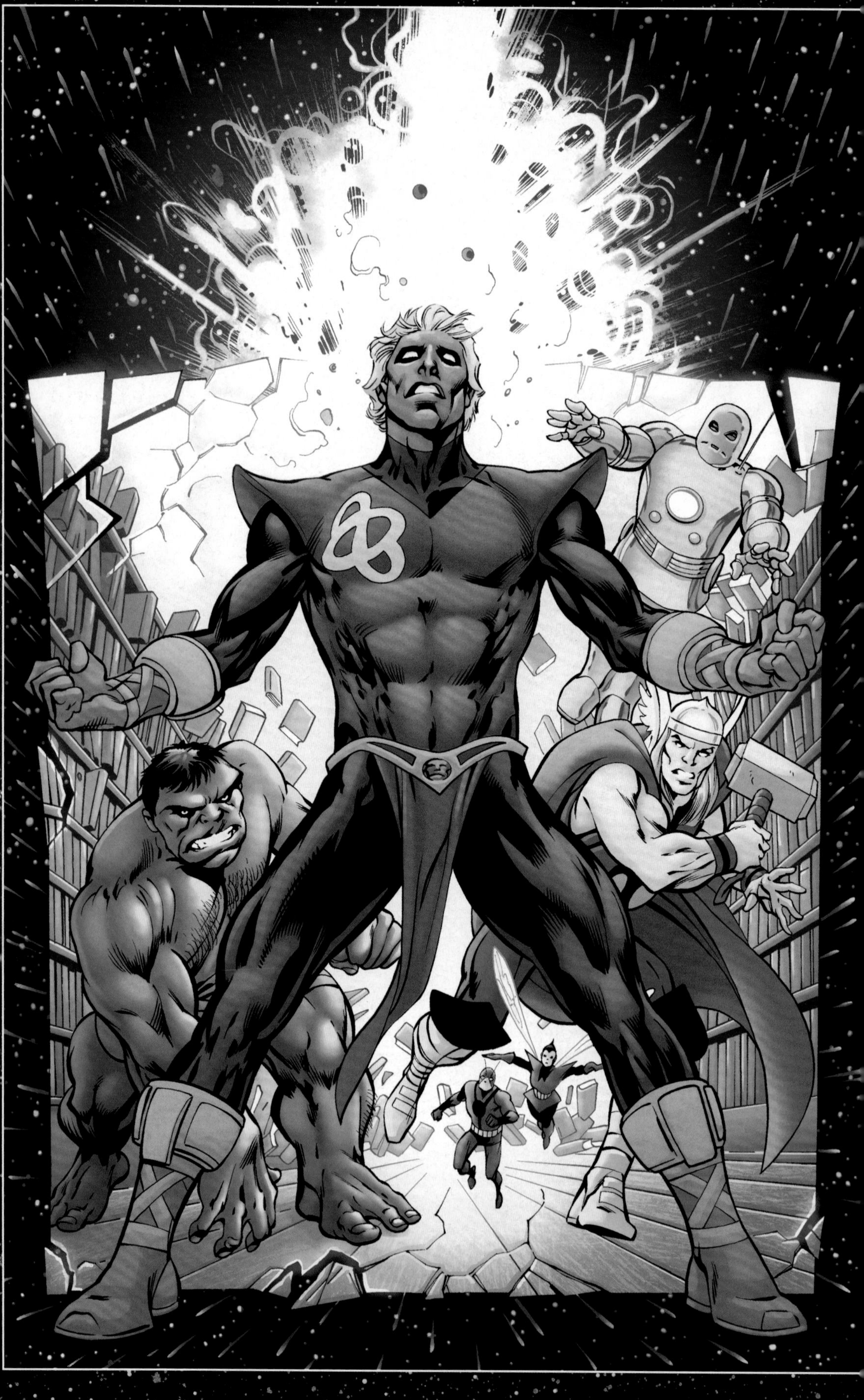

1. IN THE BEGINNING

WHERE AM I?
PERHAPS A BETTER QUESTION MIGHT BE, "WHO AM I?"
BECAUSE I CANNOT REMEMBER.
HOW DID I COME TO FIND MYSELF IN SUCH CIRCUMSTANCES?
SOMETHING FEELS TERRIBLY WRONG ABOUT ALL THIS!
CAN IT BE THAT MY BRAIN IS NOT FUNCTIONING PROPERLY?
AND WHY WOULD THAT NOT SURPRISE ME?
IN THE BEGINNING!

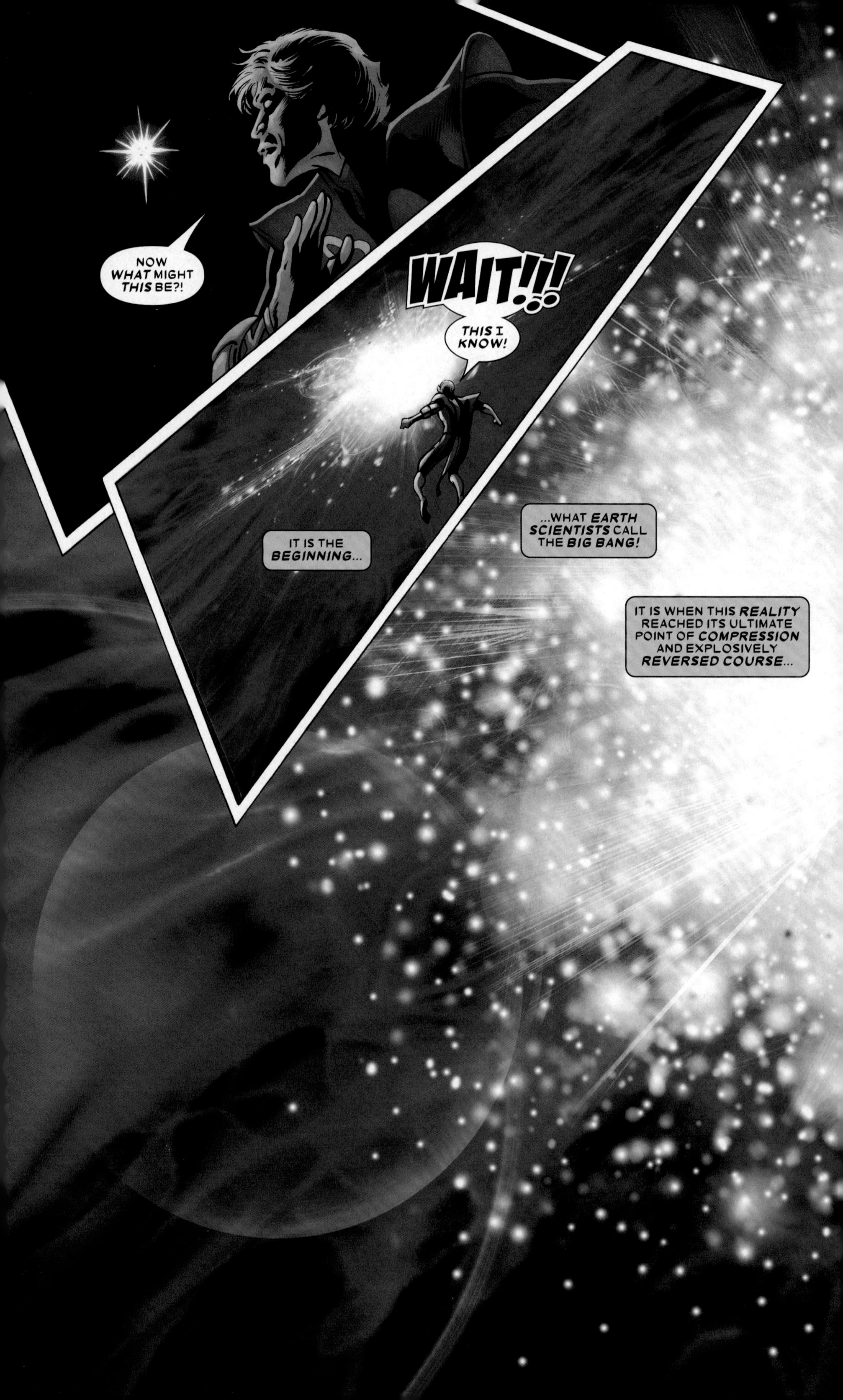

NOW WHAT MIGHT THIS BE?!
WAIT!!!
THIS I KNOW!
IT IS THE BEGINNING...
...WHAT EARTH SCIENTISTS CALL THE BIG BANG!
IT IS WHEN THIS REALITY REACHED ITS ULTIMATE POINT OF COMPRESSION AND EXPLOSIVELY REVERSED COURSE...

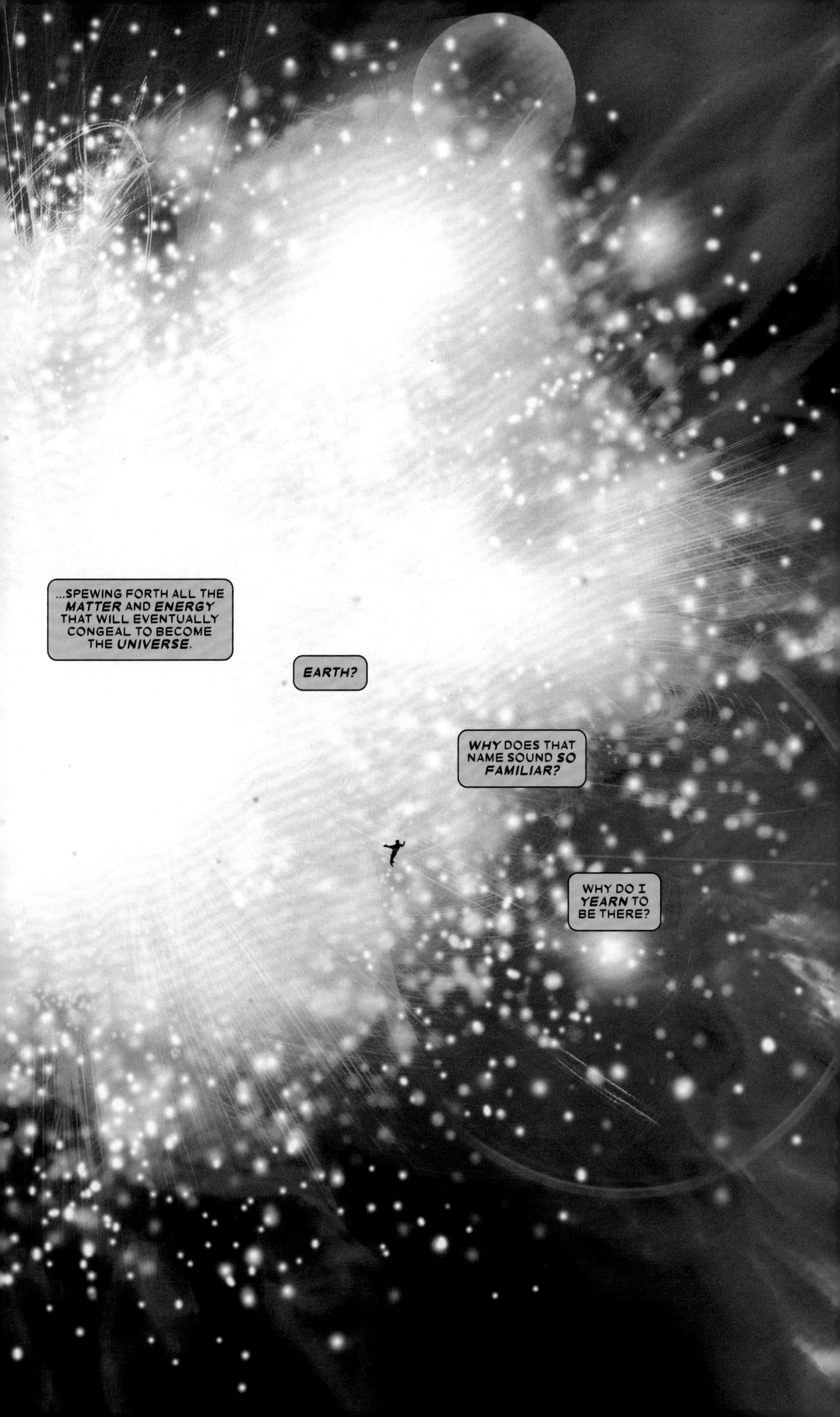
...SPEWING FORTH ALL THE MATTER AND ENERGY THAT WILL EVENTUALLY CONGEAL TO BECOME THE UNIVERSE.
EARTH?
WHY DOES THAT NAME SOUND SO FAMILIAR?
WHY DO I YEARN TO BE THERE?

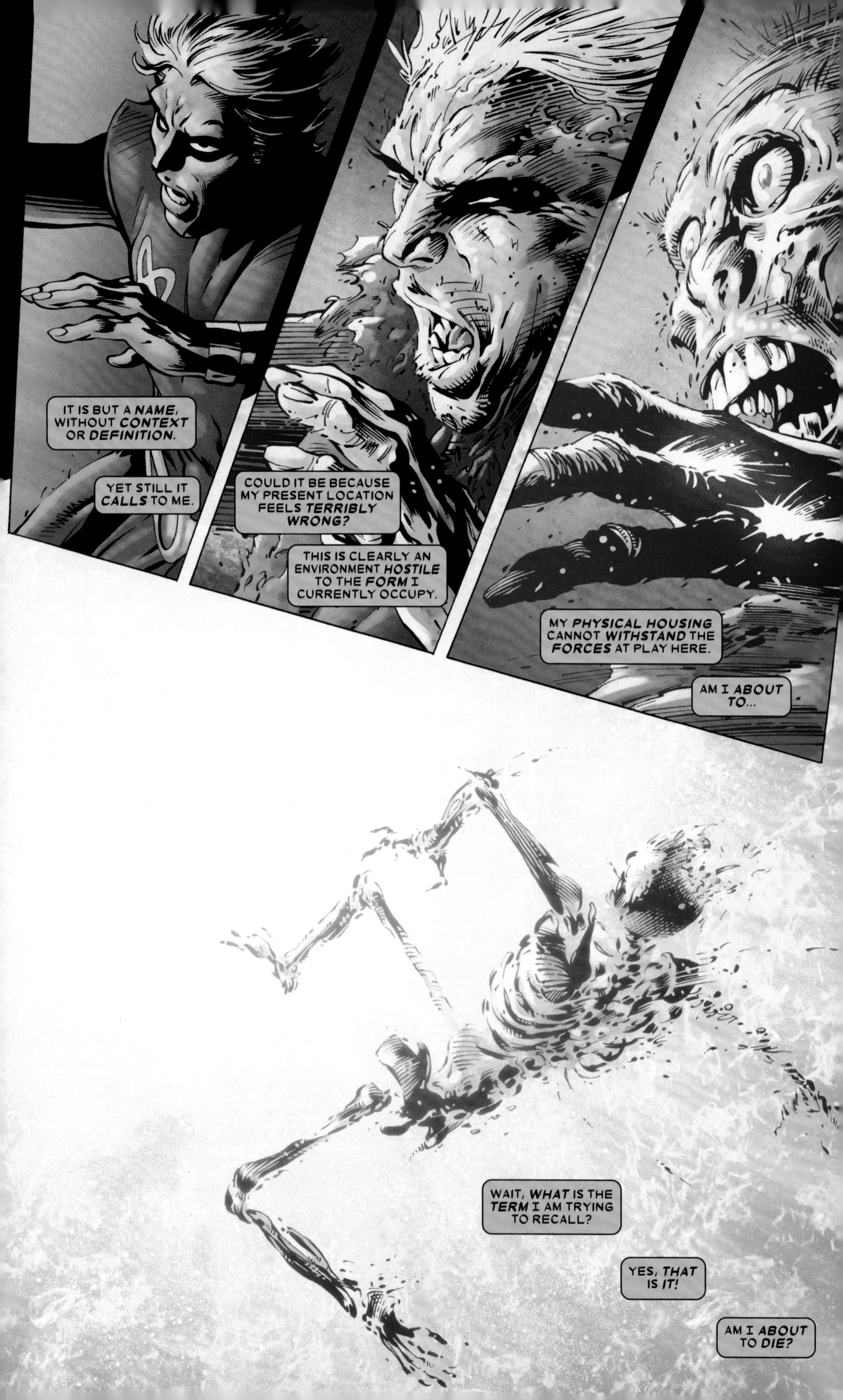

IT IS BUT A NAME, WITHOUT CONTEXT OR DEFINITION.
YET STILL IT CALLS TO ME.
COULD IT BE BECAUSE MY PRESENT LOCATION FEELS TERRIBLY WRONG?
THIS IS CLEARLY AN ENVIRONMENT HOSTILE TO THE FORM I CURRENTLY OCCUPY.
MY PHYSICAL HOUSING CANNOT WITHSTAND THE FORCES AT PLAY HERE.
AM I ABOUT TO...
WAIT, WHAT IS THE TERM I AM TRYING TO RECALL?
YES, THAT IS IT!
AM I ABOUT TO DIE?

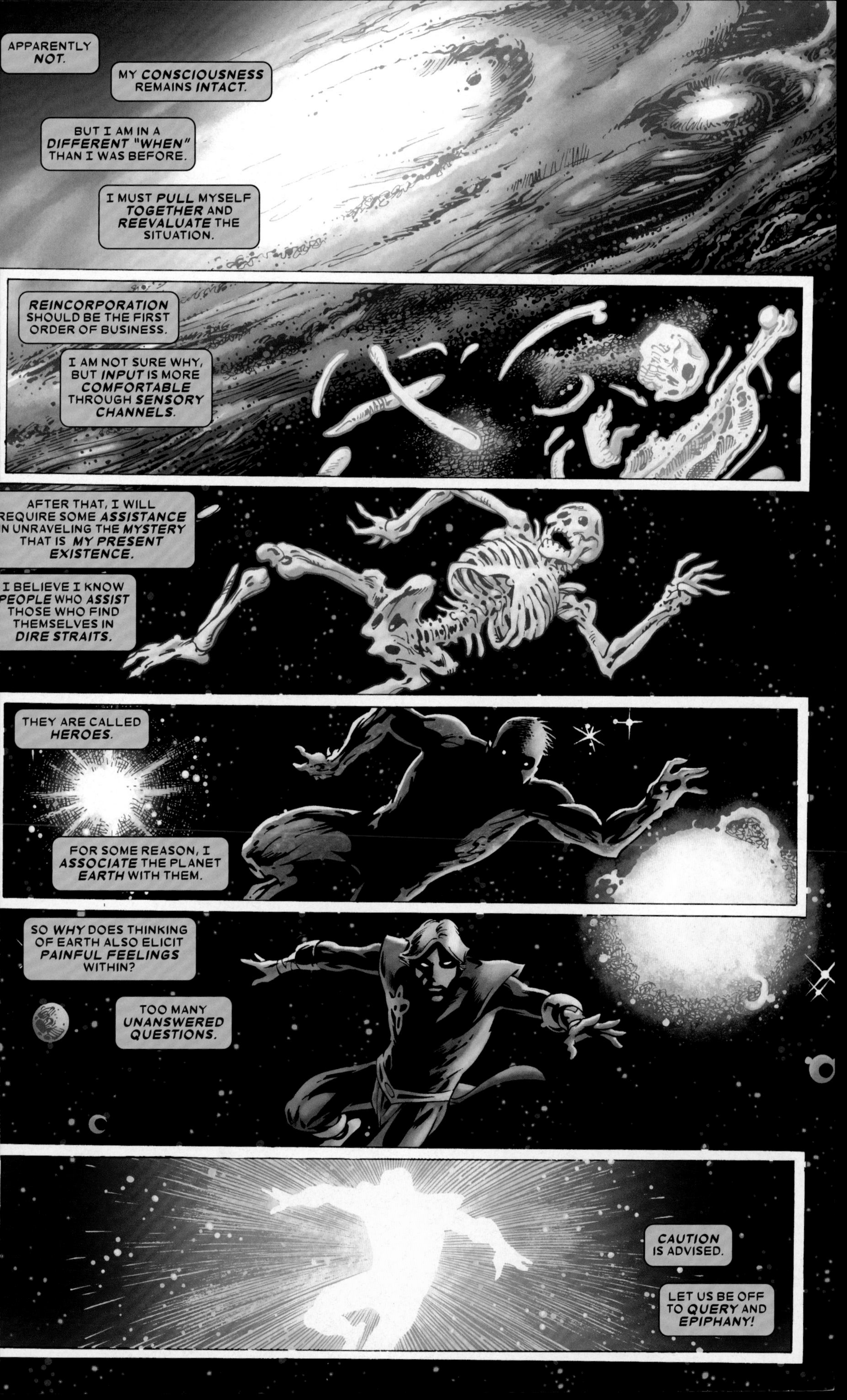

APPARENTLY NOT.
MY CONSCIOUSNESS REMAINS INTACT.
BUT I AM IN A DIFFERENT "WHEN" THAN I WAS BEFORE.
I MUST PULL MYSELF TOGETHER AND REEVALUATE THE SITUATION.
REINCORPORATION SHOULD BE THE FIRST ORDER OF BUSINESS.
I AM NOT SURE WHY, BUT INPUT IS MORE COMFORTABLE THROUGH SENSORY CHANNELS.
AFTER THAT, I WILL REQUIRE SOME ASSISTANCE IN UNRAVELING THE MYSTERY THAT IS MY PRESENT EXISTENCE.
I BELIEVE I KNOW PEOPLE WHO ASSIST THOSE WHO FIND THEMSELVES IN DIRE STRAITS.
THEY ARE CALLED HEROES.
FOR SOME REASON, I ASSOCIATE THE PLANET EARTH WITH THEM.
SO WHY DOES THINKING OF EARTH ALSO ELICIT PAINFUL FEELINGS WITHIN?
TOO MANY UNANSWERED QUESTIONS.
CAUTION IS ADVISED.
LET US BE OFF TO QUERY AND EPIPHANY!

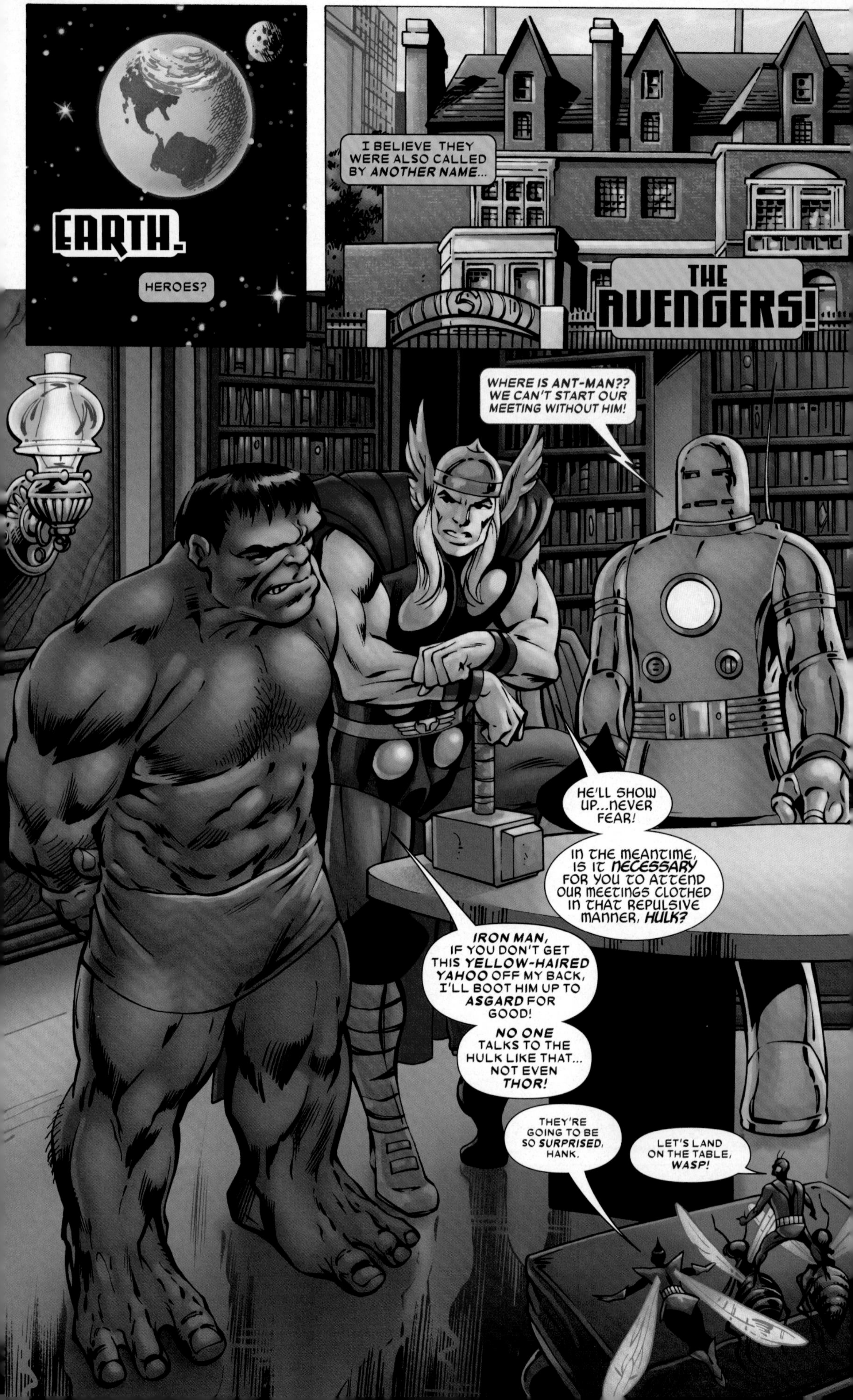

EARTH.
HEROES?
I BELIEVE THEY WERE ALSO CALLED BY ANOTHER NAME...
THE AVENGERS!
WHERE IS ANT-MAN?? WE CAN'T START OUR MEETING WITHOUT HIM!
HE'LL SHOW UP...NEVER FEAR!
IN THE MEANTIME, IS IT NECESSARY FOR YOU TO ATTEND OUR MEETINGS CLOTHED IN THAT REPULSIVE MANNER, HULK?
IRON MAN, IF YOU DON'T GET THIS YELLOW-HAIRED YAHOO OFF MY BACK, I'LL BOOT HIM UP TO ASGARD FOR GOOD!
NO ONE TALKS TO THE HULK LIKE THAT... NOT EVEN THOR!
THEY'RE GOING TO BE SO SURPRISED, HANK.
LET'S LAND ON THE TABLE, WASP!

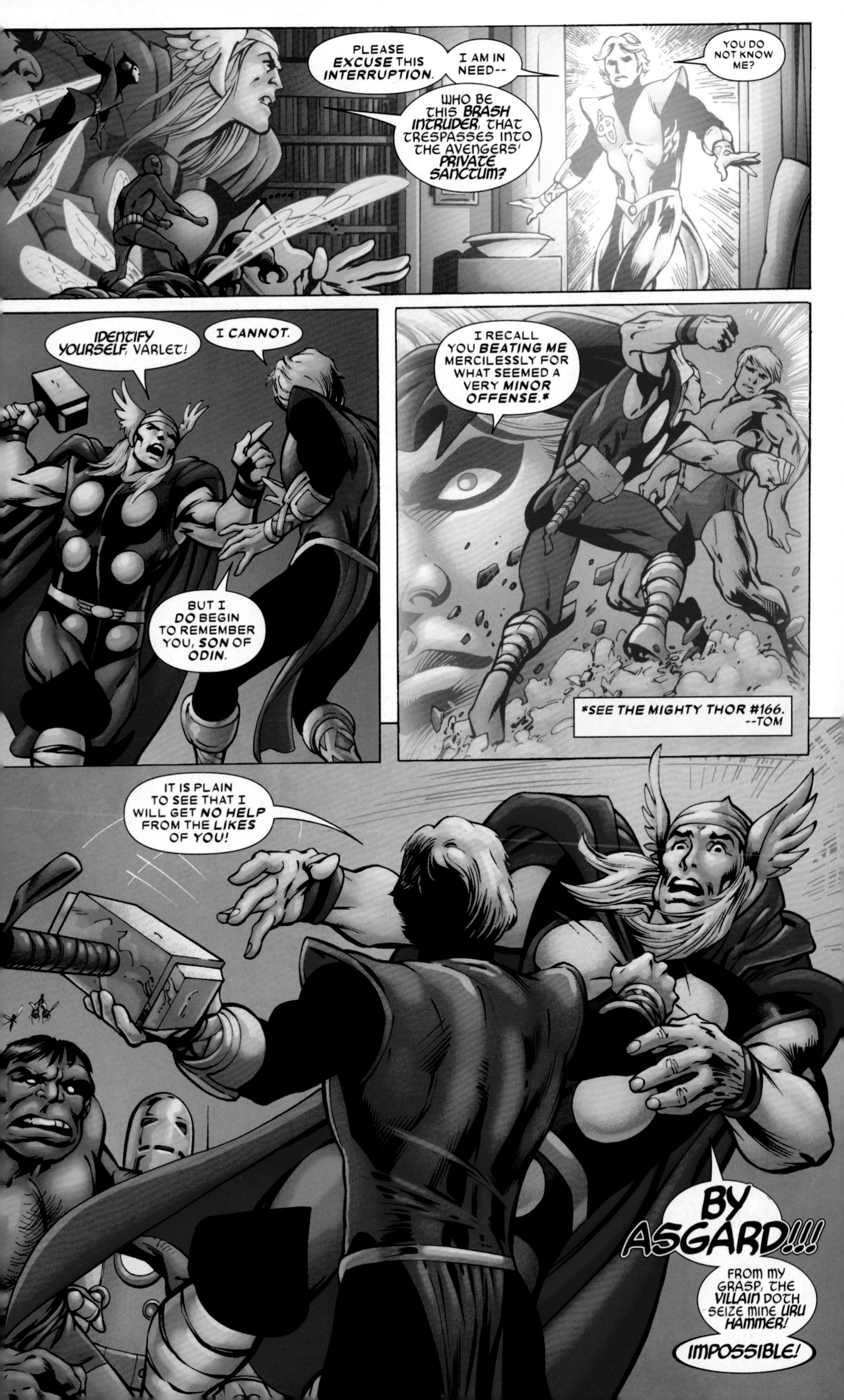
PLEASE EXCUSE THIS INTERRUPTION.
I AM IN NEED--
WHO BE THIS BRASH INTRUDER, THAT TRESPASSES INTO THE AVENGERS' PRIVATE SANCTUM?
YOU DO NOT KNOW ME?
IDENTIFY YOURSELF, VARLET!
I CANNOT.
BUT I DO BEGIN TO REMEMBER YOU, SON OF ODIN.
I RECALL YOU BEATING ME MERCILESSLY FOR WHAT SEEMED A VERY MINOR OFFENSE.*
*SEE THE MIGHTY THOR #166. --TOM
IT IS PLAIN TO SEE THAT I WILL GET NO HELP FROM THE LIKES OF YOU!
BY ASGARD!!!!
FROM MY GRASP, THE VILLAIN DOTH SEIZE MINE URU HAMMER!
IMPOSSIBLE!

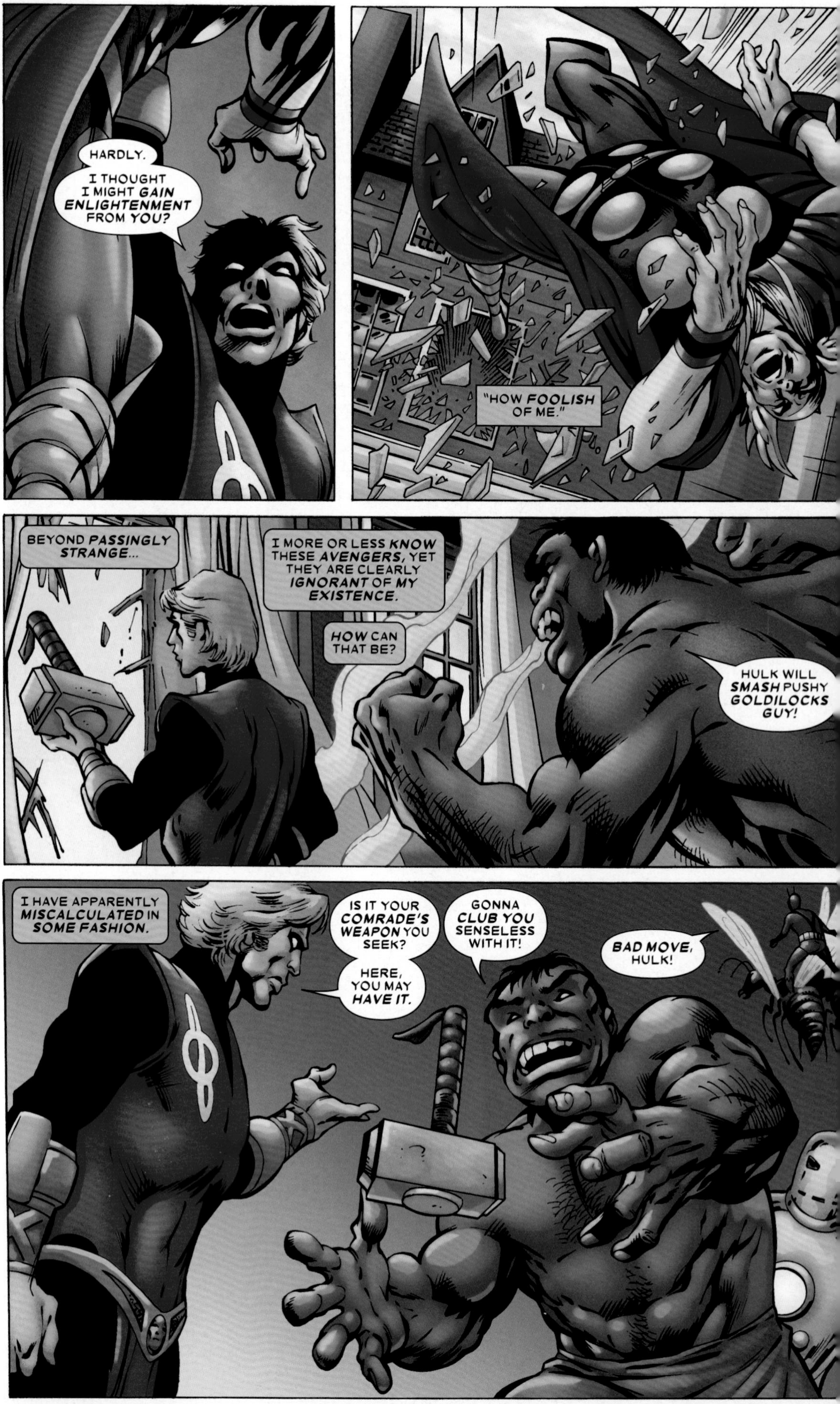
HARDLY.
I THOUGHT I MIGHT GAIN ENLIGHTENMENT FROM YOU?
"HOW FOOLISH OF ME."
BEYOND PASSINGLY STRANGE...
I MORE OR LESS KNOW THESE AVENGERS, YET THEY ARE CLEARLY IGNORANT OF MY EXISTENCE.
HOW CAN THAT BE?
HULK WILL SMASH PUSHY GOLDILOCKS GUY!
I HAVE APPARENTLY MISCALCULATED IN SOME FASHION.
IS IT YOUR COMRADE'S WEAPON YOU SEEK?
HERE, YOU MAY HAVE IT.
GONNA CLUB YOU SENSELESS WITH IT!
BAD MOVE, HULK!

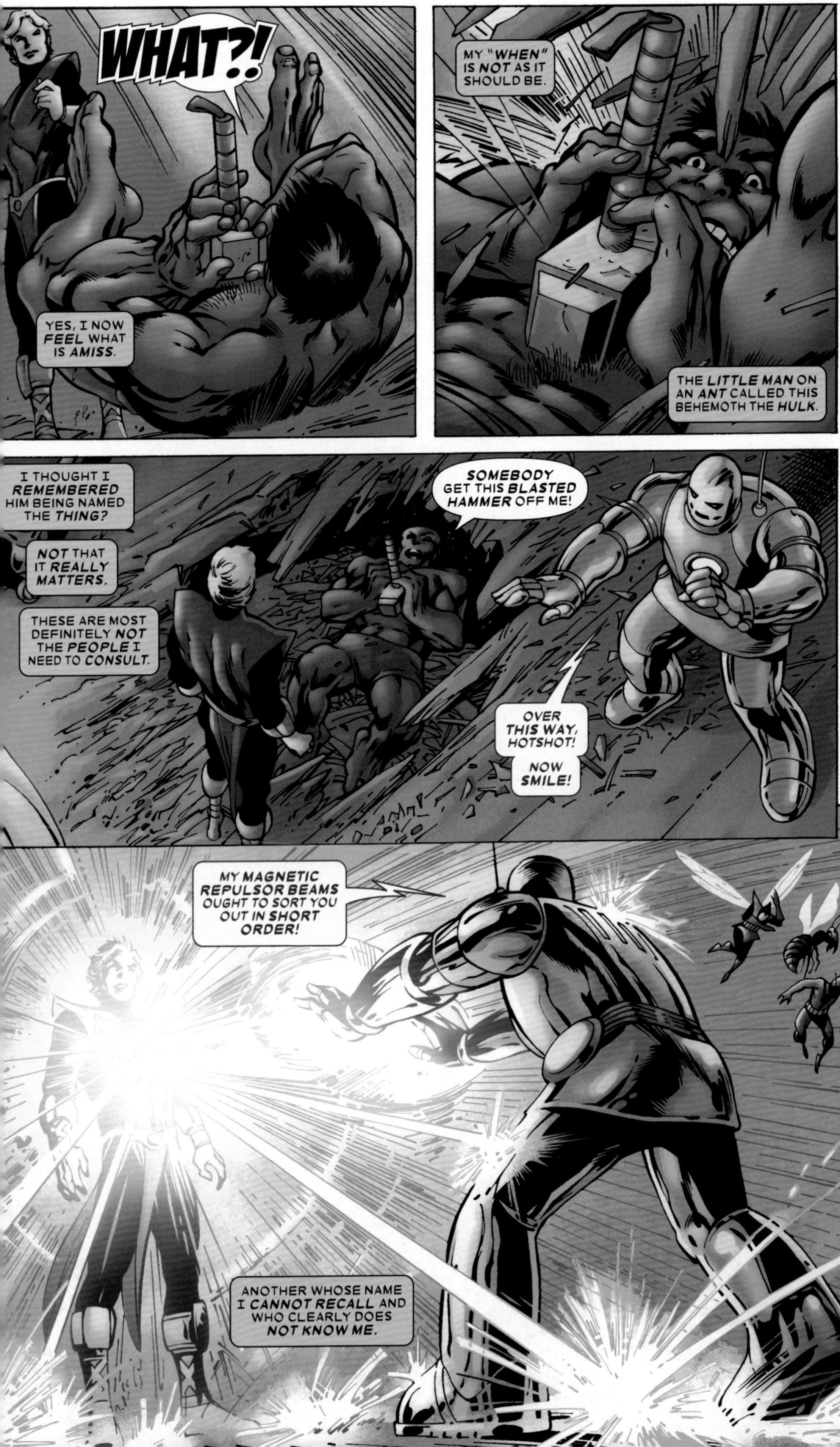

WHAT?!
YES, I NOW FEEL WHAT IS AMISS.
MY "WHEN" IS NOT AS IT SHOULD BE.
THE LITTLE MAN ON AN ANT CALLED THIS BEHEMOTH THE HULK.
I THOUGHT I REMEMBERED HIM BEING NAMED THE THING?
NOT THAT IT REALLY MATTERS.
THESE ARE MOST DEFINITELY NOT THE PEOPLE I NEED TO CONSULT.
SOMEBODY GET THIS BLASTED HAMMER OFF ME!
OVER THIS WAY, HOTSHOT!
NOW SMILE!
MY MAGNETIC REPULSOR BEAMS OUGHT TO SORT YOU OUT IN SHORT ORDER!
ANOTHER WHOSE NAME I CANNOT RECALL AND WHO CLEARLY DOES NOT KNOW ME.

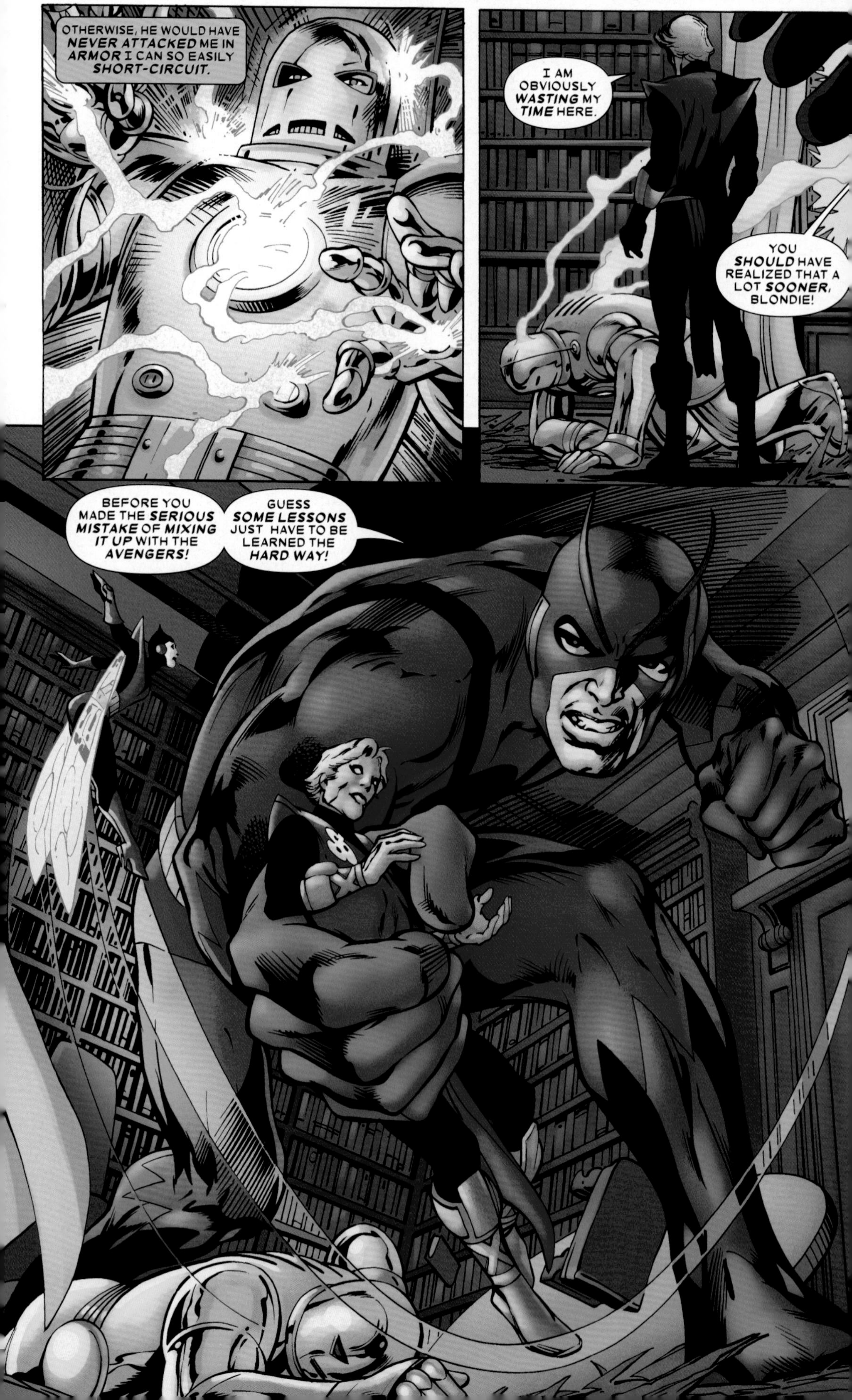
OTHERWISE, HE WOULD HAVE NEVER ATTACKED ME IN ARMOR I CAN SO EASILY SHORT-CIRCUIT.
I AM OBVIOUSLY WASTING MY TIME HERE.
YOU SHOULD HAVE REALIZED THAT A LOT SOONER, BLONDIE!
BEFORE YOU MADE THE SERIOUS MISTAKE OF MIXING IT UP WITH THE AVENGERS!
GUESS SOME LESSONS JUST HAVE TO BE LEARNED THE HARD WAY!

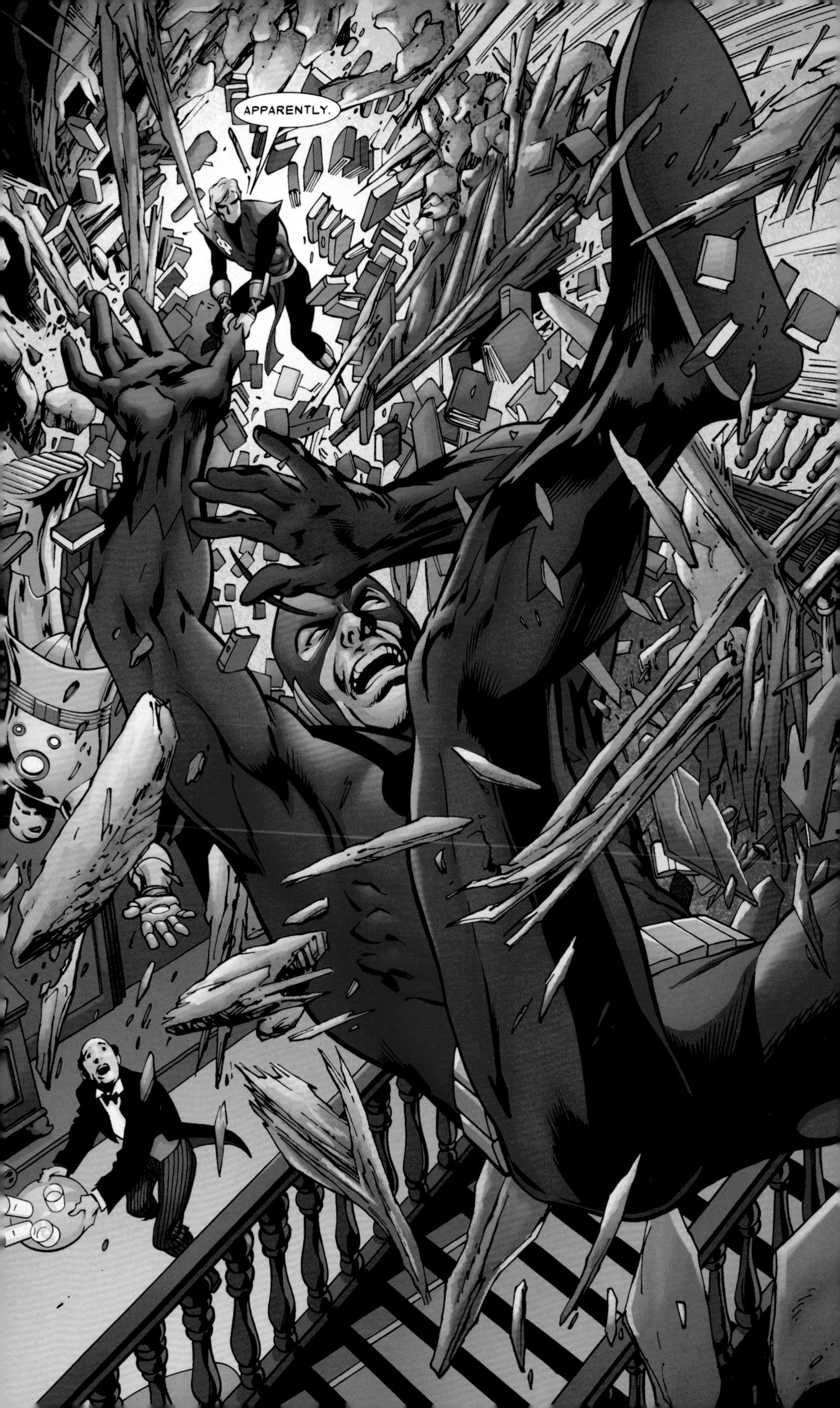
APPARENTLY.

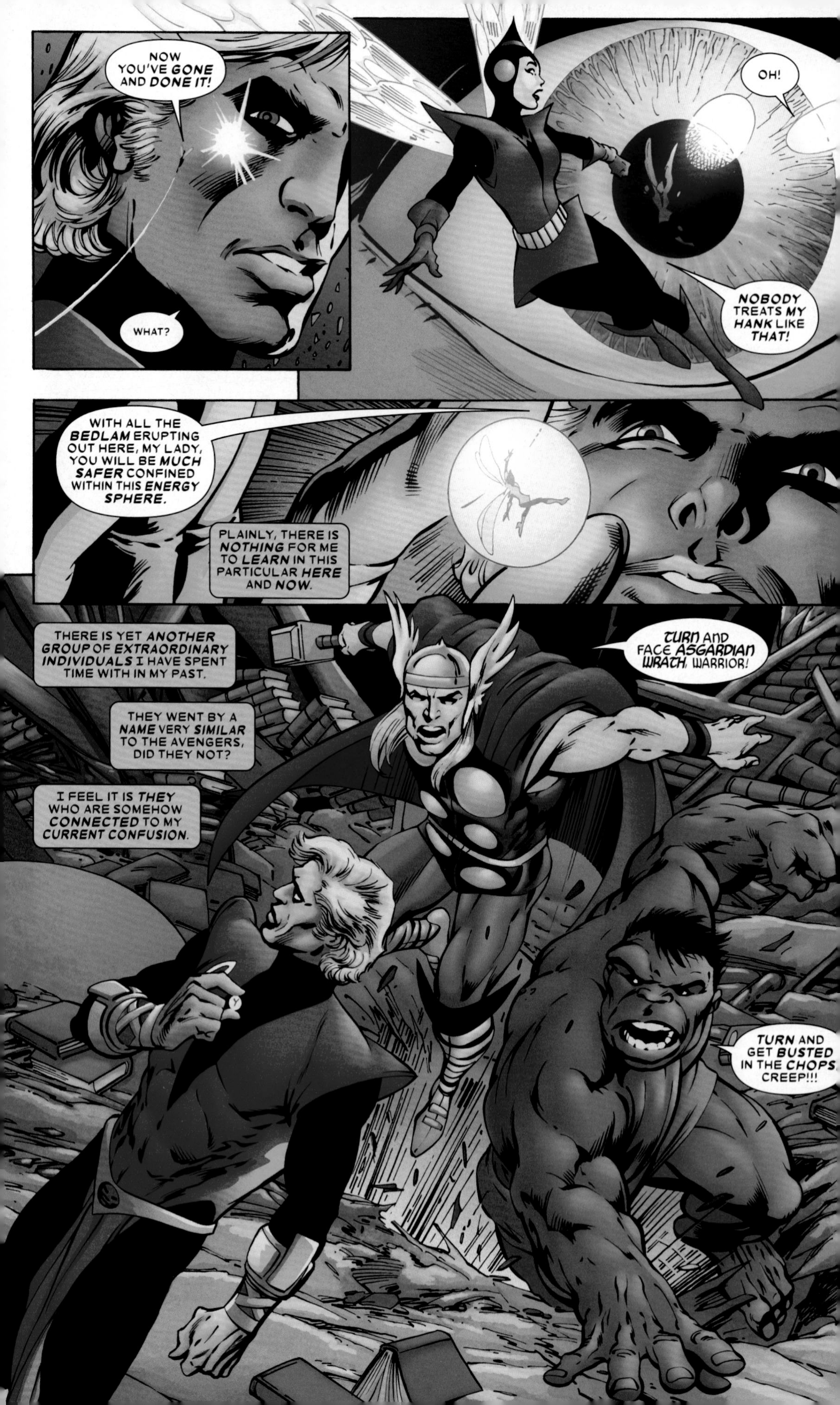
NOW YOU'VE GONE AND DONE IT!
WHAT?
OH!
NOBODY TREATS MY HANK LIKE THAT!
WITH ALL THE BEDLAM ERUPTING OUT HERE, MY LADY, YOU WILL BE MUCH SAFER CONFINED WITHIN THIS ENERGY SPHERE.
PLAINLY, THERE IS NOTHING FOR ME TO LEARN IN THIS PARTICULAR HERE AND NOW.
THERE IS YET ANOTHER GROUP OF EXTRAORDINARY INDIVIDUALS I HAVE SPENT TIME WITH IN MY PAST.
THEY WENT BY A NAME VERY SIMILAR TO THE AVENGERS, DID THEY NOT?
I FEEL IT IS THEY WHO ARE SOMEHOW CONNECTED TO MY CURRENT CONFUSION.
TURN AND FACE ASGARDIAN WRATH, WARRIOR!
TURN AND GET BUSTED IN THE CHOPS, CREEP!!!

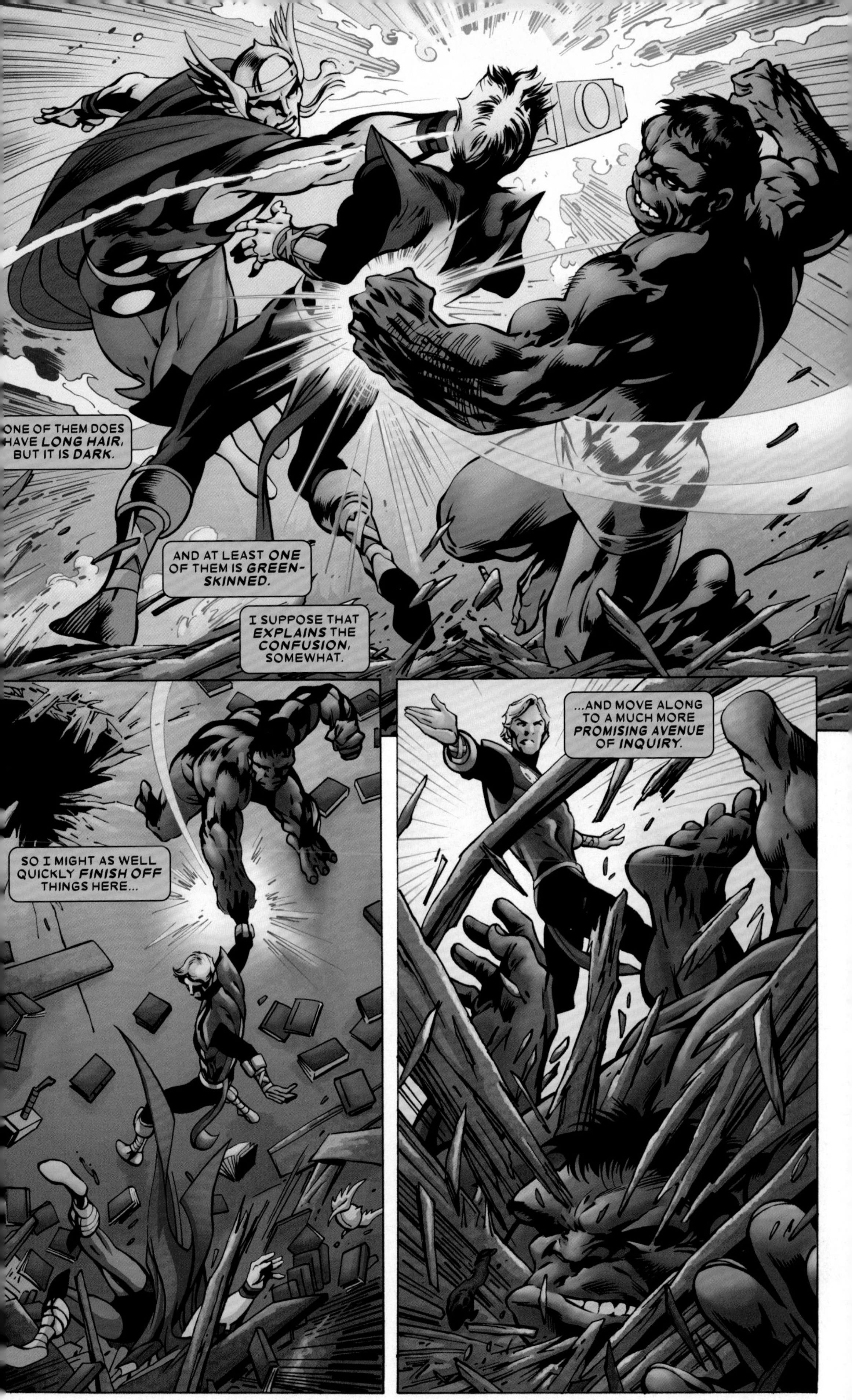
ONE OF THEM DOES HAVE LONG HAIR, BUT IT IS DARK.
AND AT LEAST ONE OF THEM IS GREEN-SKINNED.
I SUPPOSE THAT EXPLAINS THE CONFUSION, SOMEWHAT.
SO I MIGHT AS WELL QUICKLY FINISH OFF THINGS HERE...
...AND MOVE ALONG TO A MUCH MORE PROMISING AVENUE OF INQUIRY.

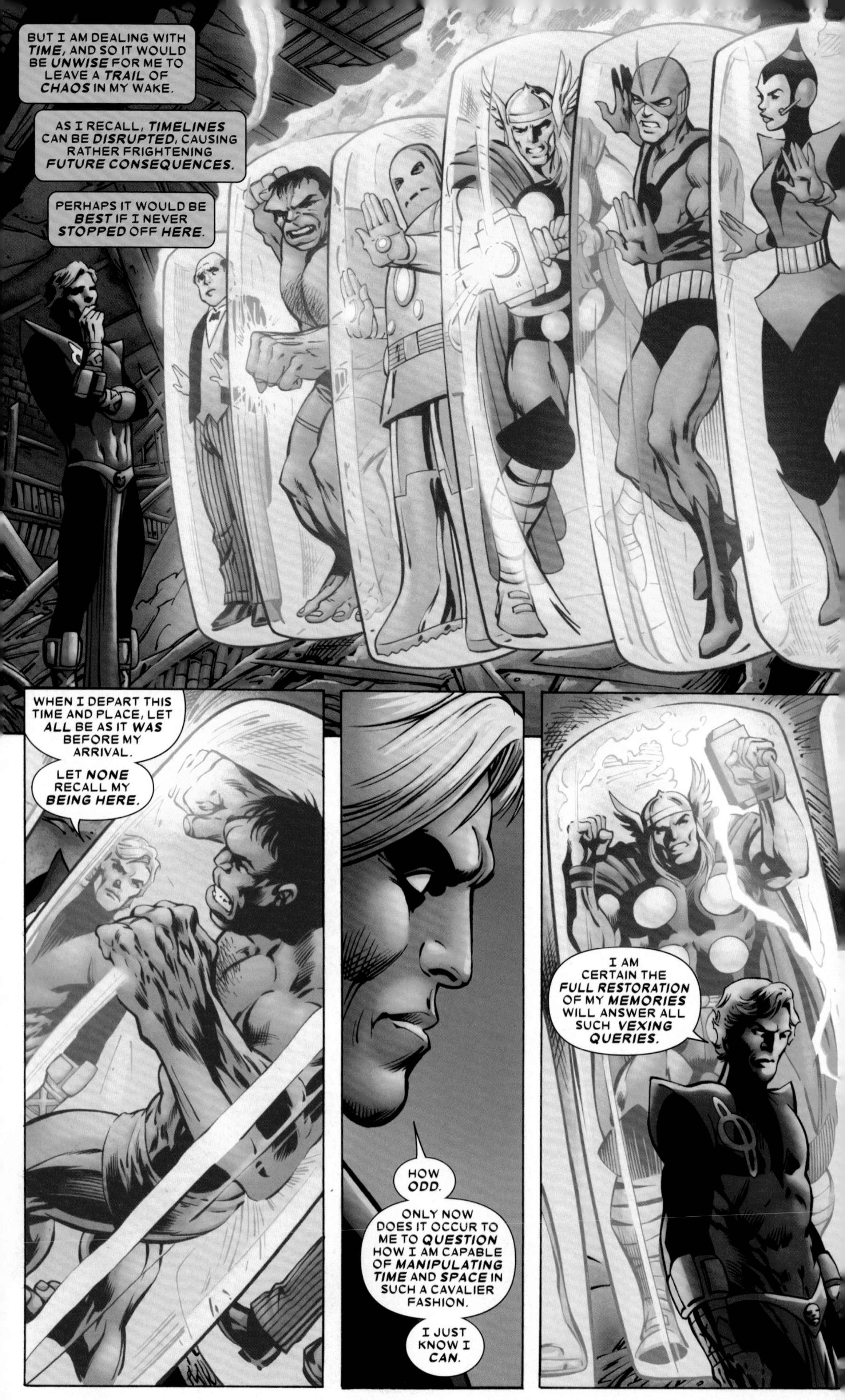
BUT I AM DEALING WITH TIME, AND SO IT WOULD BE UNWISE FOR ME TO LEAVE A TRAIL OF CHAOS IN MY WAKE.
AS I RECALL, TIMELINES CAN BE DISRUPTED, CAUSING RATHER FRIGHTENING FUTURE CONSEQUENCES.
PERHAPS IT WOULD BE BEST IF I NEVER STOPPED OFF HERE.
WHEN I DEPART THIS TIME AND PLACE, LET ALL BE AS IT WAS BEFORE MY ARRIVAL.
LET NONE RECALL MY BEING HERE.
HOW ODD.
ONLY NOW DOES IT OCCUR TO ME TO QUESTION HOW I AM CAPABLE OF MANIPULATING TIME AND SPACE IN SUCH A CAVALIER FASHION.
I JUST KNOW I CAN.
I AM CERTAIN THE FULL RESTORATION OF MY MEMORIES WILL ANSWER ALL SUCH VEXING QUERIES.

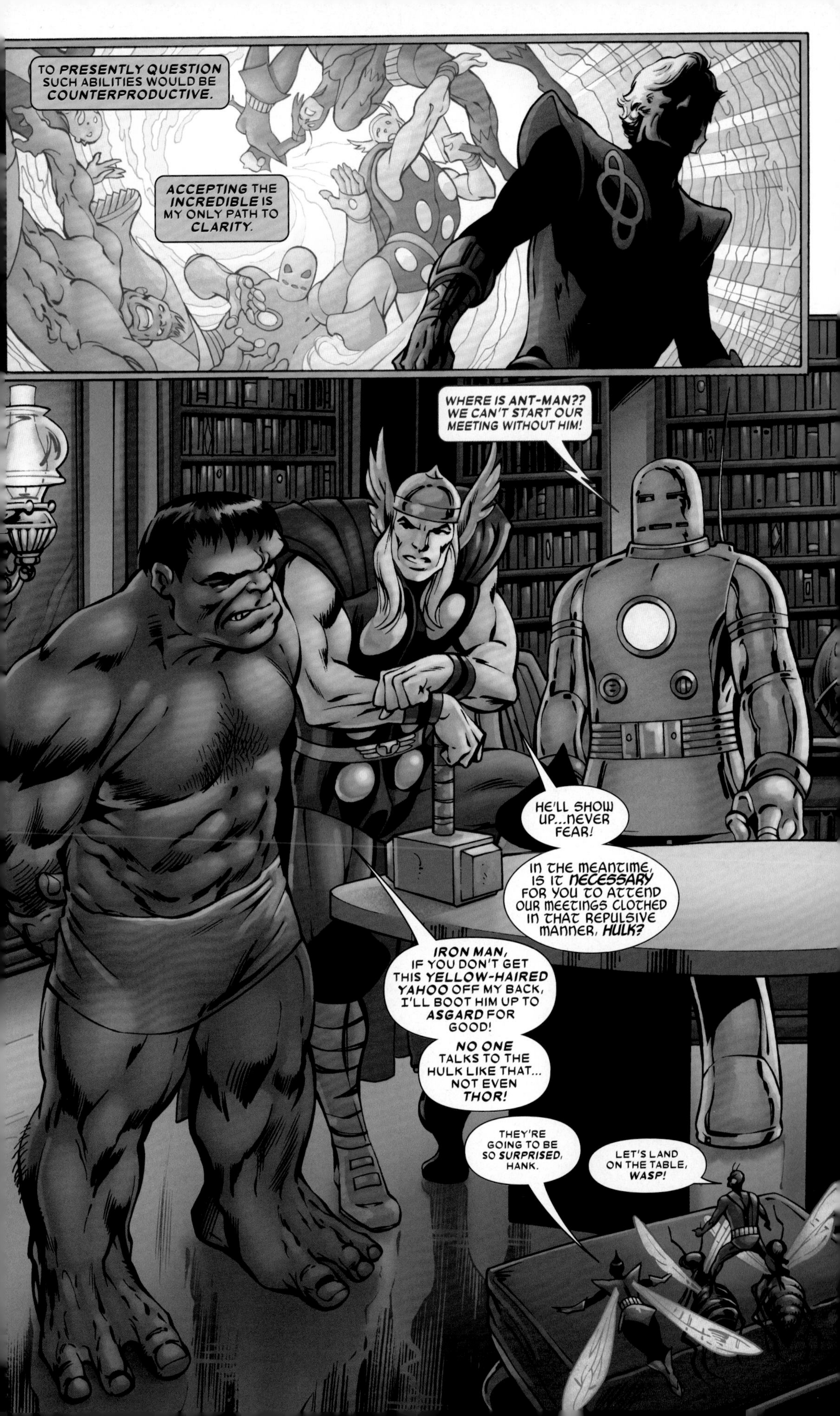
TO PRESENTLY QUESTION SUCH ABILITIES WOULD BE COUNTERPRODUCTIVE.
ACCEPTING THE INCREDIBLE IS MY ONLY PATH TO CLARITY.
WHERE IS ANT-MAN?? WE CAN'T START OUR MEETING WITHOUT HIM!
HE'LL SHOW UP...NEVER FEAR!
IN THE MEANTIME, IS IT NECESSARY FOR YOU TO ATTEND OUR MEETINGS CLOTHED IN THAT REPULSIVE MANNER, HULK?
IRON MAN, IF YOU DON'T GET THIS YELLOW-HAIRED YAHOO OFF MY BACK, I'LL BOOT HIM UP TO ASGARD FOR GOOD!
NO ONE TALKS TO THE HULK LIKE THAT... NOT EVEN THOR!
THEY'RE GOING TO BE SO SURPRISED, HANK.
LET'S LAND ON THE TABLE, WASP!

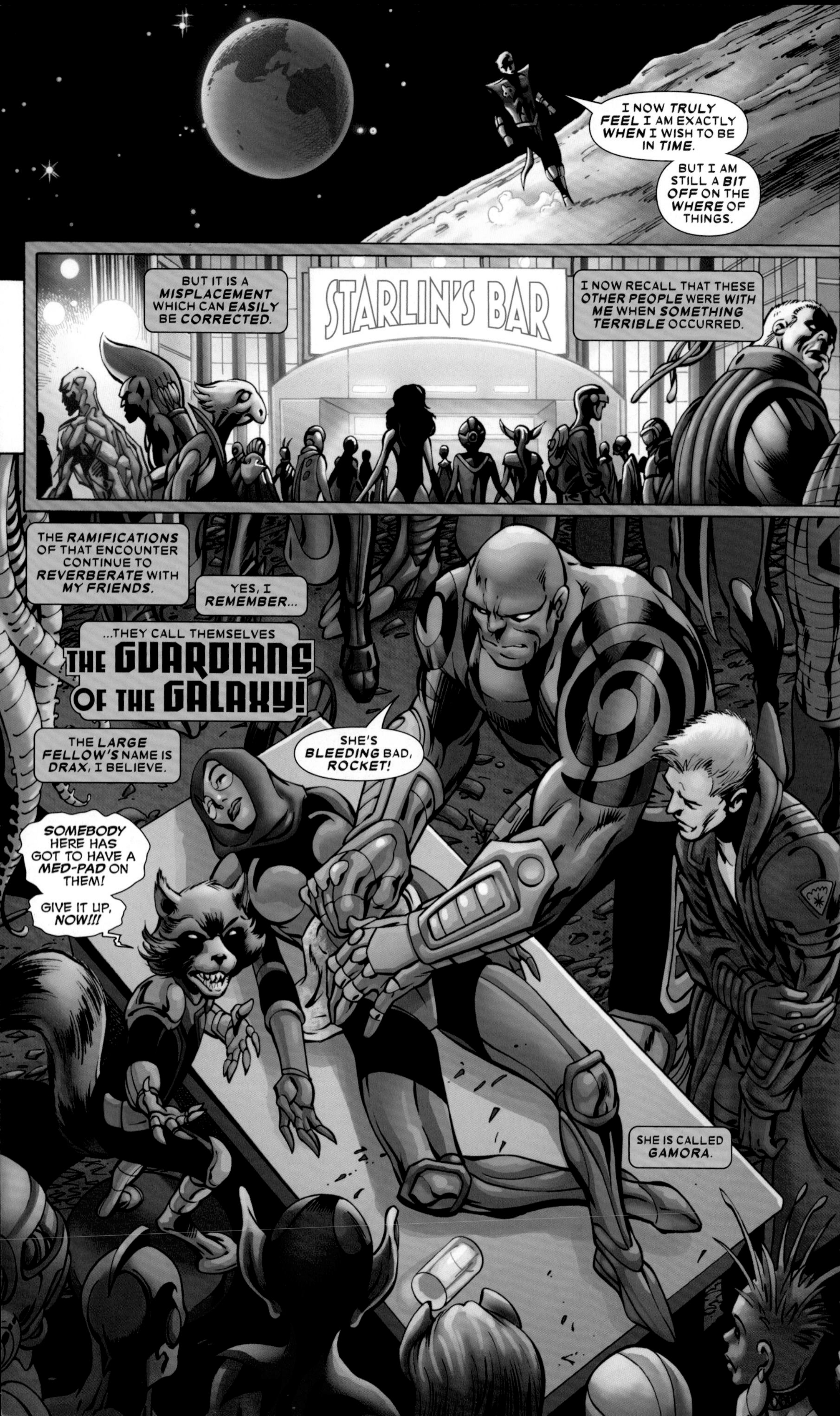
I NOW TRULY FEEL I AM EXACTLY WHEN I WISH TO BE IN TIME.
BUT I AM STILL A BIT OFF ON THE WHERE OF THINGS.
BUT IT IS A MISPLACEMENT WHICH CAN EASILY BE CORRECTED.
STARLIN'S BAR
I NOW RECALL THAT THESE OTHER PEOPLE WERE WITH ME WHEN SOMETHING TERRIBLE OCCURRED.
THE RAMIFICATIONS OF THAT ENCOUNTER CONTINUE TO REVERBERATE WITH MY FRIENDS.
YES, I REMEMBER...
...THEY CALL THEMSELVES THE GUARDIANS OF THE GALAXY!
THE LARGE FELLOW'S NAME IS DRAX, I BELIEVE.
SHE'S BLEEDING BAD, ROCKET!
SOMEBODY HERE HAS GOT TO HAVE A MED-PAD ON THEM!
GIVE IT UP, NOW!!!
SHE IS CALLED GAMORA.

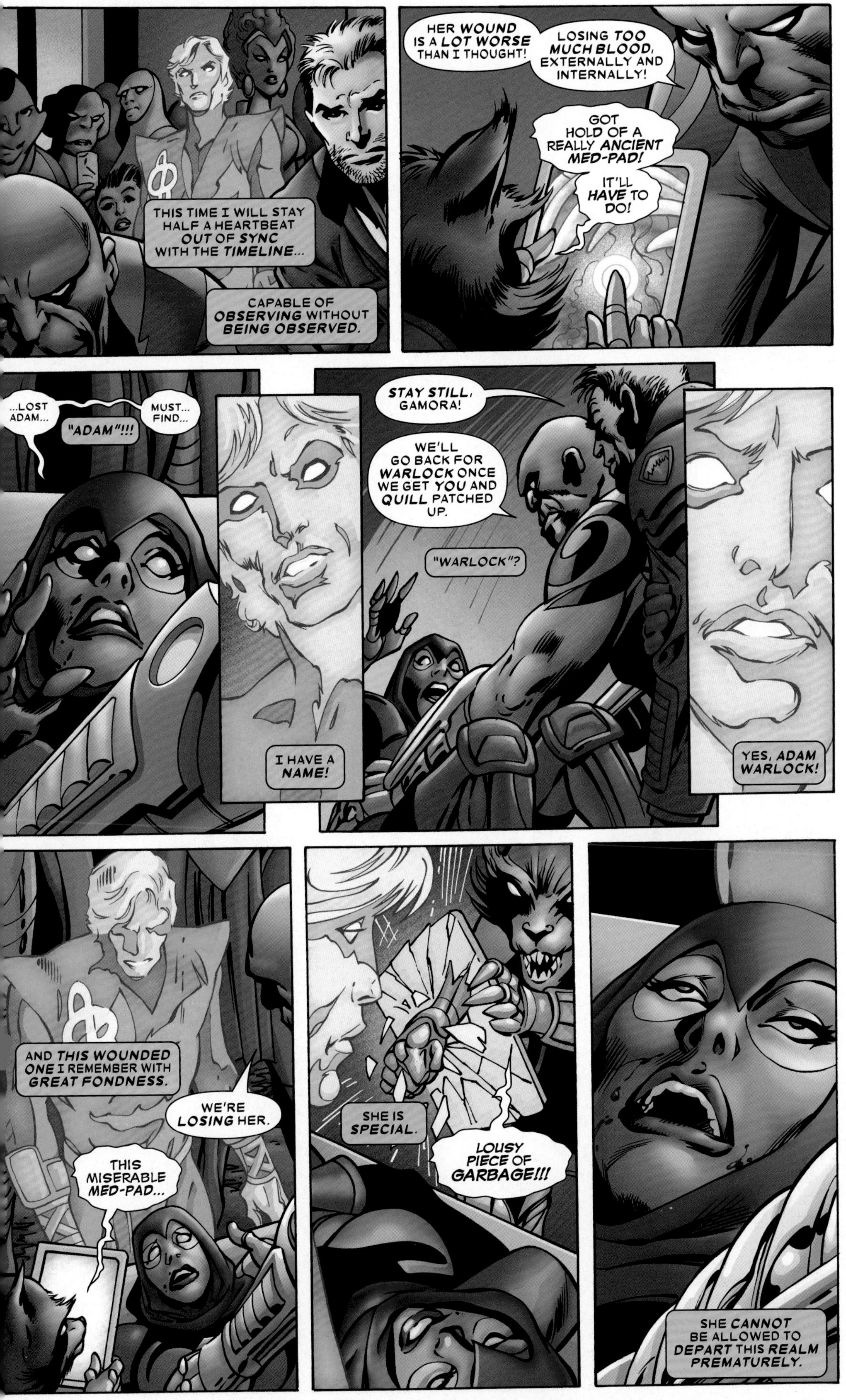

THIS TIME I WILL STAY HALF A HEARTBEAT OUT OF SYNC WITH THE TIMELINE...
CAPABLE OF OBSERVING WITHOUT BEING OBSERVED.
HER WOUND IS A LOT WORSE THAN I THOUGHT!
LOSING TOO MUCH BLOOD, EXTERNALLY AND INTERNALLY!
GOT HOLD OF A REALLY ANCIENT MED-PAD!
IT'LL HAVE TO DO!
...LOST ADAM...
MUST... FIND...
"ADAM"!!!
I HAVE A NAME!
STAY STILL, GAMORA!
WE'LL GO BACK FOR WARLOCK ONCE WE GET YOU AND QUILL PATCHED UP.
"WARLOCK"?
YES, ADAM WARLOCK!
AND THIS WOUNDED ONE I REMEMBER WITH GREAT FONDNESS.
WE'RE LOSING HER.
THIS MISERABLE MED-PAD...
SHE IS SPECIAL.
LOUSY PIECE OF GARBAGE!!!
SHE CANNOT BE ALLOWED TO DEPART THIS REALM PREMATURELY.

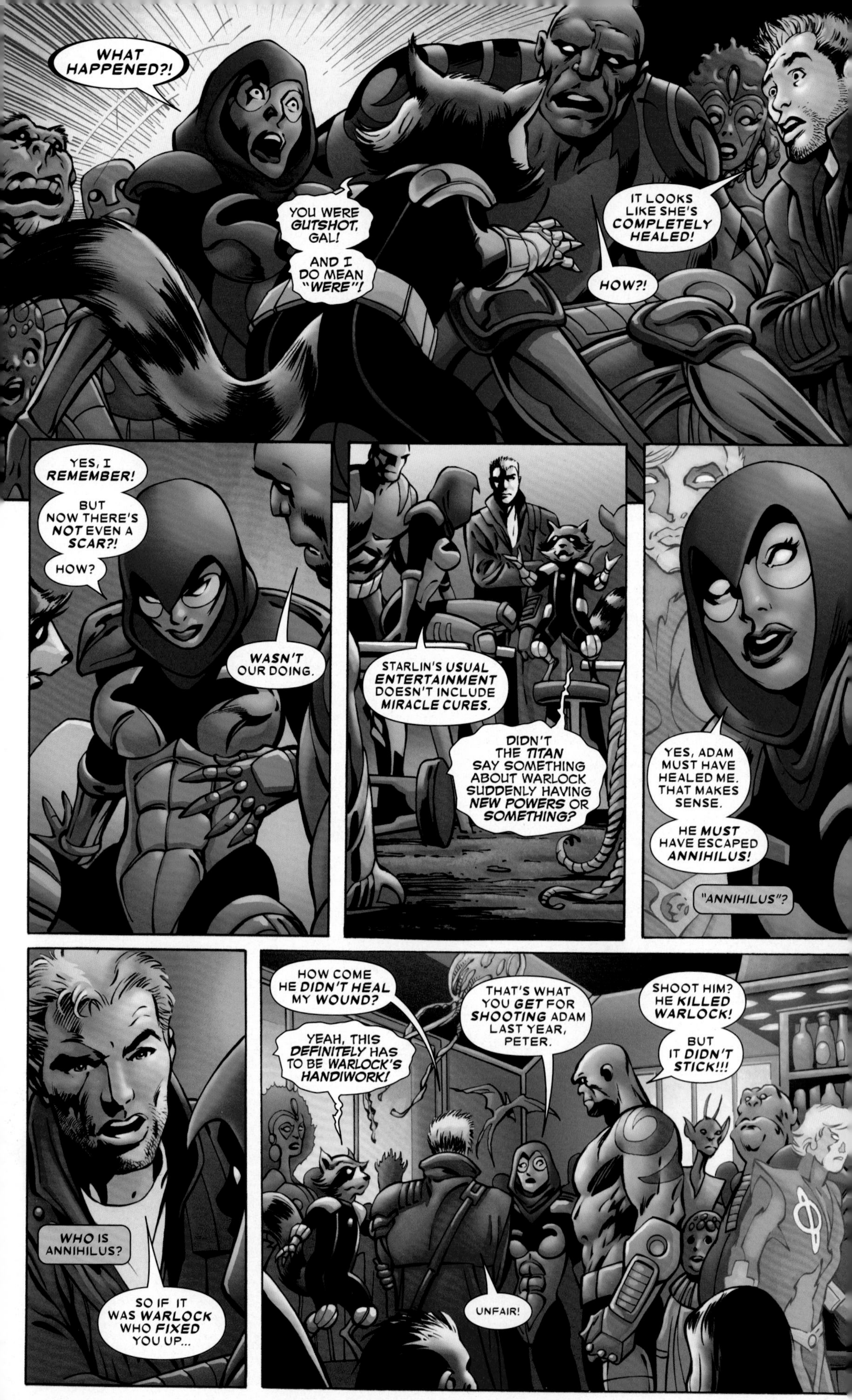

WHAT HAPPENED?!
YOU WERE GUTSHOT, GAL!
AND I DO MEAN "WERE"!
IT LOOKS LIKE SHE'S COMPLETELY HEALED!
HOW?!
YES, I REMEMBER!
BUT NOW THERE'S NOT EVEN A SCAR?!
HOW?
WASN'T OUR DOING.
STARLIN'S USUAL ENTERTAINMENT DOESN'T INCLUDE MIRACLE CURES.
DIDN'T THE TITAN SAY SOMETHING ABOUT WARLOCK SUDDENLY HAVING NEW POWERS OR SOMETHING?
YES, ADAM MUST HAVE HEALED ME. THAT MAKES SENSE.
HE MUST HAVE ESCAPED ANNIHILUS!
"ANNIHILUS"?
WHO IS ANNIHILUS?
SO IF IT WAS WARLOCK WHO FIXED YOU UP...
HOW COME HE DIDN'T HEAL MY WOUND?
YEAH, THIS DEFINITELY HAS TO BE WARLOCK'S HANDIWORK!
THAT'S WHAT YOU GET FOR SHOOTING ADAM LAST YEAR, PETER.
UNFAIR!
SHOOT HIM? HE KILLED WARLOCK!
BUT IT DIDN'T STICK!!!

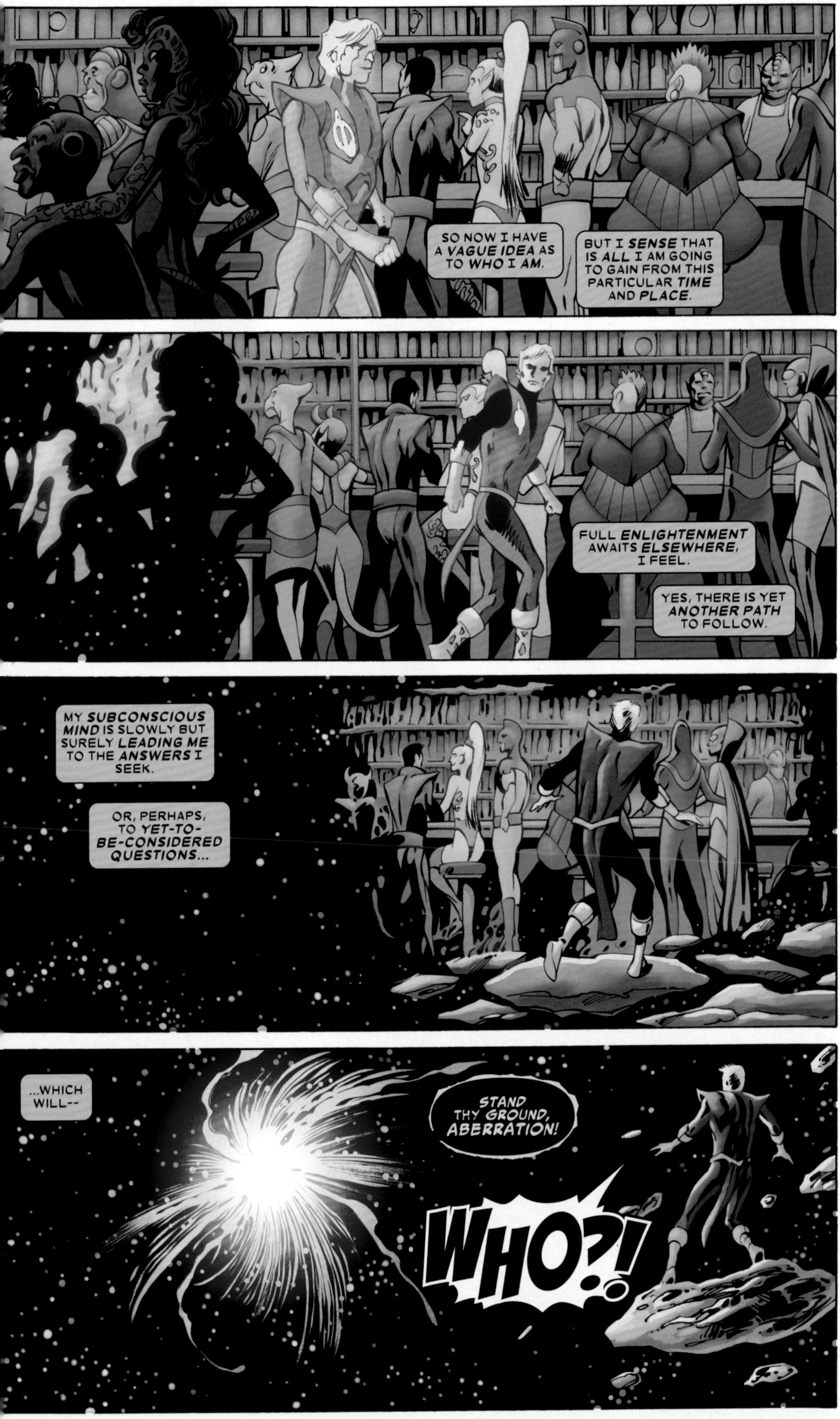
SO NOW I HAVE A VAGUE IDEA AS TO WHO I AM.
BUT I SENSE THAT IS ALL I AM GOING TO GAIN FROM THIS PARTICULAR TIME AND PLACE.
FULL ENLIGHTENMENT AWAITS ELSEWHERE, I FEEL.
YES, THERE IS YET ANOTHER PATH TO FOLLOW.
MY SUBCONSCIOUS MIND IS SLOWLY BUT SURELY LEADING ME TO THE ANSWERS I SEEK.
OR, PERHAPS, TO YET-TO-BE-CONSIDERED QUESTIONS...
...WHICH WILL--
STAND THY GROUND, ABERRATION!
WHO?!

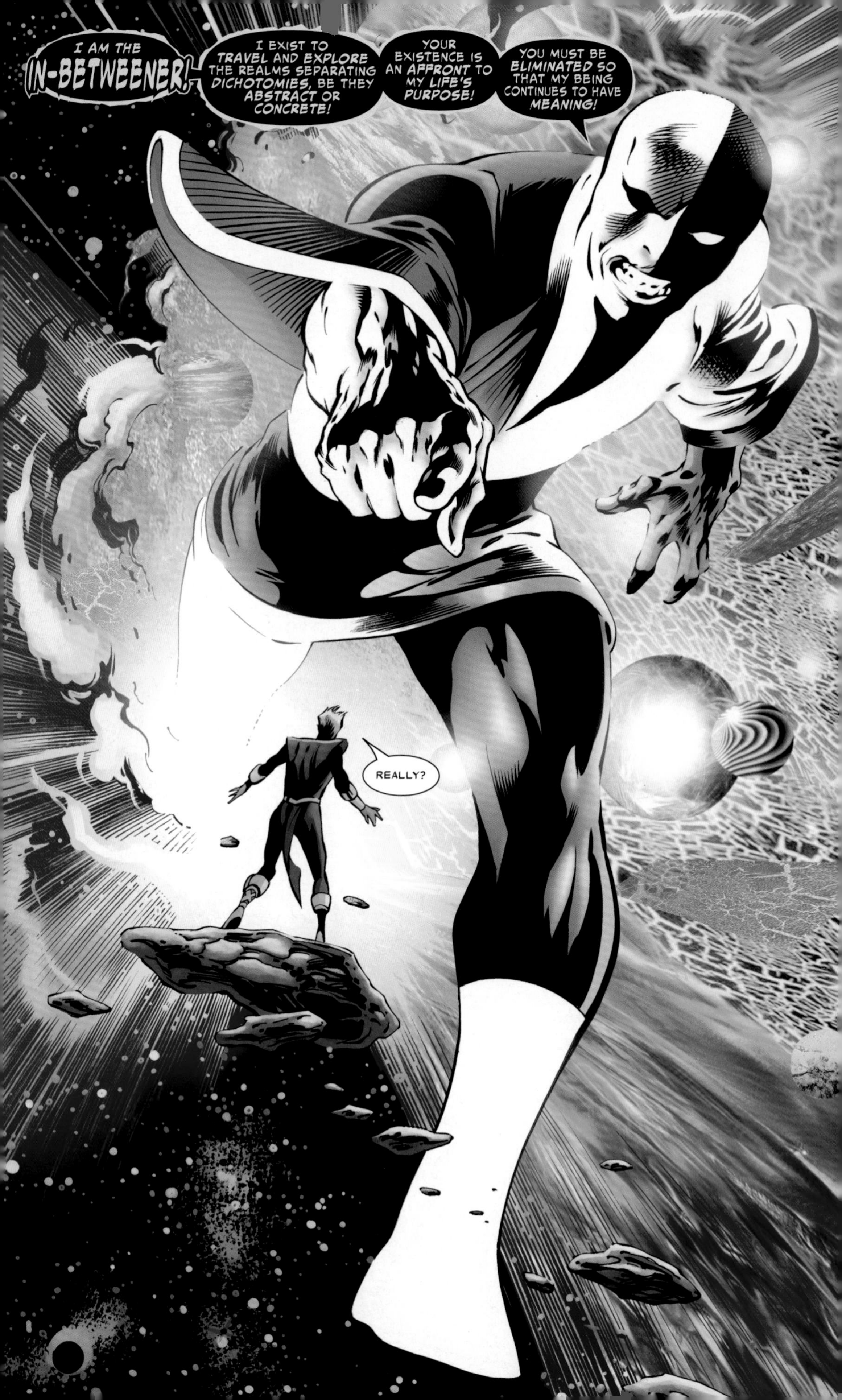
I AM THE IN-BETWEENER!
I EXIST TO TRAVEL AND EXPLORE THE REALMS SEPARATING DICHOTOMIES, BE THEY ABSTRACT OR CONCRETE!
YOUR EXISTENCE IS AN AFFRONT TO MY LIFE'S PURPOSE!
YOU MUST BE ELIMINATED SO THAT MY BEING CONTINUES TO HAVE MEANING!
REALLY?

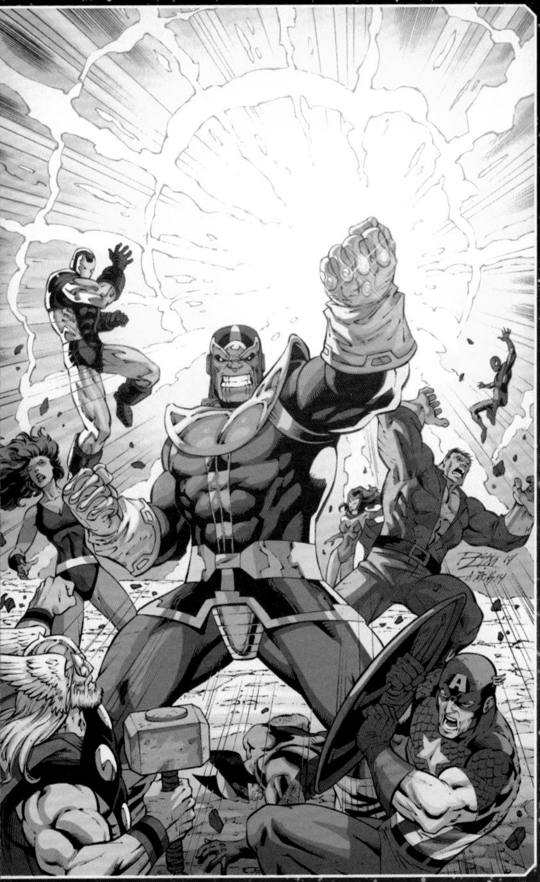

Thanos Annual 1 variant by Ron Lim, Andy Smith & Brad Anderson

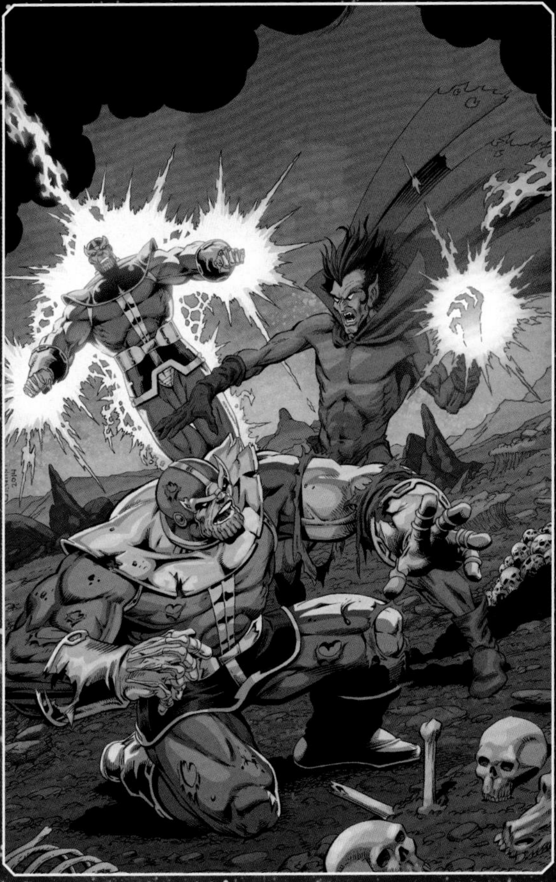

Thanos Annual 1 variant by Jim Starlin, Al Milgrom & Brad Anderson

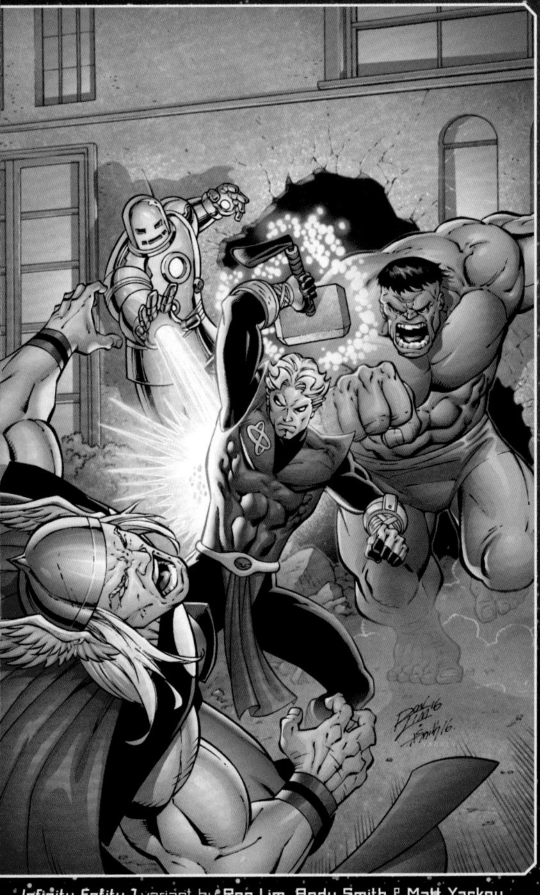

Infinity Entity 1 variant by Ron Lim, Andy Smith & Matt Yackey

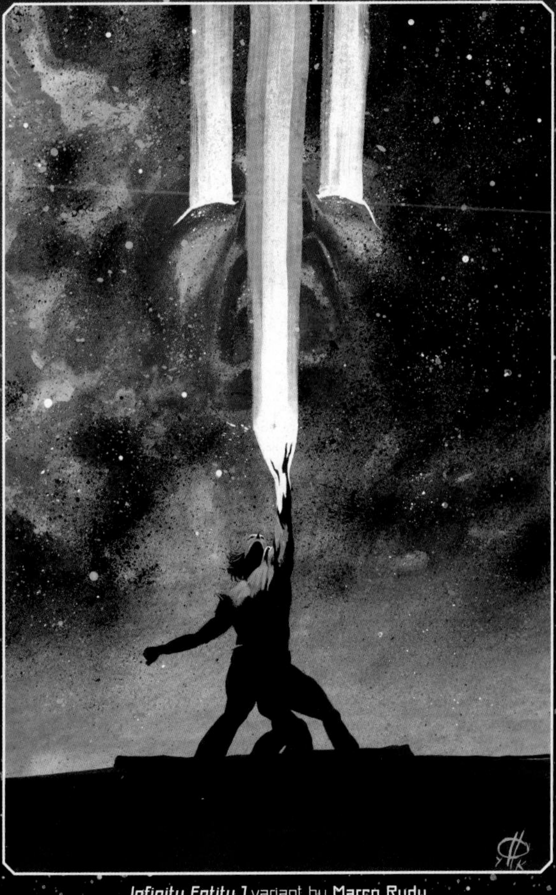

Infinity Entity 1 variant by Marco Rudy

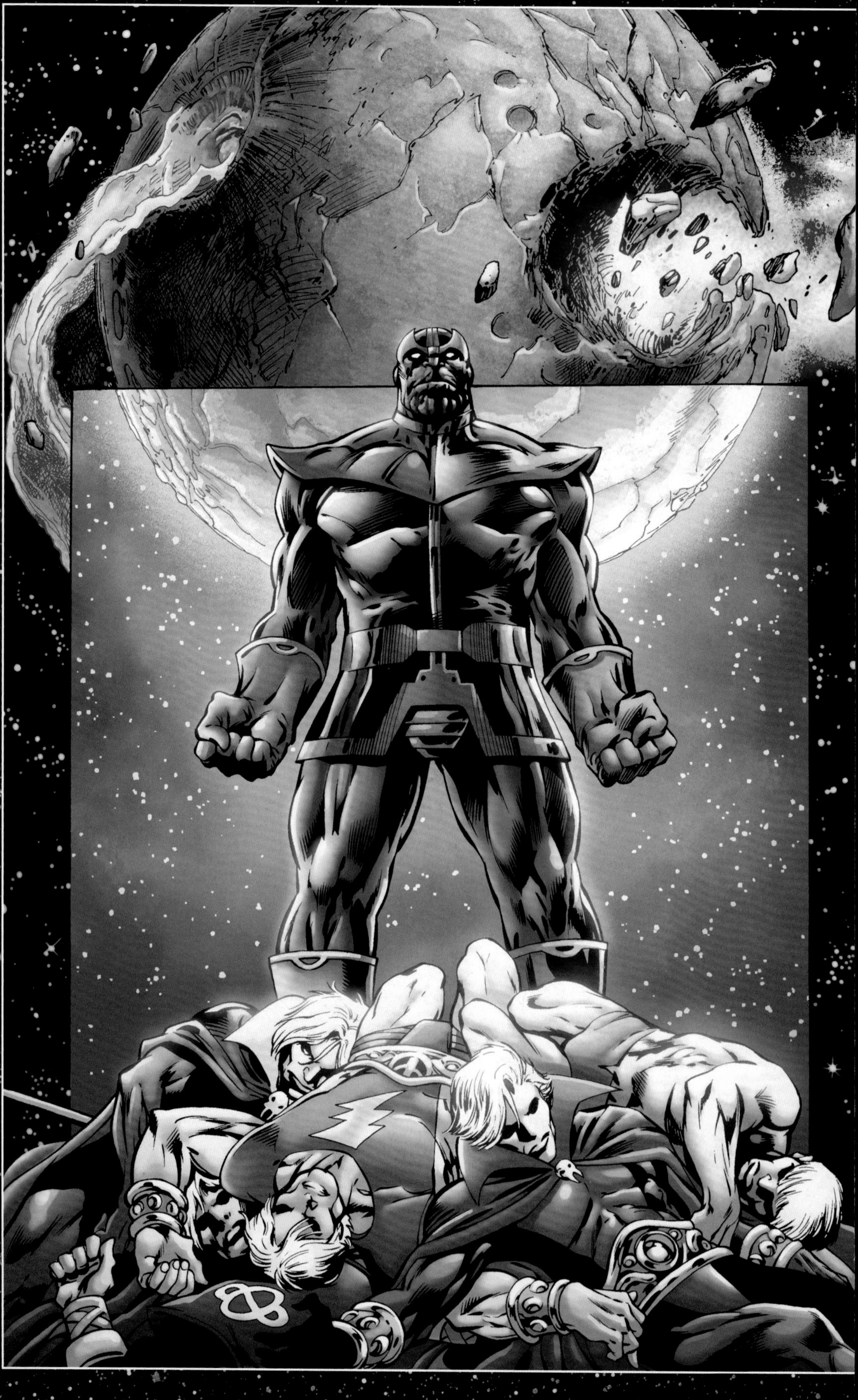

2: OVERLOAD

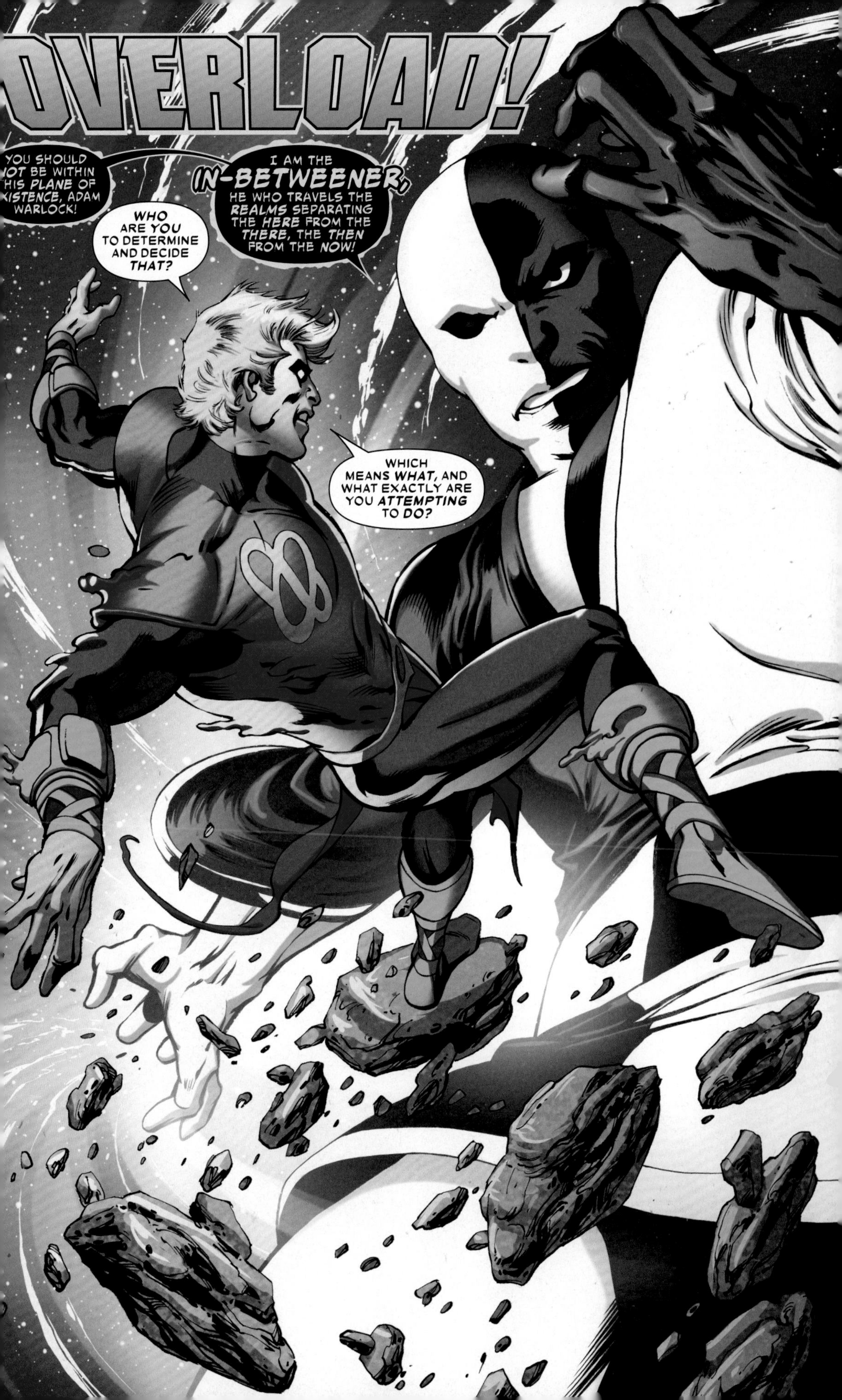
OVERLOAD!
YOU SHOULD NOT BE WITHIN THIS PLANE OF EXISTENCE, ADAM WARLOCK!
I AM THE IN-BETWEENER, HE WHO TRAVELS THE REALMS SEPARATING THE HERE FROM THE THERE, THE THEN FROM THE NOW!
WHO ARE YOU TO DETERMINE AND DECIDE THAT?
WHICH MEANS WHAT, AND WHAT EXACTLY ARE YOU ATTEMPTING TO DO?

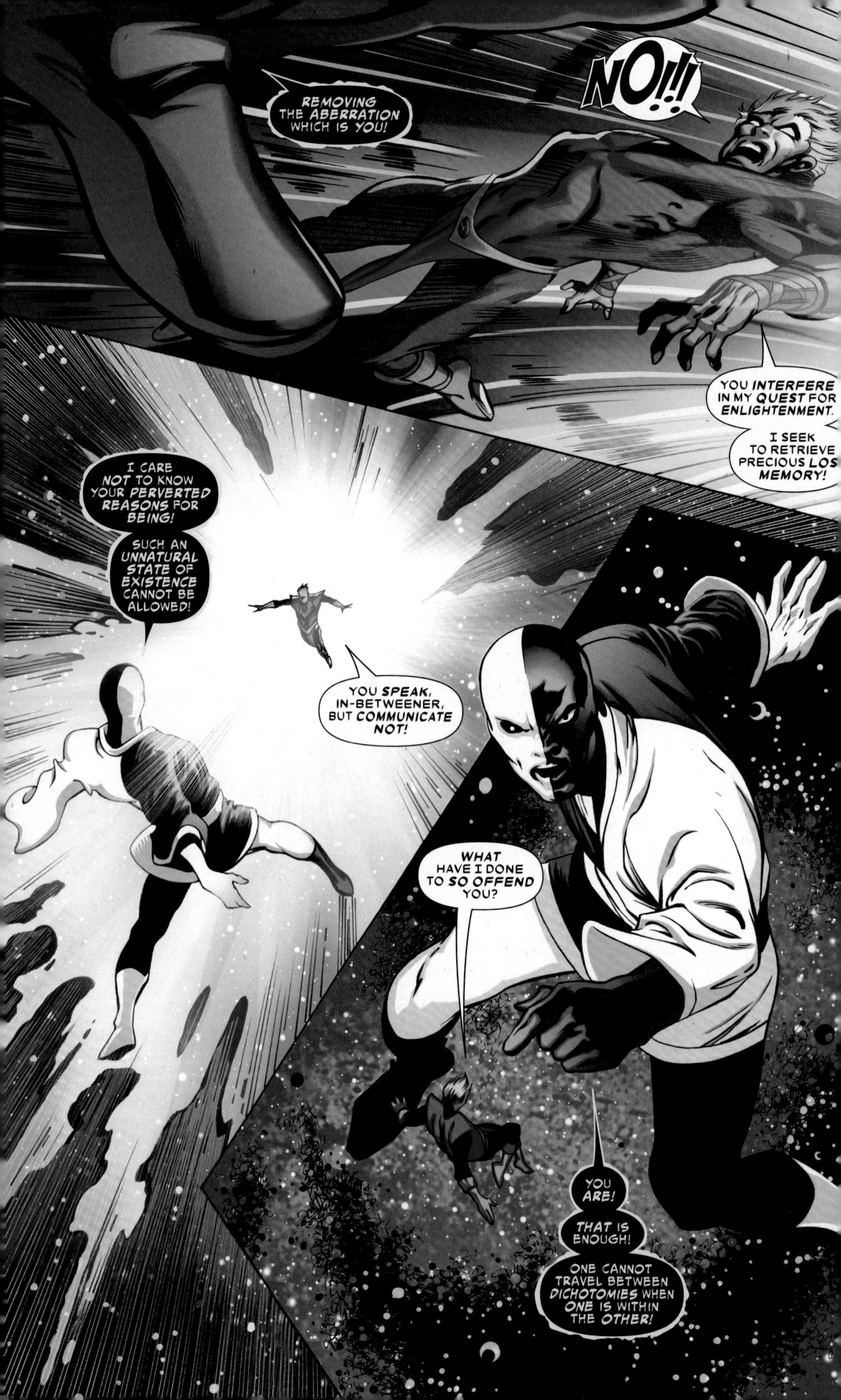

REMOVING THE ABERRATION WHICH IS YOU!
NO!!!
YOU INTERFERE IN MY QUEST FOR ENLIGHTENMENT.
I SEEK TO RETRIEVE PRECIOUS LOS MEMORY!
I CARE NOT TO KNOW YOUR PERVERTED REASONS FOR BEING!
SUCH AN UNNATURAL STATE OF EXISTENCE CANNOT BE ALLOWED!
YOU SPEAK, IN-BETWEENER, BUT COMMUNICATE NOT!
WHAT HAVE I DONE TO SO OFFEND YOU?
YOU ARE!
THAT IS ENOUGH!
ONE CANNOT TRAVEL BETWEEN DICHOTOMIES WHEN ONE IS WITHIN THE OTHER!

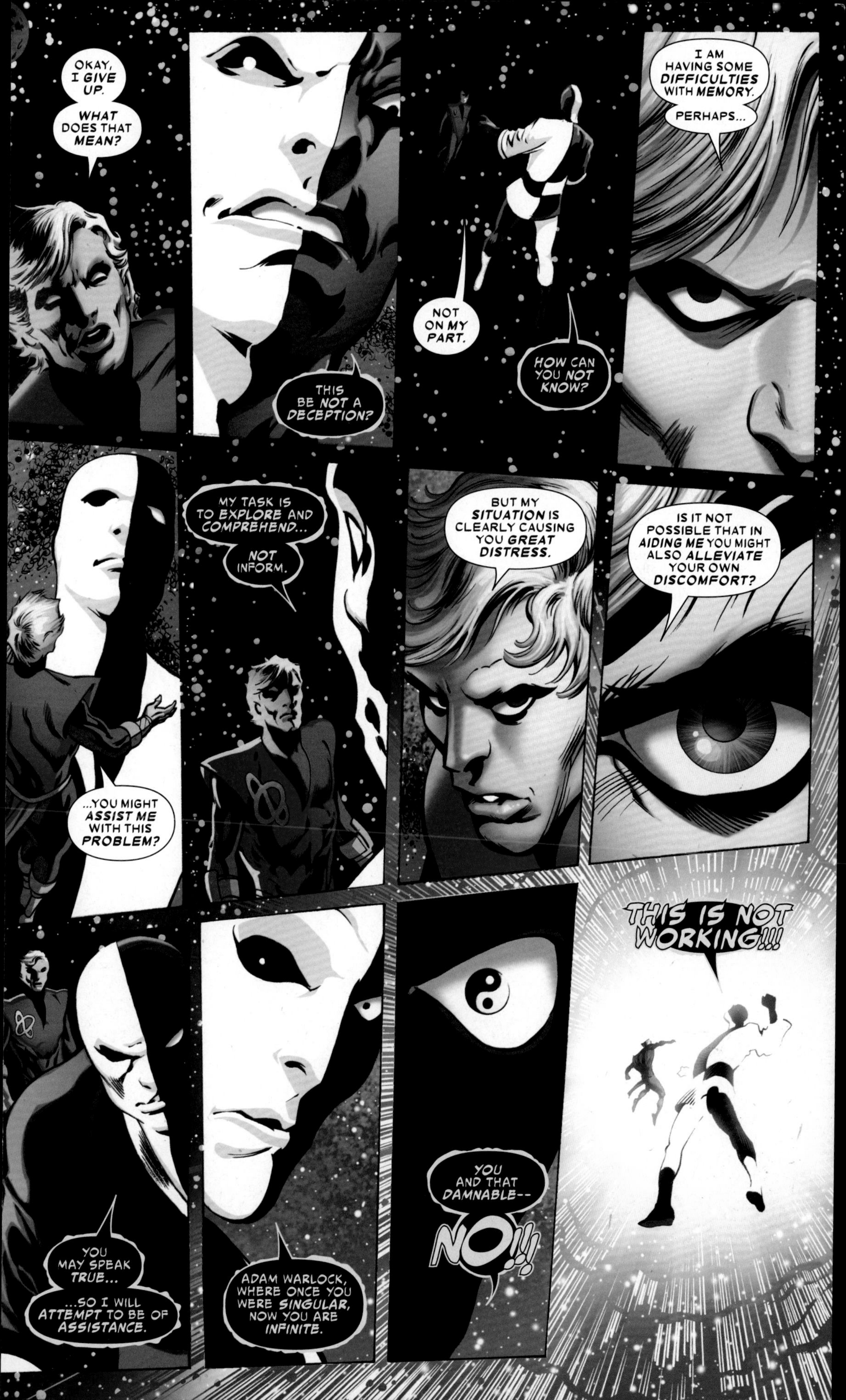
OKAY, I GIVE UP.
WHAT DOES THAT MEAN?
THIS BE NOT A DECEPTION?
NOT ON MY PART.
HOW CAN YOU NOT KNOW?
I AM HAVING SOME DIFFICULTIES WITH MEMORY.
PERHAPS...
...YOU MIGHT ASSIST ME WITH THIS PROBLEM?
MY TASK IS TO EXPLORE AND COMPREHEND...
NOT INFORM.
BUT MY SITUATION IS CLEARLY CAUSING YOU GREAT DISTRESS.
IS IT NOT POSSIBLE THAT IN AIDING ME YOU MIGHT ALSO ALLEVIATE YOUR OWN DISCOMFORT?
YOU MAY SPEAK TRUE...
...SO I WILL ATTEMPT TO BE OF ASSISTANCE.
ADAM WARLOCK, WHERE ONCE YOU WERE SINGULAR, NOW YOU ARE INFINITE.
YOU AND THAT DAMNABLE--
NO!!!
THIS IS NOT WORKING!!!

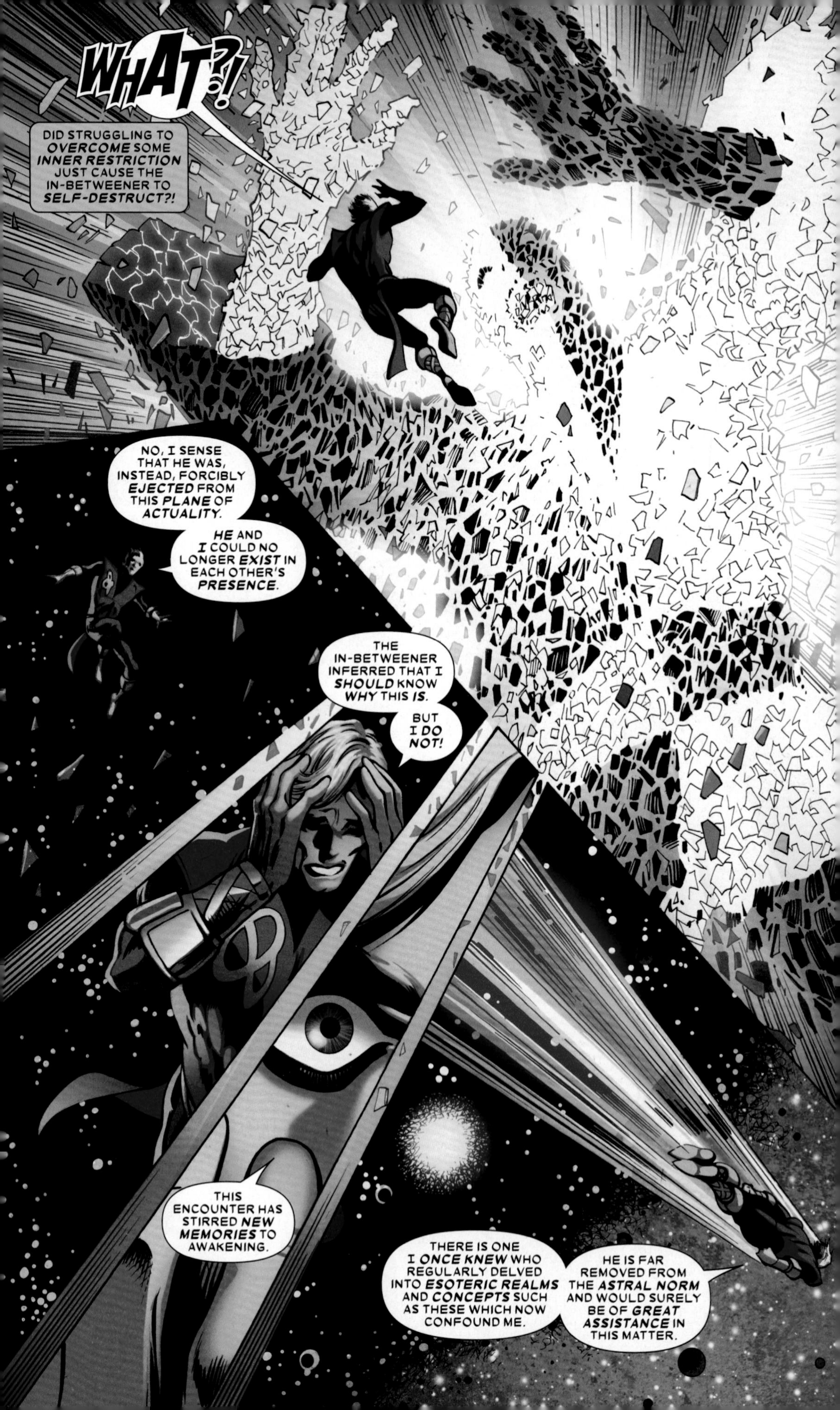
WHAT?!
DID STRUGGLING TO OVERCOME SOME INNER RESTRICTION JUST CAUSE THE IN-BETWEENER TO SELF-DESTRUCT?!
NO, I SENSE THAT HE WAS, INSTEAD, FORCIBLY EJECTED FROM THIS PLANE OF ACTUALITY.
HE AND I COULD NO LONGER EXIST IN EACH OTHER'S PRESENCE.
THE IN-BETWEENER INFERRED THAT I SHOULD KNOW WHY THIS IS.
BUT I DO NOT!
THIS ENCOUNTER HAS STIRRED NEW MEMORIES TO AWAKENING.
THERE IS ONE I ONCE KNEW WHO REGULARLY DELVED INTO ESOTERIC REALMS AND CONCEPTS SUCH AS THESE WHICH NOW CONFOUND ME.
HE IS FAR REMOVED FROM THE ASTRAL NORM AND WOULD SURELY BE OF GREAT ASSISTANCE IN THIS MATTER.

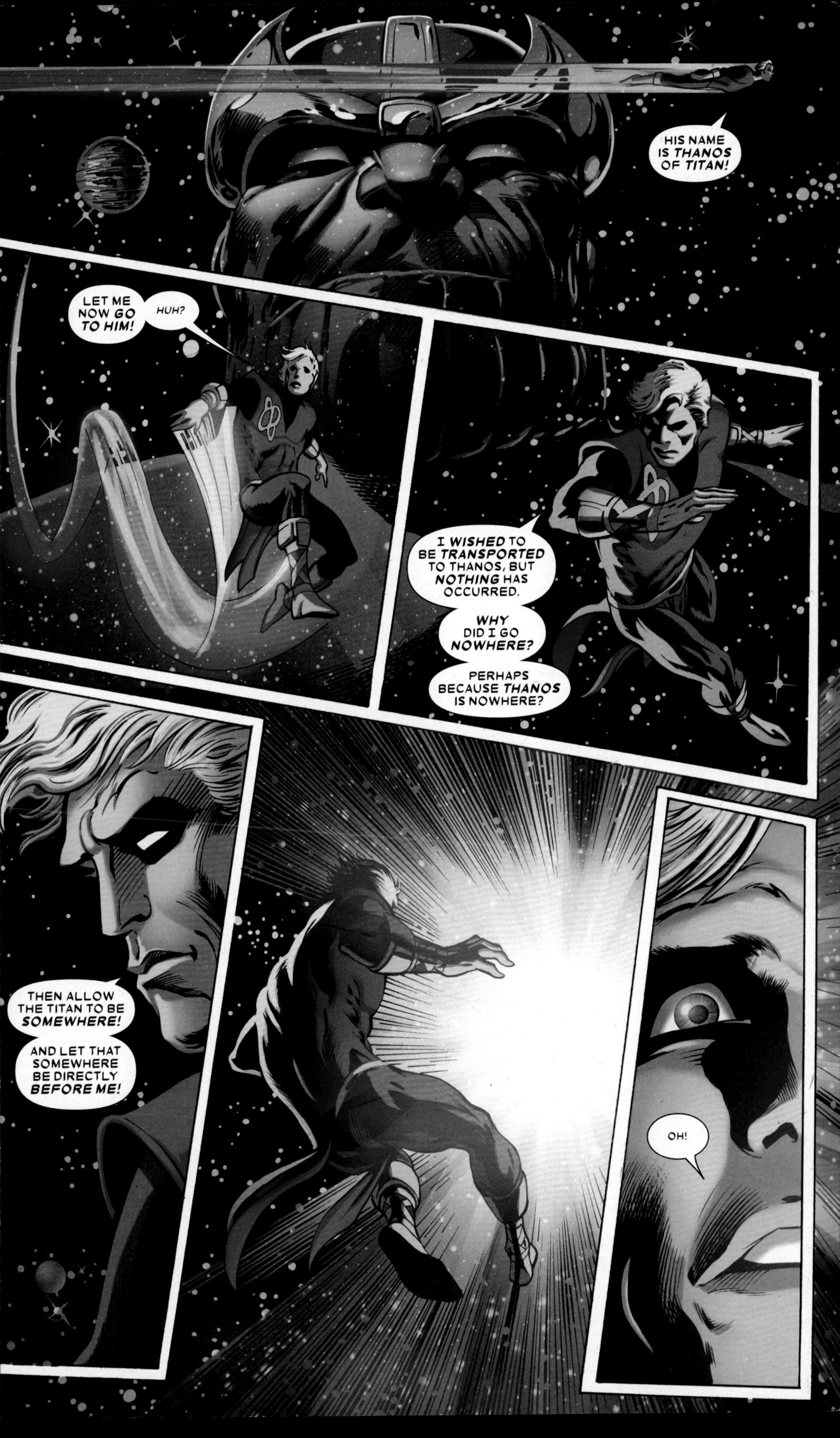
HIS NAME IS THANOS OF TITAN!
LET ME NOW GO TO HIM!
HUH?
I WISHED TO BE TRANSPORTED TO THANOS, BUT NOTHING HAS OCCURRED.
WHY DID I GO NOWHERE?
PERHAPS BECAUSE THANOS IS NOWHERE?
THEN ALLOW THE TITAN TO BE SOMEWHERE!
AND LET THAT SOMEWHERE BE DIRECTLY BEFORE ME!
OH!

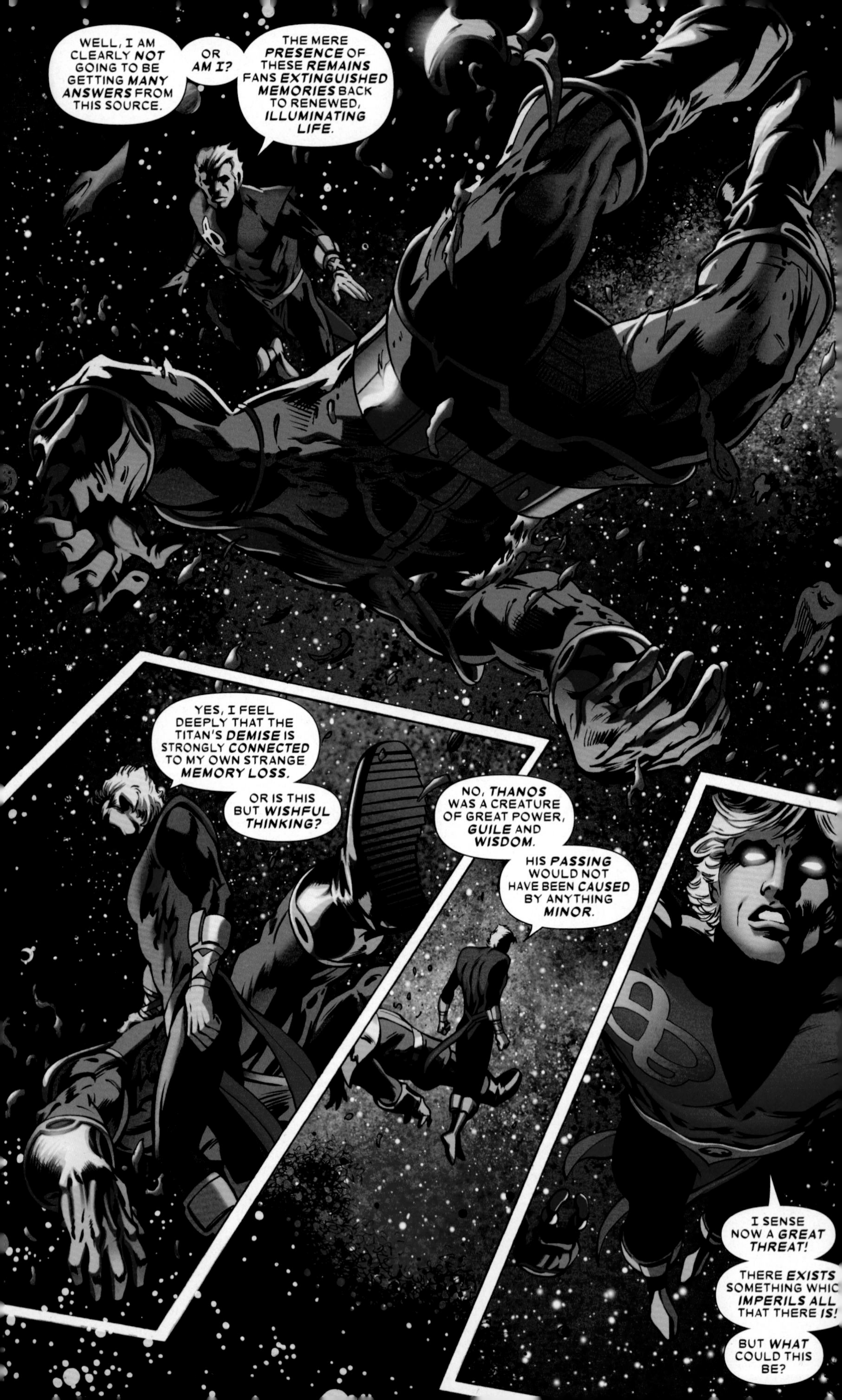
WELL, I AM CLEARLY NOT GOING TO BE GETTING MANY ANSWERS FROM THIS SOURCE.
OR AM I?
THE MERE PRESENCE OF THESE REMAINS FANS EXTINGUISHED MEMORIES BACK TO RENEWED, ILLUMINATING LIFE.
YES, I FEEL DEEPLY THAT THE TITAN'S DEMISE IS STRONGLY CONNECTED TO MY OWN STRANGE MEMORY LOSS.
OR IS THIS BUT WISHFUL THINKING?
NO, THANOS WAS A CREATURE OF GREAT POWER, GUILE AND WISDOM.
HIS PASSING WOULD NOT HAVE BEEN CAUSED BY ANYTHING MINOR.
I SENSE NOW A GREAT THREAT!
THERE EXISTS SOMETHING WHIC IMPERILS ALL THAT THERE IS!
BUT WHAT COULD THIS BE?

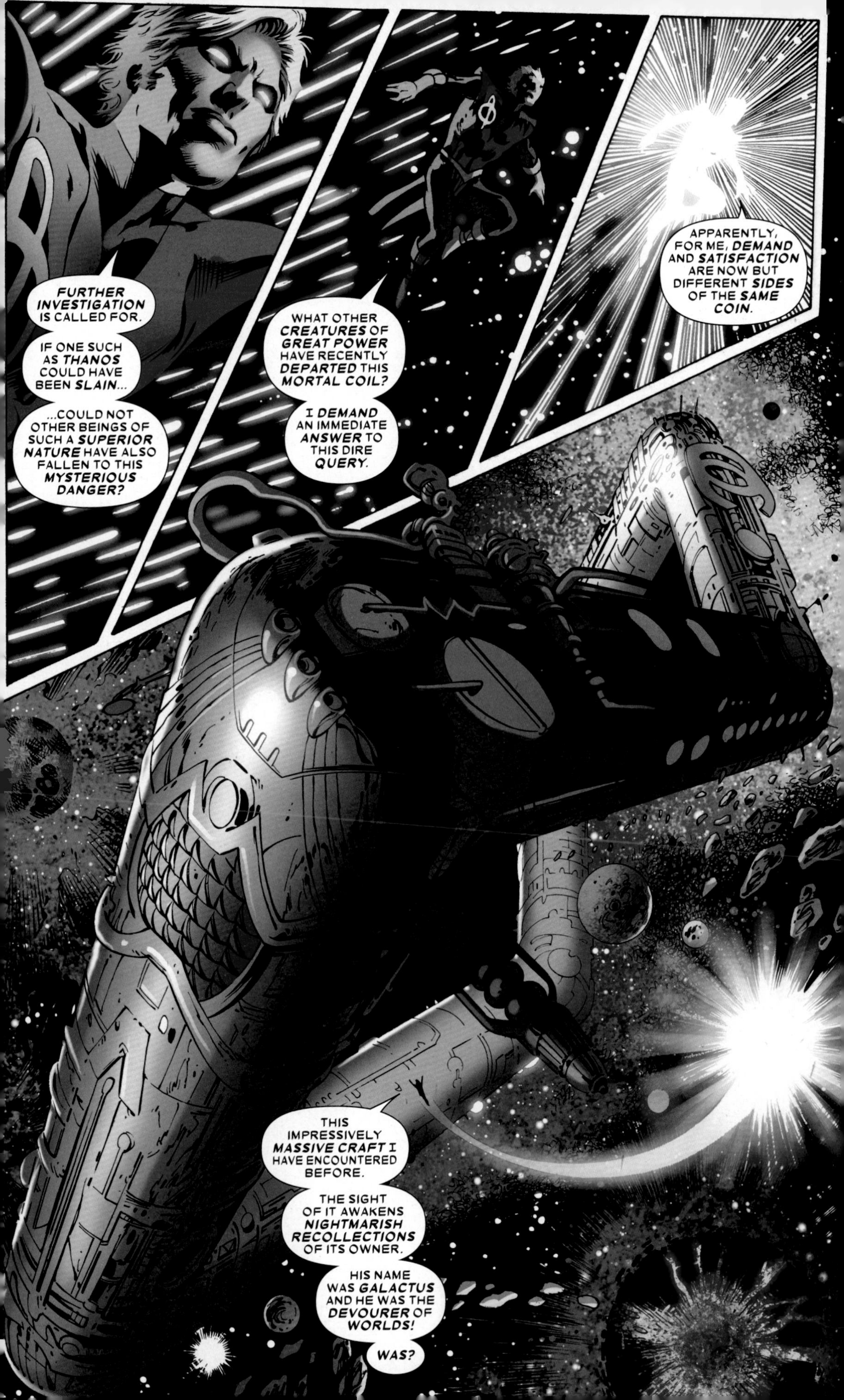
FURTHER INVESTIGATION IS CALLED FOR.
IF ONE SUCH AS THANOS COULD HAVE BEEN SLAIN...
...COULD NOT OTHER BEINGS OF SUCH A SUPERIOR NATURE HAVE ALSO FALLEN TO THIS MYSTERIOUS DANGER?
WHAT OTHER CREATURES OF GREAT POWER HAVE RECENTLY DEPARTED THIS MORTAL COIL?
I DEMAND AN IMMEDIATE ANSWER TO THIS DIRE QUERY.
APPARENTLY, FOR ME, DEMAND AND SATISFACTION ARE NOW BUT DIFFERENT SIDES OF THE SAME COIN.
THIS IMPRESSIVELY MASSIVE CRAFT I HAVE ENCOUNTERED BEFORE.
THE SIGHT OF IT AWAKENS NIGHTMARISH RECOLLECTIONS OF ITS OWNER.
HIS NAME WAS GALACTUS AND HE WAS THE DEVOURER OF WORLDS!
WAS?

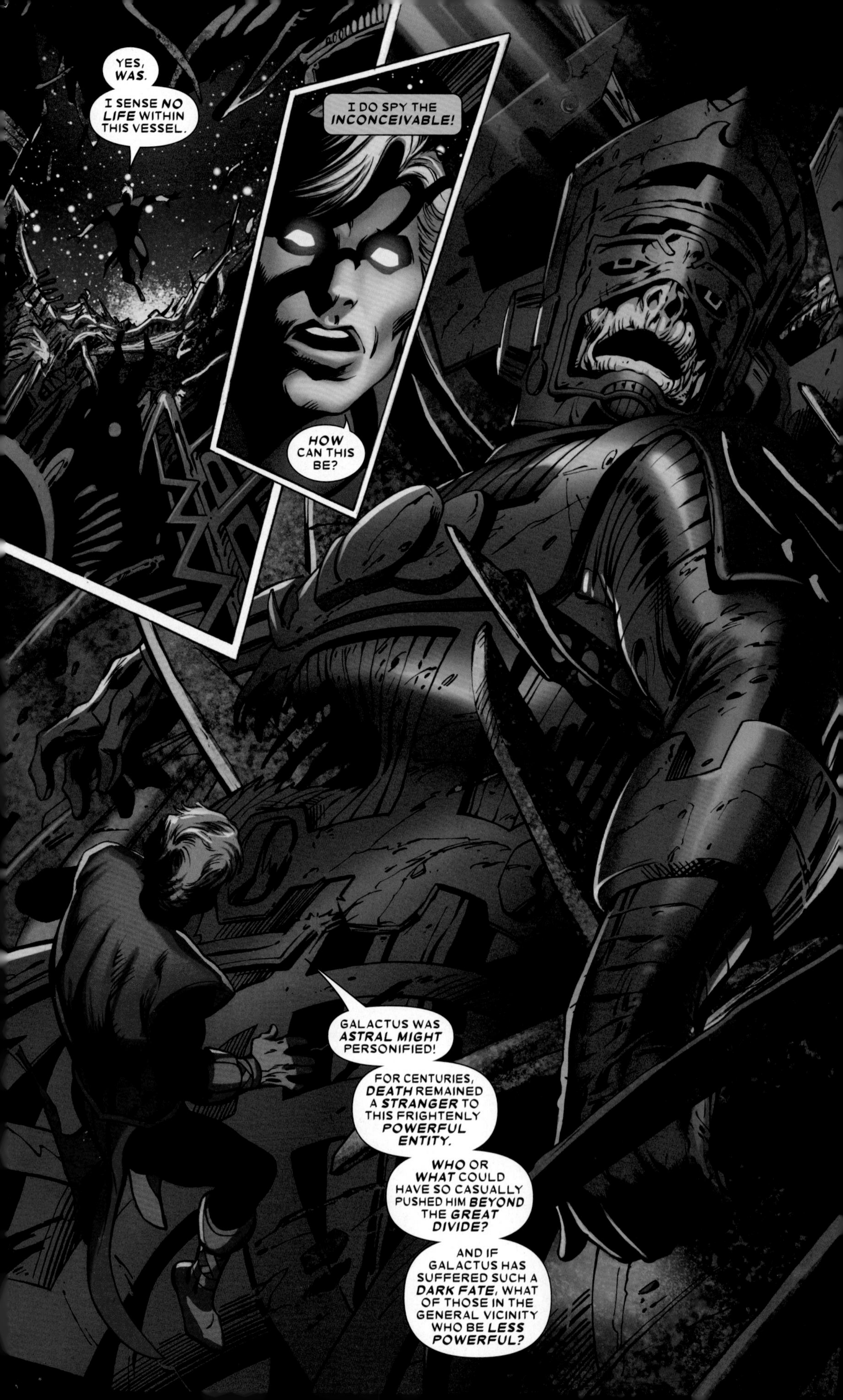
YES, WAS.
I SENSE NO LIFE WITHIN THIS VESSEL.
I DO SPY THE INCONCEIVABLE!
HOW CAN THIS BE?
GALACTUS WAS ASTRAL MIGHT PERSONIFIED!
FOR CENTURIES, DEATH REMAINED A STRANGER TO THIS FRIGHTENLY POWERFUL ENTITY.
WHO OR WHAT COULD HAVE SO CASUALLY PUSHED HIM BEYOND THE GREAT DIVIDE?
AND IF GALACTUS HAS SUFFERED SUCH A DARK FATE, WHAT OF THOSE IN THE GENERAL VICINITY WHO BE LESS POWERFUL?

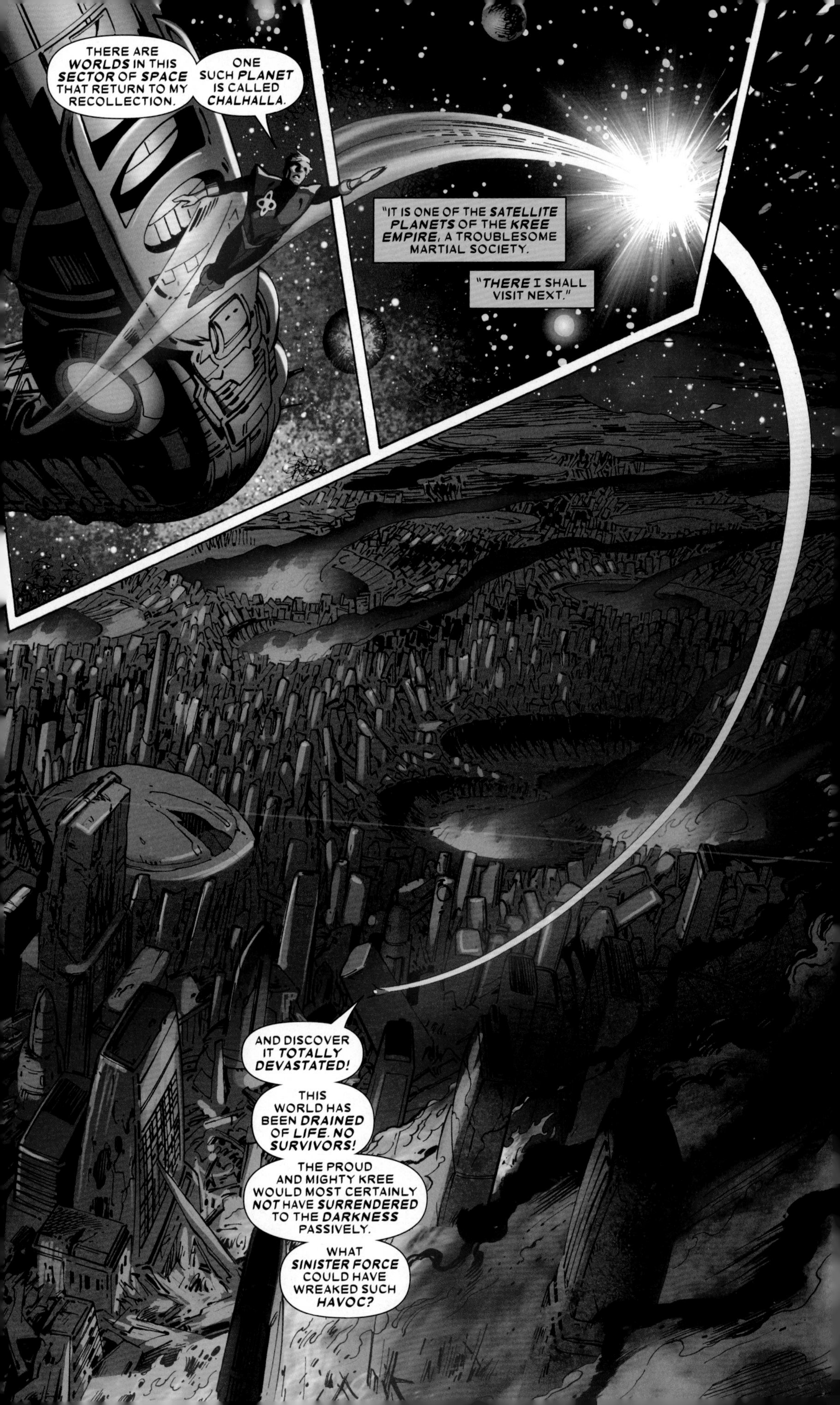
THERE ARE WORLDS IN THIS SECTOR OF SPACE THAT RETURN TO MY RECOLLECTION.
ONE SUCH PLANET IS CALLED CHALHALLA.
"IT IS ONE OF THE SATELLITE PLANETS OF THE KREE EMPIRE, A TROUBLESOME MARTIAL SOCIETY.
"THERE I SHALL VISIT NEXT."
AND DISCOVER IT TOTALLY DEVASTATED!
THIS WORLD HAS BEEN DRAINED OF LIFE. NO SURVIVORS!
THE PROUD AND MIGHTY KREE WOULD MOST CERTAINLY NOT HAVE SURRENDERED TO THE DARKNESS PASSIVELY.
WHAT SINISTER FORCE COULD HAVE WREAKED SUCH HAVOC?

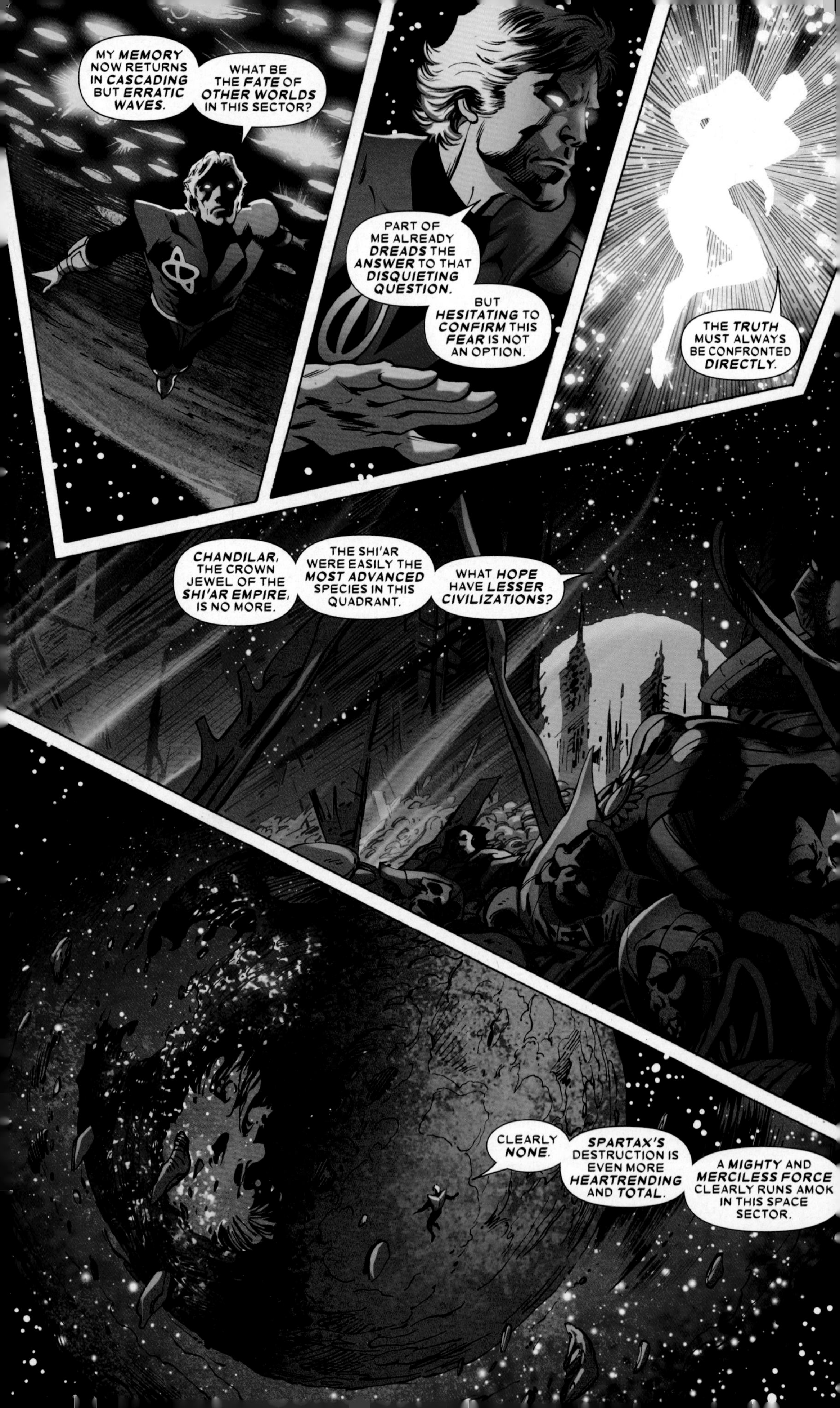
MY MEMORY NOW RETURNS IN CASCADING BUT ERRATIC WAVES.
WHAT BE THE FATE OF OTHER WORLDS IN THIS SECTOR?
PART OF ME ALREADY DREADS THE ANSWER TO THAT DISQUIETING QUESTION.
BUT HESITATING TO CONFIRM THIS FEAR IS NOT AN OPTION.
THE TRUTH MUST ALWAYS BE CONFRONTED DIRECTLY.
CHANDILAR, THE CROWN JEWEL OF THE SHI'AR EMPIRE, IS NO MORE.
THE SHI'AR WERE EASILY THE MOST ADVANCED SPECIES IN THIS QUADRANT.
WHAT HOPE HAVE LESSER CIVILIZATIONS?
CLEARLY NONE.
SPARTAX'S DESTRUCTION IS EVEN MORE HEARTRENDING AND TOTAL.
A MIGHTY AND MERCILESS FORCE CLEARLY RUNS AMOK IN THIS SPACE SECTOR.

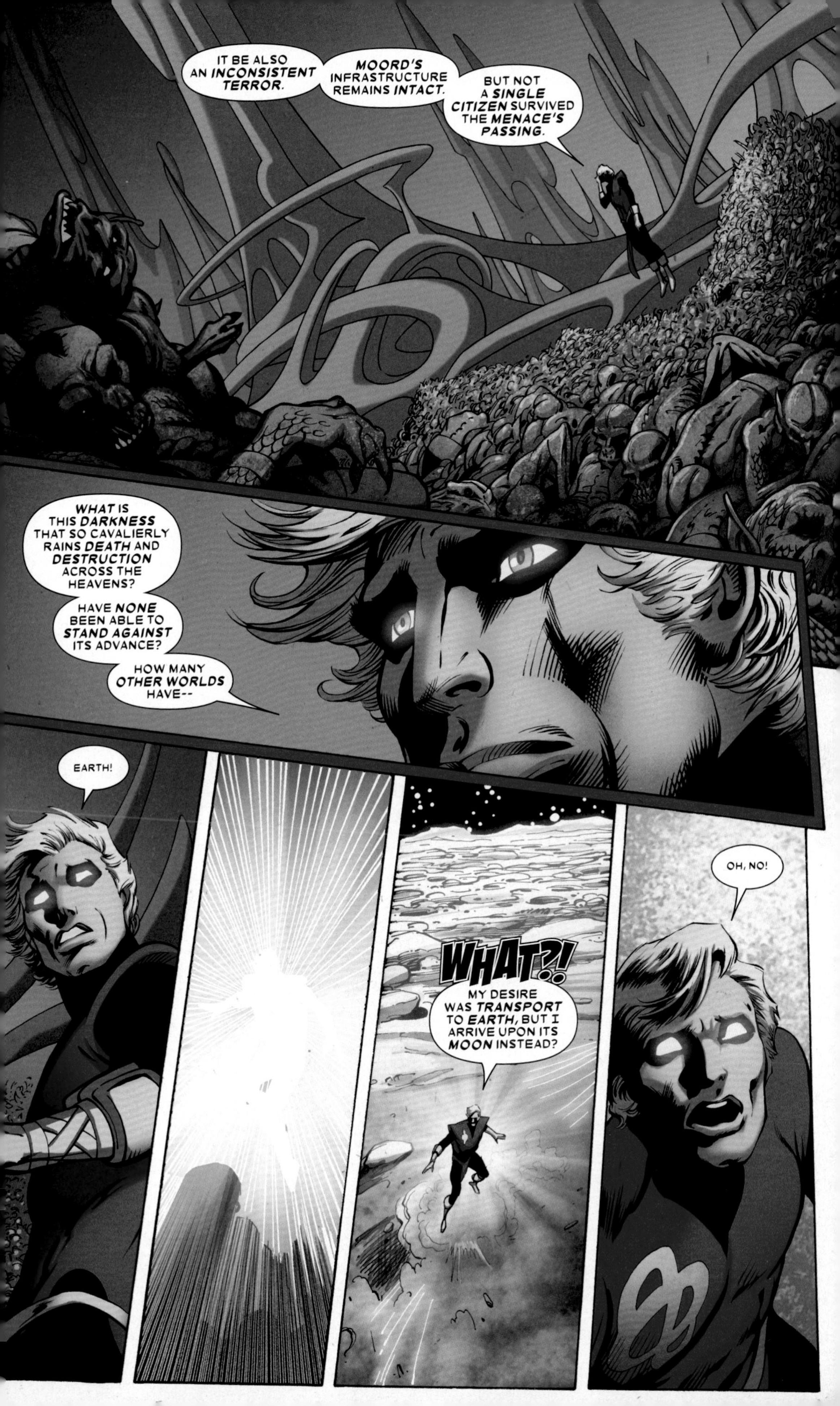
IT BE ALSO AN INCONSISTENT TERROR.
MOORD'S INFRASTRUCTURE REMAINS INTACT.
BUT NOT A SINGLE CITIZEN SURVIVED THE MENACE'S PASSING.
WHAT IS THIS DARKNESS THAT SO CAVALIERLY RAINS DEATH AND DESTRUCTION ACROSS THE HEAVENS?
HAVE NONE BEEN ABLE TO STAND AGAINST ITS ADVANCE?
HOW MANY OTHER WORLDS HAVE--
EARTH!
WHAT?!
MY DESIRE WAS TRANSPORT TO EARTH, BUT I ARRIVE UPON ITS MOON INSTEAD?
OH, NO!

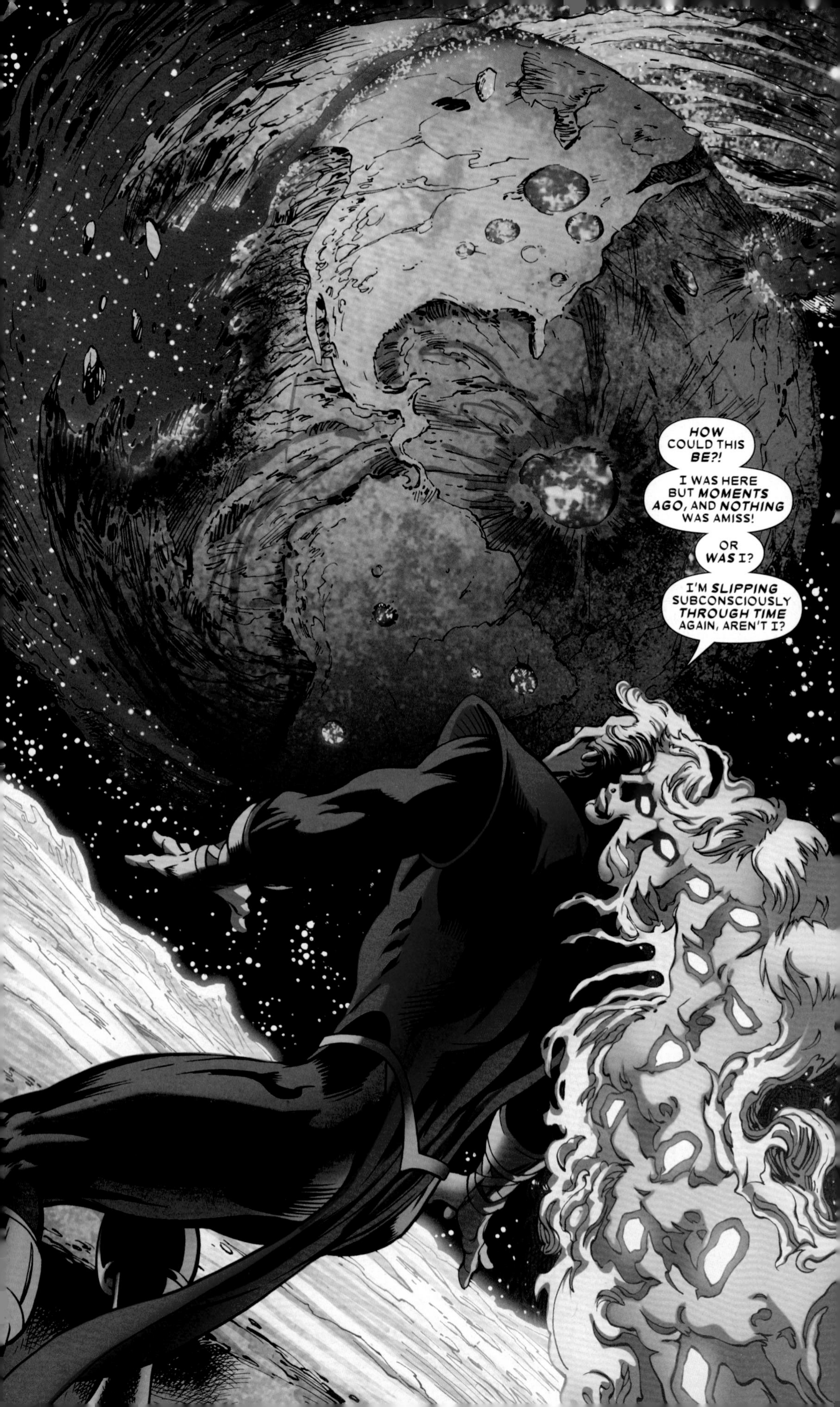

HOW COULD THIS BE?!
I WAS HERE BUT MOMENTS AGO, AND NOTHING WAS AMISS!
OR WAS I?
I'M SLIPPING SUBCONSCIOUSLY THROUGH TIME AGAIN, AREN'T I?

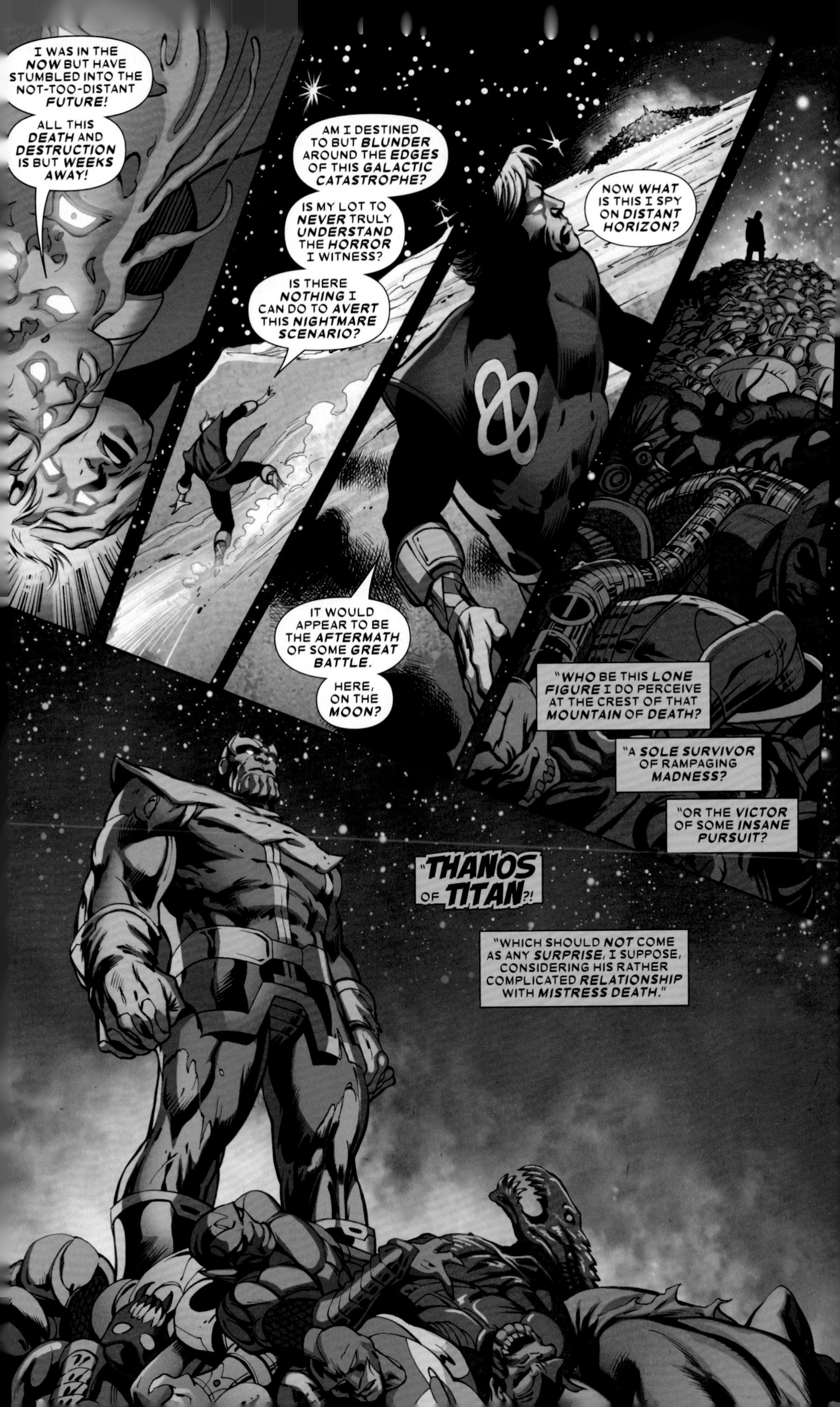
I WAS IN THE NOW BUT HAVE STUMBLED INTO THE NOT-TOO-DISTANT FUTURE!
ALL THIS DEATH AND DESTRUCTION IS BUT WEEKS AWAY!
AM I DESTINED TO BUT BLUNDER AROUND THE EDGES OF THIS GALACTIC CATASTROPHE?
IS MY LOT TO NEVER TRULY UNDERSTAND THE HORROR I WITNESS?
IS THERE NOTHING I CAN DO TO AVERT THIS NIGHTMARE SCENARIO?
NOW WHAT IS THIS I SPY ON DISTANT HORIZON?
IT WOULD APPEAR TO BE THE AFTERMATH OF SOME GREAT BATTLE.
HERE, ON THE MOON?
"WHO BE THIS LONE FIGURE I DO PERCEIVE AT THE CREST OF THAT MOUNTAIN OF DEATH?
"A SOLE SURVIVOR OF RAMPAGING MADNESS?
"OR THE VICTOR OF SOME INSANE PURSUIT?
"THANOS OF TITAN?!
"WHICH SHOULD NOT COME AS ANY SURPRISE, I SUPPOSE, CONSIDERING HIS RATHER COMPLICATED RELATIONSHIP WITH MISTRESS DEATH."

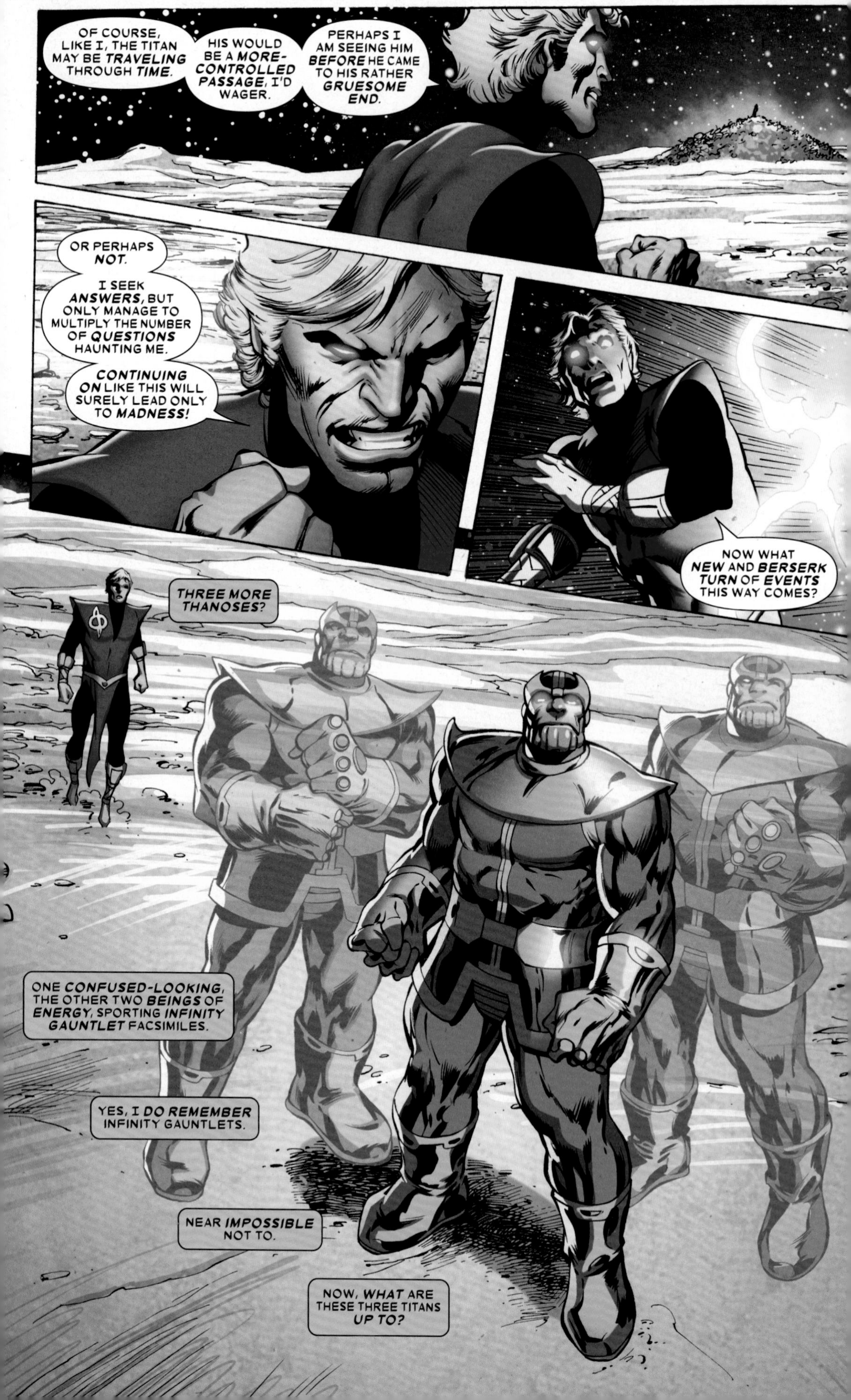
OF COURSE, LIKE I, THE TITAN MAY BE TRAVELING THROUGH TIME.
HIS WOULD BE A MORE-CONTROLLED PASSAGE, I'D WAGER.
PERHAPS I AM SEEING HIM BEFORE HE CAME TO HIS RATHER GRUESOME END.
OR PERHAPS NOT.
I SEEK ANSWERS, BUT ONLY MANAGE TO MULTIPLY THE NUMBER OF QUESTIONS HAUNTING ME.
CONTINUING ON LIKE THIS WILL SURELY LEAD ONLY TO MADNESS!
NOW WHAT NEW AND BERSERK TURN OF EVENTS THIS WAY COMES?
THREE MORE THANOSES?
ONE CONFUSED-LOOKING, THE OTHER TWO BEINGS OF ENERGY, SPORTING INFINITY GAUNTLET FACSIMILES.
YES, I DO REMEMBER INFINITY GAUNTLETS.
NEAR IMPOSSIBLE NOT TO.
NOW, WHAT ARE THESE THREE TITANS UP TO?

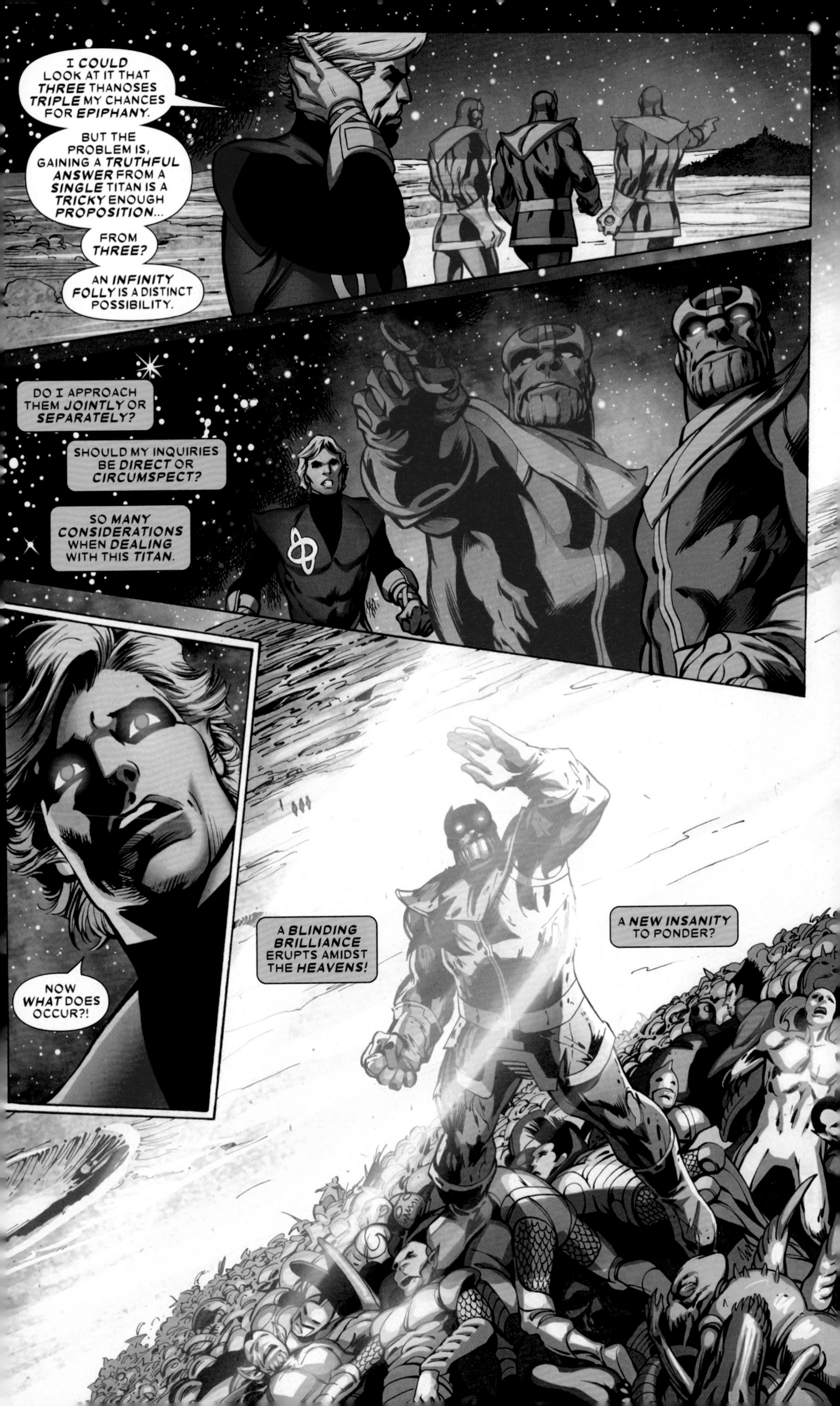
I COULD LOOK AT IT THAT THREE THANOSES TRIPLE MY CHANCES FOR EPIPHANY.
BUT THE PROBLEM IS, GAINING A TRUTHFUL ANSWER FROM A SINGLE TITAN IS A TRICKY ENOUGH PROPOSITION...
FROM THREE?
AN INFINITY FOLLY IS A DISTINCT POSSIBILITY.
DO I APPROACH THEM JOINTLY OR SEPARATELY?
SHOULD MY INQUIRIES BE DIRECT OR CIRCUMSPECT?
SO MANY CONSIDERATIONS WHEN DEALING WITH THIS TITAN.
NOW WHAT DOES OCCUR?!
A BLINDING BRILLIANCE ERUPTS AMIDST THE HEAVENS!
A NEW INSANITY TO PONDER?

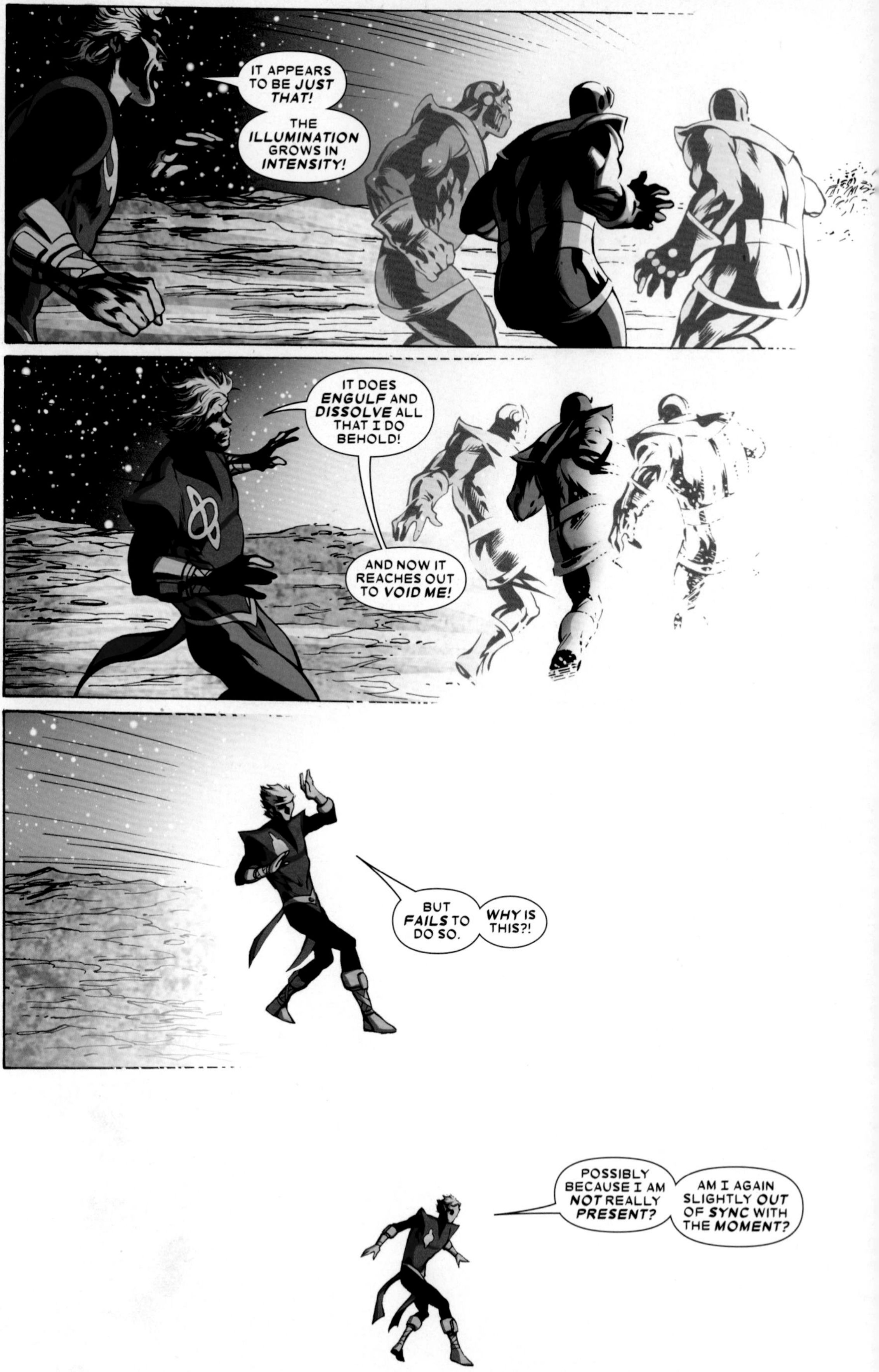
IT APPEARS TO BE JUST THAT!
THE ILLUMINATION GROWS IN INTENSITY!
IT DOES ENGULF AND DISSOLVE ALL THAT I DO BEHOLD!
AND NOW IT REACHES OUT TO VOID ME!
BUT FAILS TO DO SO.
WHY IS THIS?!
POSSIBLY BECAUSE I AM NOT REALLY PRESENT?
AM I AGAIN SLIGHTLY OUT OF SYNC WITH THE MOMENT?

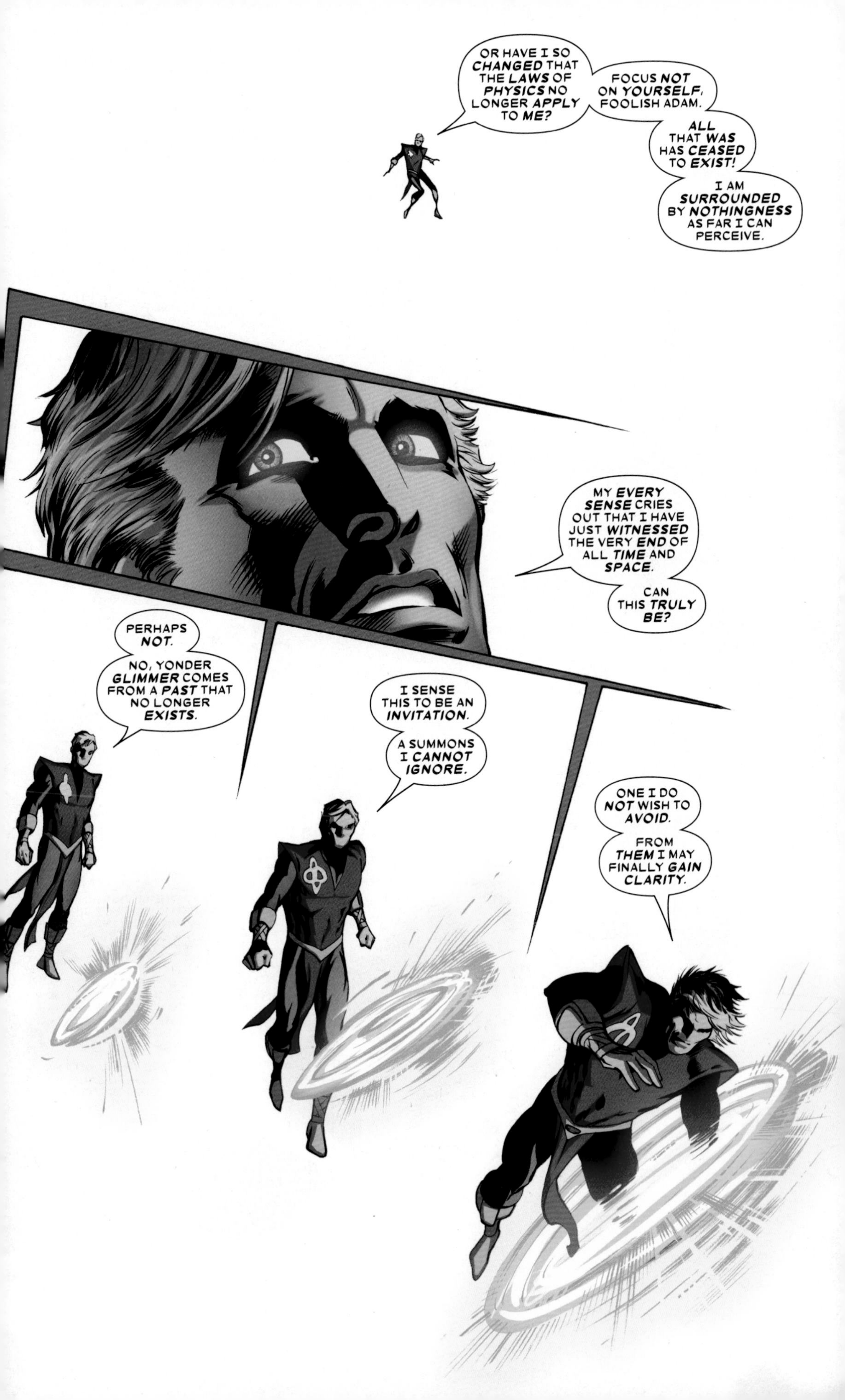
OR HAVE I SO CHANGED THAT THE LAWS OF PHYSICS NO LONGER APPLY TO ME?
FOCUS NOT ON YOURSELF, FOOLISH ADAM.
ALL THAT WAS HAS CEASED TO EXIST!
I AM SURROUNDED BY NOTHINGNESS AS FAR I CAN PERCEIVE.
MY EVERY SENSE CRIES OUT THAT I HAVE JUST WITNESSED THE VERY END OF ALL TIME AND SPACE.
CAN THIS TRULY BE?
PERHAPS NOT.
NO, YONDER GLIMMER COMES FROM A PAST THAT NO LONGER EXISTS.
I SENSE THIS TO BE AN INVITATION.
A SUMMONS I CANNOT IGNORE.
ONE I DO NOT WISH TO AVOID.
FROM THEM I MAY FINALLY GAIN CLARITY.

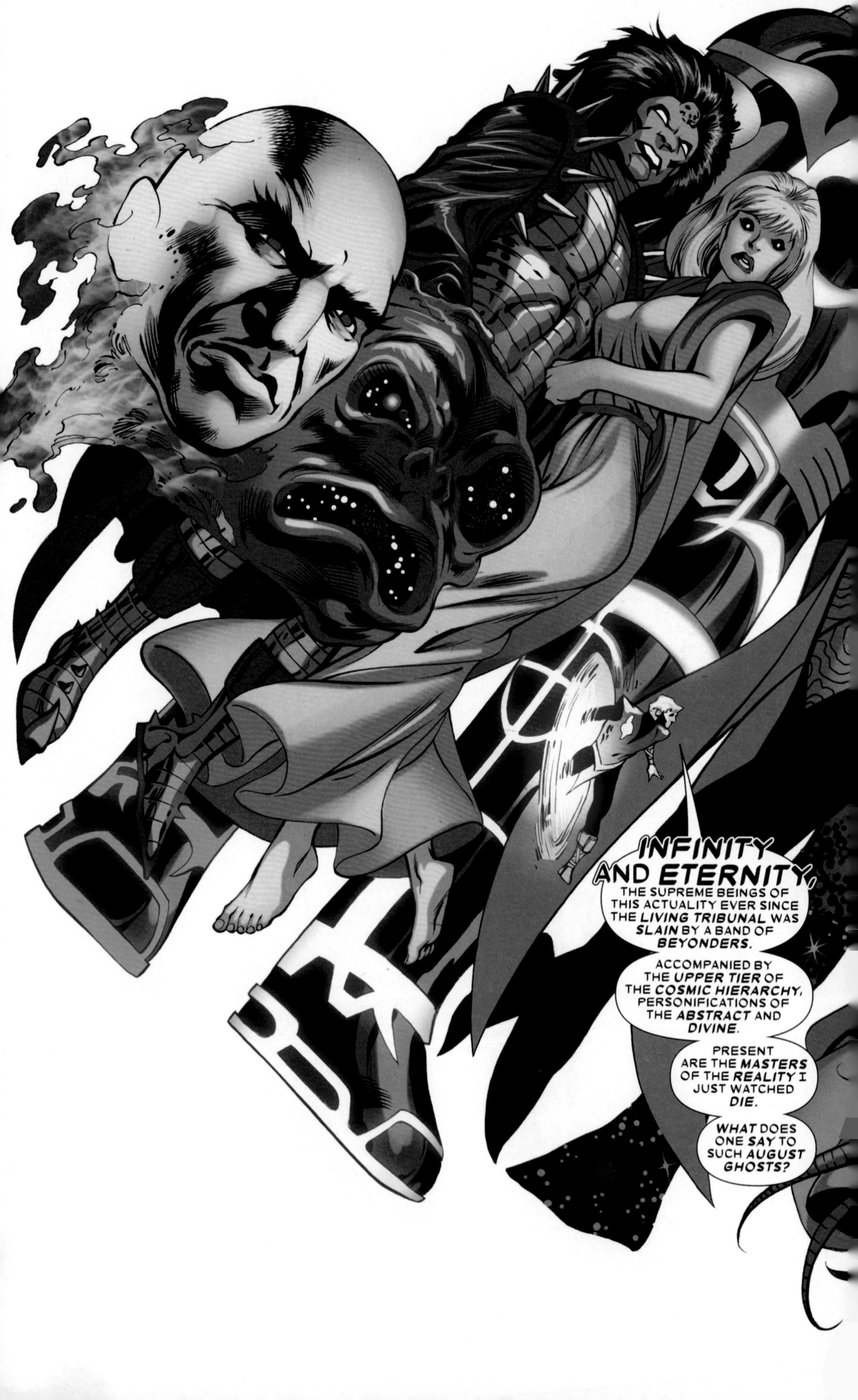
INFINITY AND ETERNITY,
THE SUPREME BEINGS OF THIS ACTUALITY EVER SINCE THE LIVING TRIBUNAL WAS SLAIN BY A BAND OF BEYONDERS.
ACCOMPANIED BY THE UPPER TIER OF THE COSMIC HIERARCHY, PERSONIFICATIONS OF THE ABSTRACT AND DIVINE.
PRESENT ARE THE MASTERS OF THE REALITY I JUST WATCHED DIE.
WHAT DOES ONE SAY TO SUCH AUGUST GHOSTS?

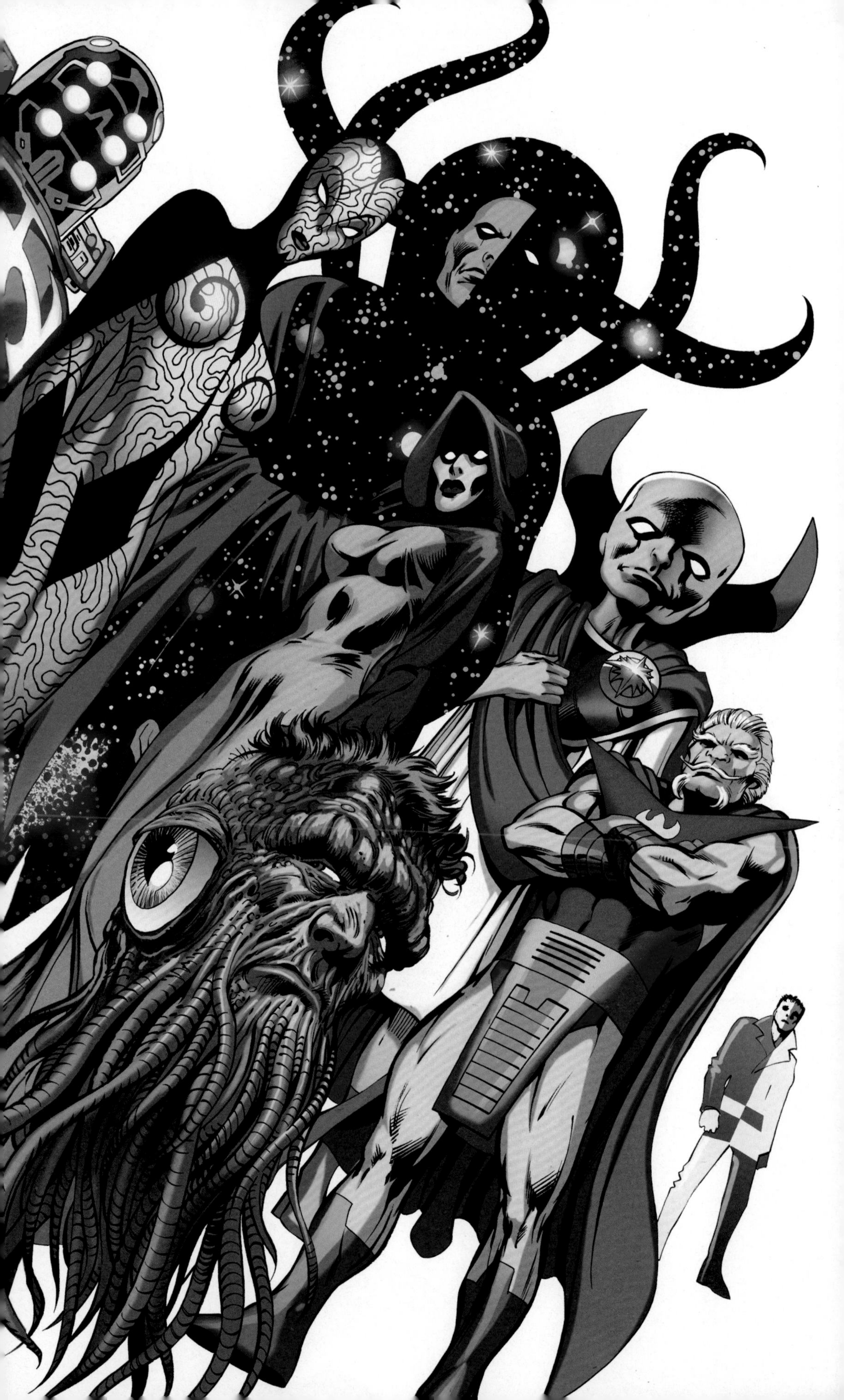

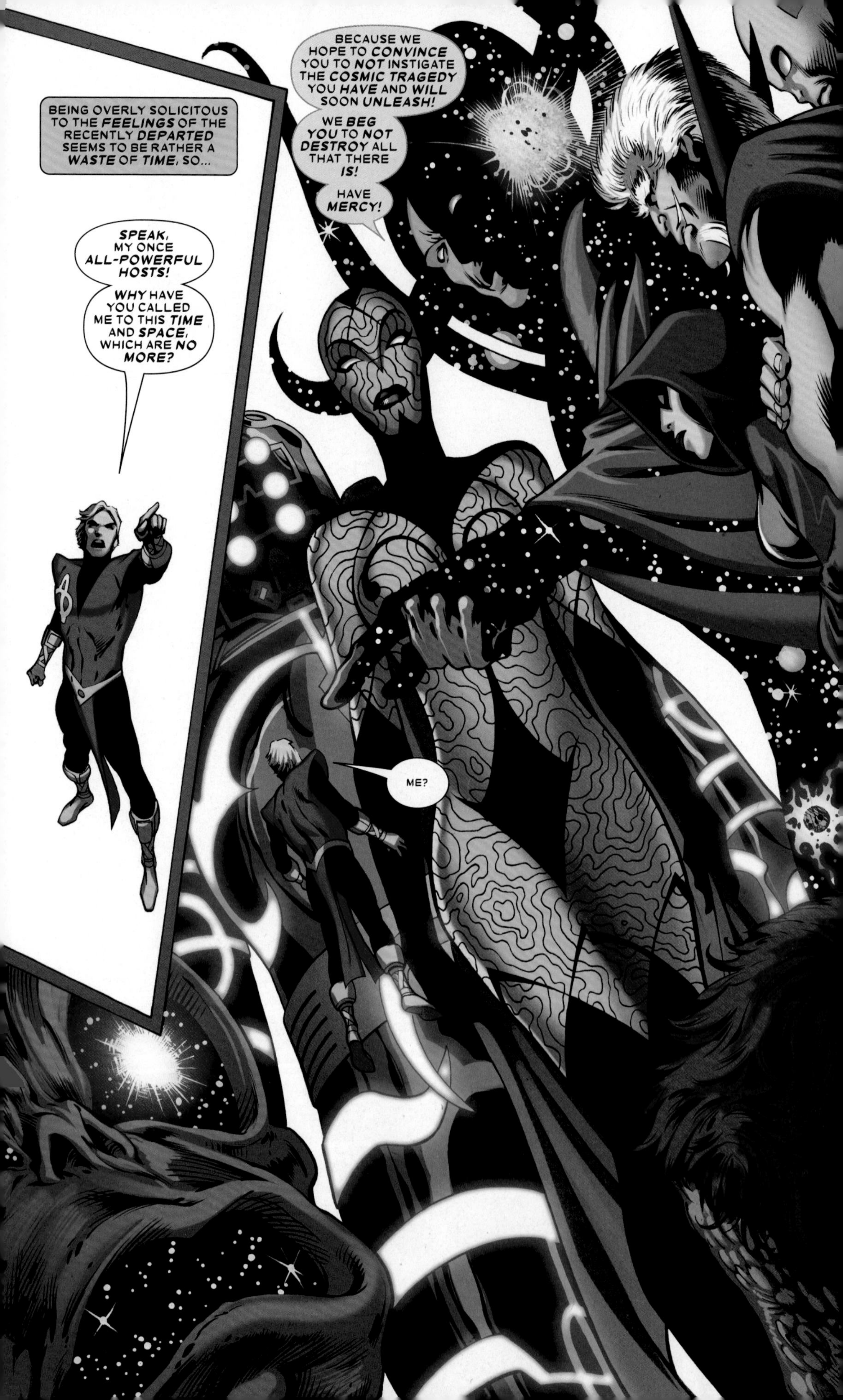
BEING OVERLY SOLICITOUS TO THE FEELINGS OF THE RECENTLY DEPARTED SEEMS TO BE RATHER A WASTE OF TIME, SO...
SPEAK, MY ONCE ALL-POWERFUL HOSTS!
WHY HAVE YOU CALLED ME TO THIS TIME AND SPACE, WHICH ARE NO MORE?
BECAUSE WE HOPE TO CONVINCE YOU TO NOT INSTIGATE THE COSMIC TRAGEDY YOU HAVE AND WILL SOON UNLEASH!
WE BEG YOU TO NOT DESTROY ALL THAT THERE IS!
HAVE MERCY!
ME?

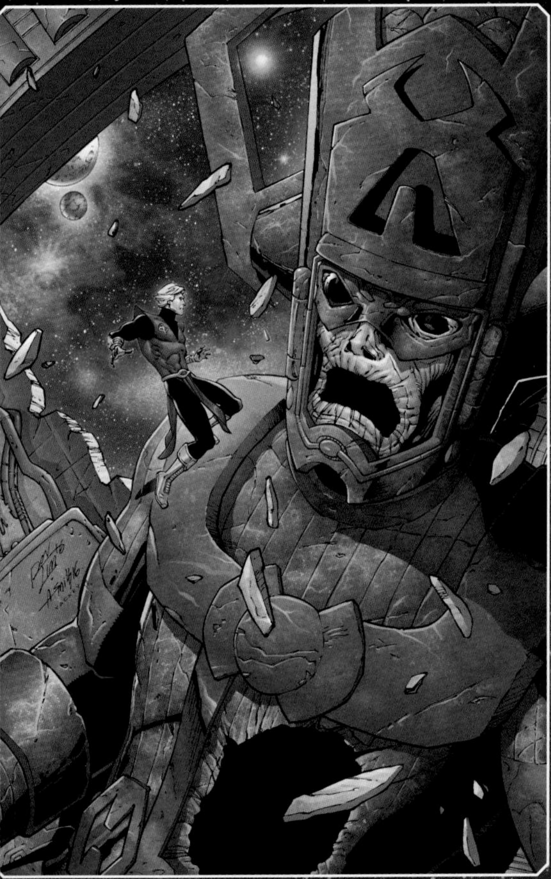

Infinity Entity 2 variant by Ron Lim, Andy Smith & Matt Yackey

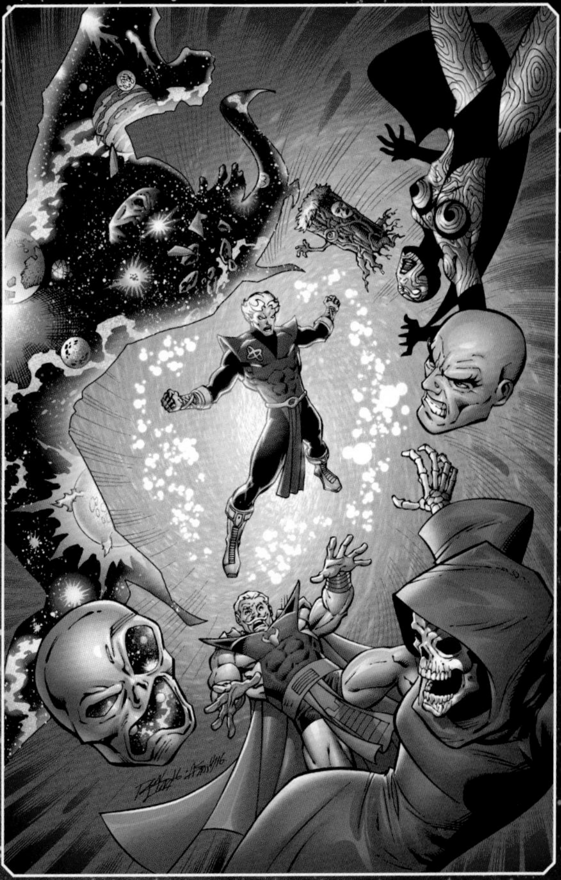

Infinity Entity 3 variant by Ron Lim, Andy Smith & Matt Yackey

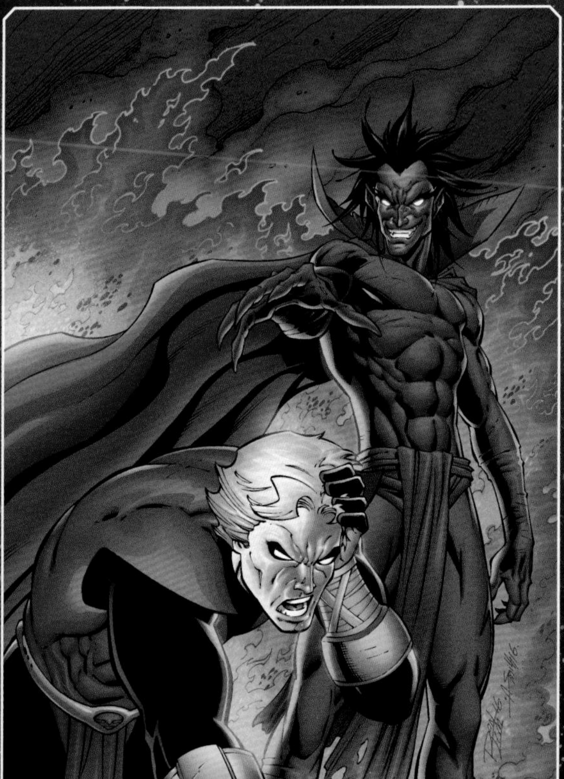

Infinity Entity 4 variant by Ron Lim, Andy Smith & Matt Yackey

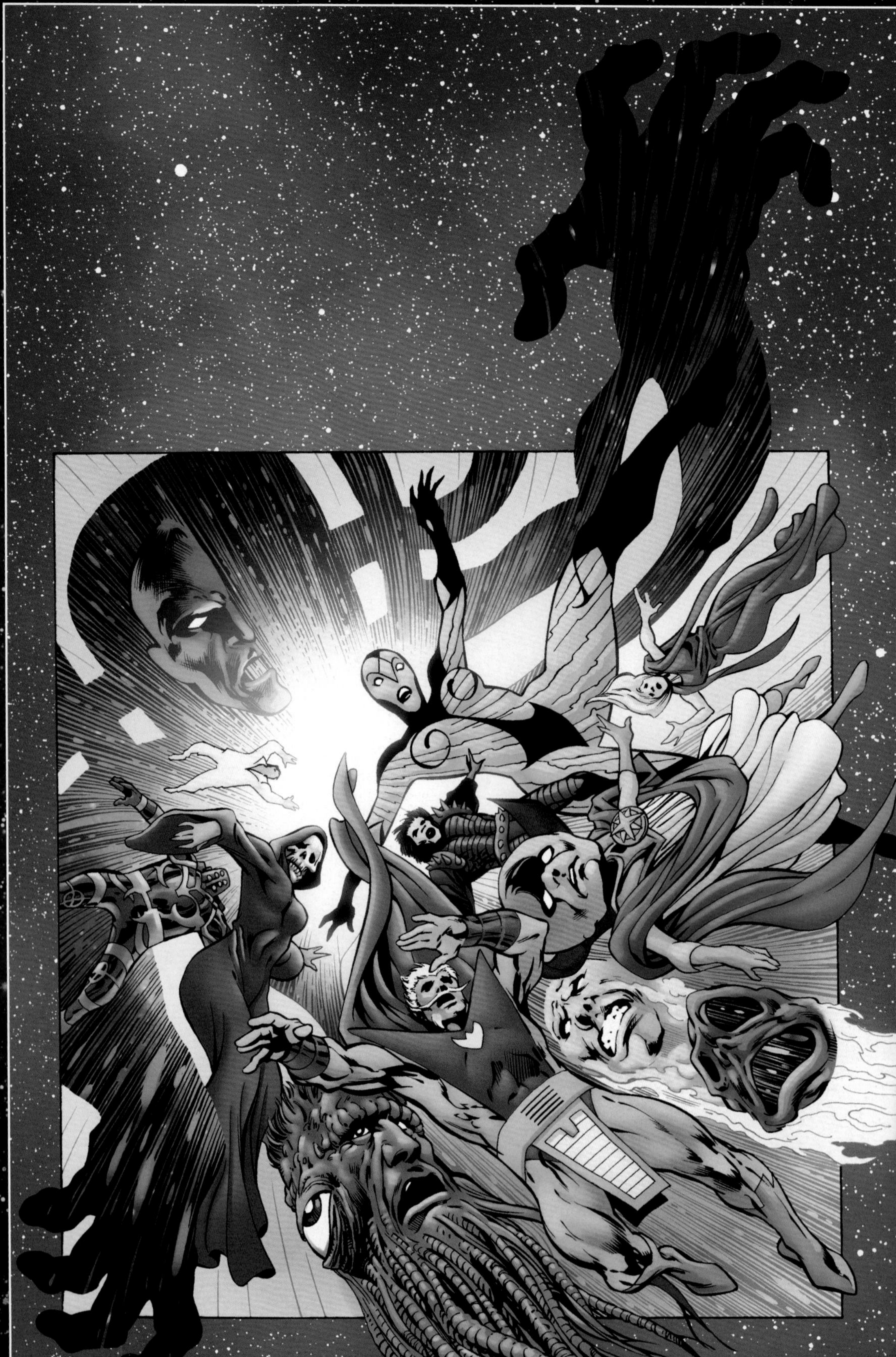

3: ANSWERS?

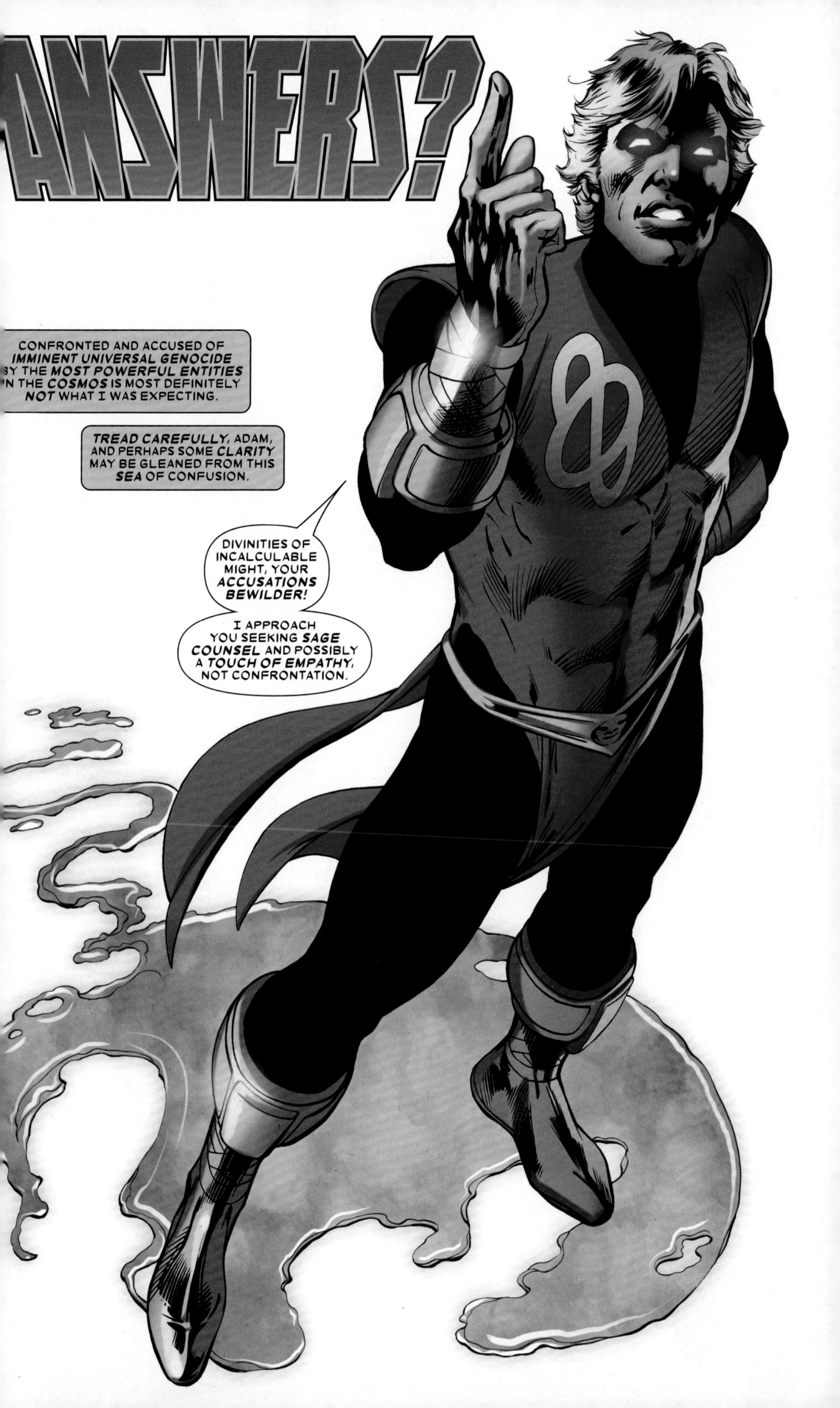
ANSWERS?
CONFRONTED AND ACCUSED OF IMMINENT UNIVERSAL GENOCIDE BY THE MOST POWERFUL ENTITIES IN THE COSMOS IS MOST DEFINITELY NOT WHAT I WAS EXPECTING.
TREAD CAREFULLY, ADAM, AND PERHAPS SOME CLARITY MAY BE GLEANED FROM THIS SEA OF CONFUSION.
DIVINITIES OF INCALCULABLE MIGHT, YOUR ACCUSATIONS BEWILDER!
I APPROACH YOU SEEKING SAGE COUNSEL AND POSSIBLY A TOUCH OF EMPATHY, NOT CONFRONTATION.

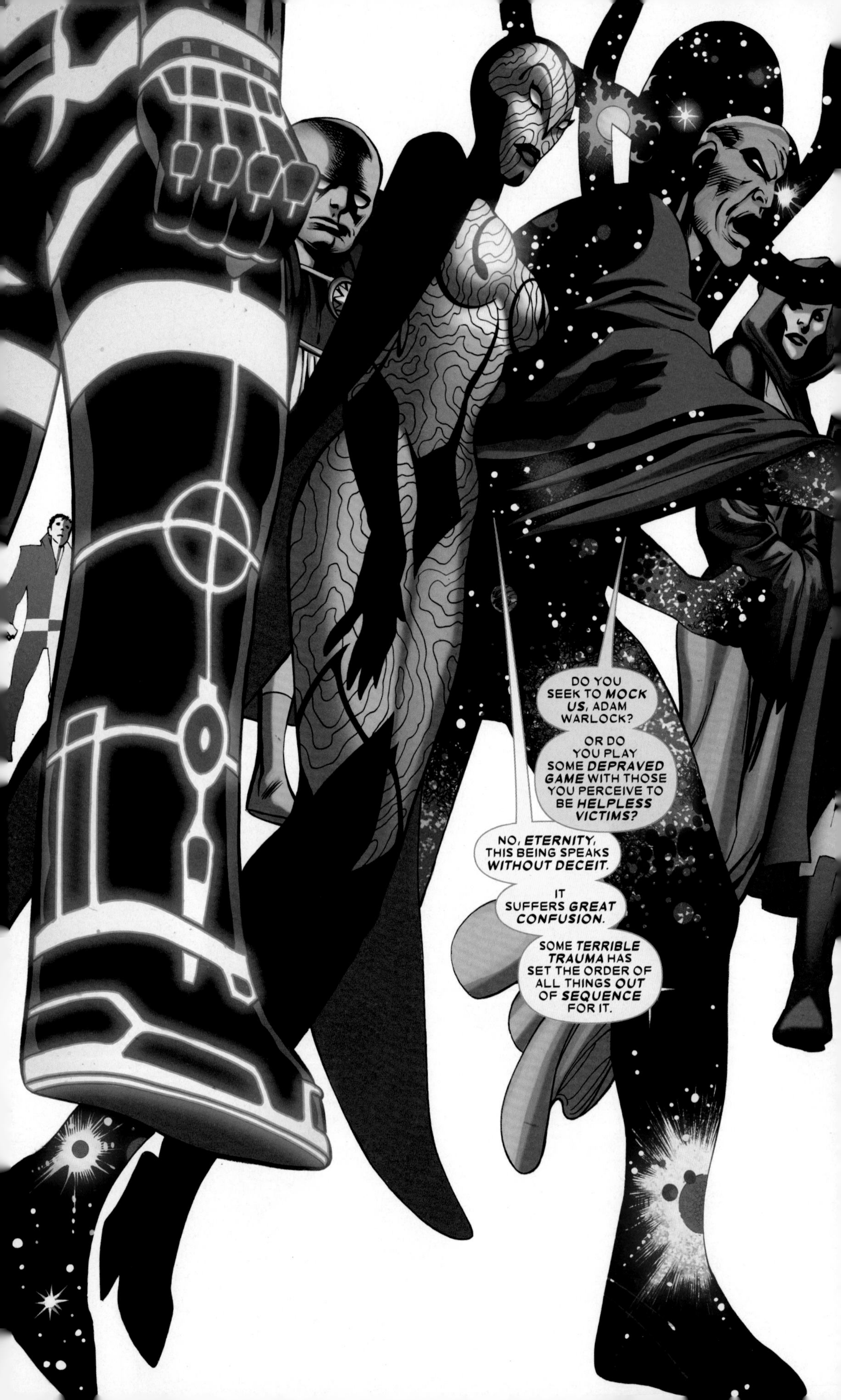
DO YOU SEEK TO MOCK US, ADAM WARLOCK?
OR DO YOU PLAY SOME DEPRAVED GAME WITH THOSE YOU PERCEIVE TO BE HELPLESS VICTIMS?
NO, ETERNITY, THIS BEING SPEAKS WITHOUT DECEIT.
IT SUFFERS GREAT CONFUSION.
SOME TERRIBLE TRAUMA HAS SET THE ORDER OF ALL THINGS OUT OF SEQUENCE FOR IT.

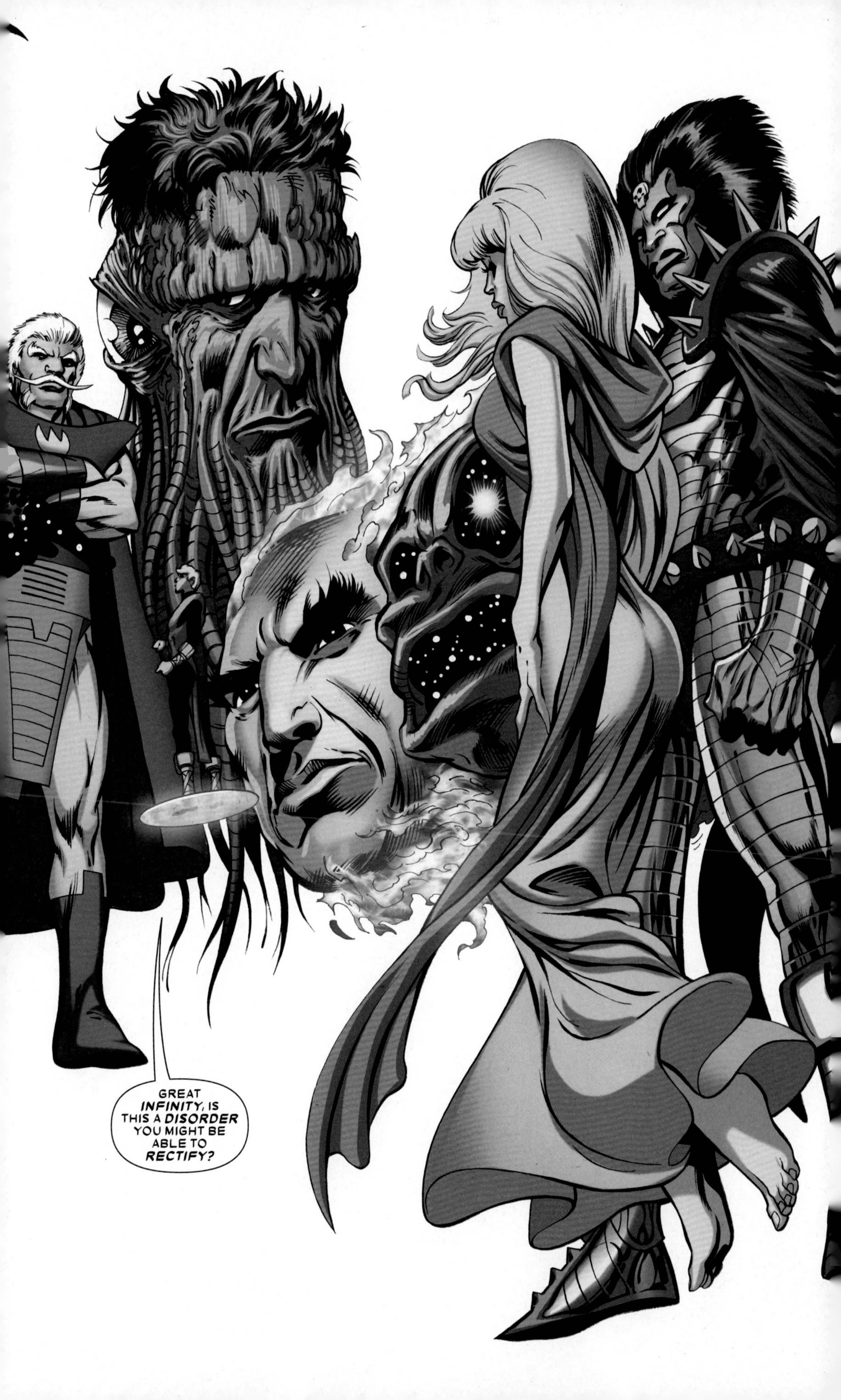
GREAT *INFINITY*, IS THIS A *DISORDER* YOU MIGHT BE ABLE TO *RECTIFY?*

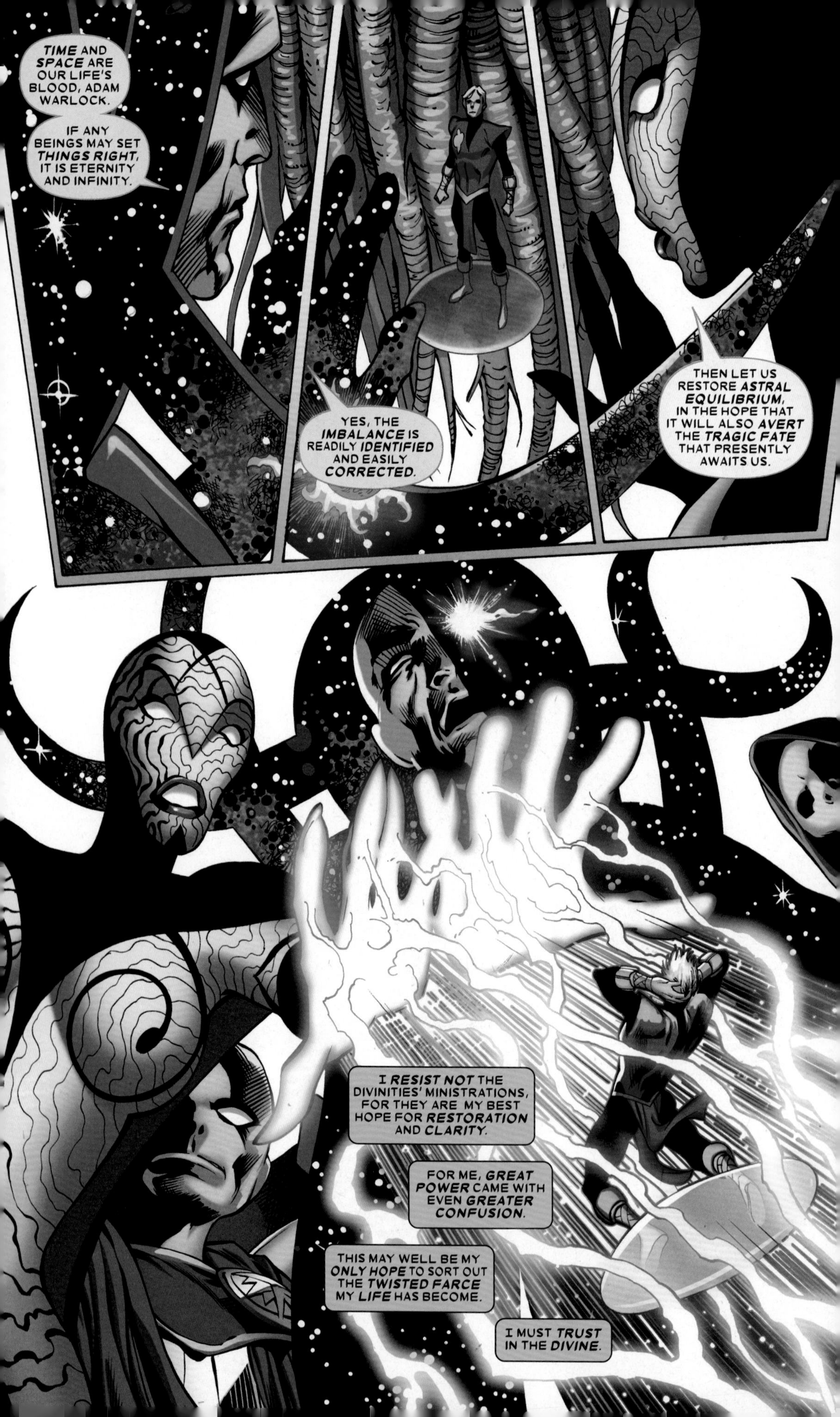

TIME AND SPACE ARE OUR LIFE'S BLOOD, ADAM WARLOCK.
IF ANY BEINGS MAY SET THINGS RIGHT, IT IS ETERNITY AND INFINITY.
YES, THE IMBALANCE IS READILY IDENTIFIED AND EASILY CORRECTED.
THEN LET US RESTORE ASTRAL EQUILIBRIUM, IN THE HOPE THAT IT WILL ALSO AVERT THE TRAGIC FATE THAT PRESENTLY AWAITS US.
I RESIST NOT THE DIVINITIES' MINISTRATIONS, FOR THEY ARE MY BEST HOPE FOR RESTORATION AND CLARITY.
FOR ME, GREAT POWER CAME WITH EVEN GREATER CONFUSION.
THIS MAY WELL BE MY ONLY HOPE TO SORT OUT THE TWISTED FARCE MY LIFE HAS BECOME.
I MUST TRUST IN THE DIVINE.

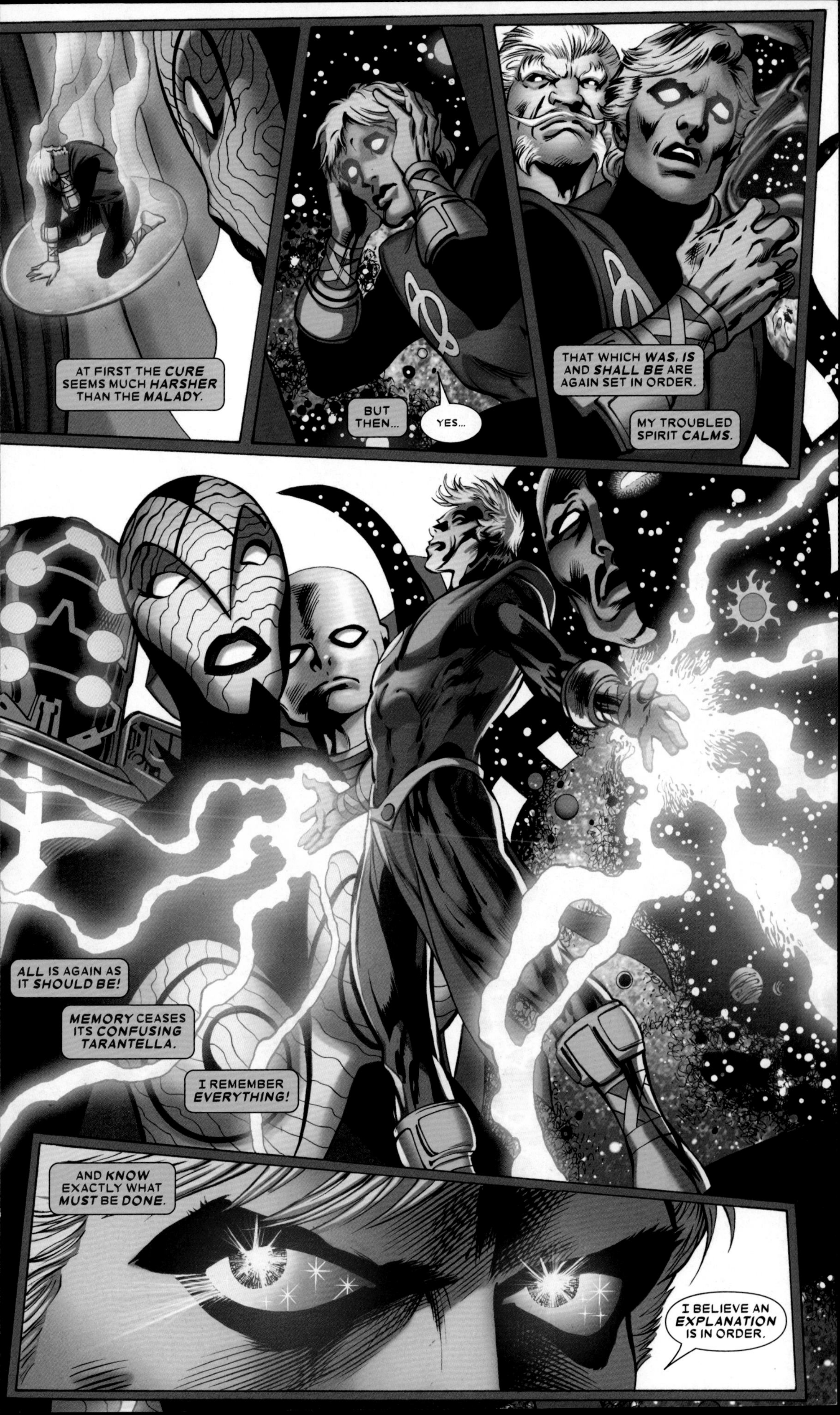
AT FIRST THE CURE SEEMS MUCH HARSHER THAN THE MALADY.
BUT THEN...
YES...
THAT WHICH WAS, IS AND SHALL BE ARE AGAIN SET IN ORDER.
MY TROUBLED SPIRIT CALMS.
ALL IS AGAIN AS IT SHOULD BE!
MEMORY CEASES ITS CONFUSING TARANTELLA.
I REMEMBER EVERYTHING!
AND KNOW EXACTLY WHAT MUST BE DONE.
I BELIEVE AN EXPLANATION IS IN ORDER.

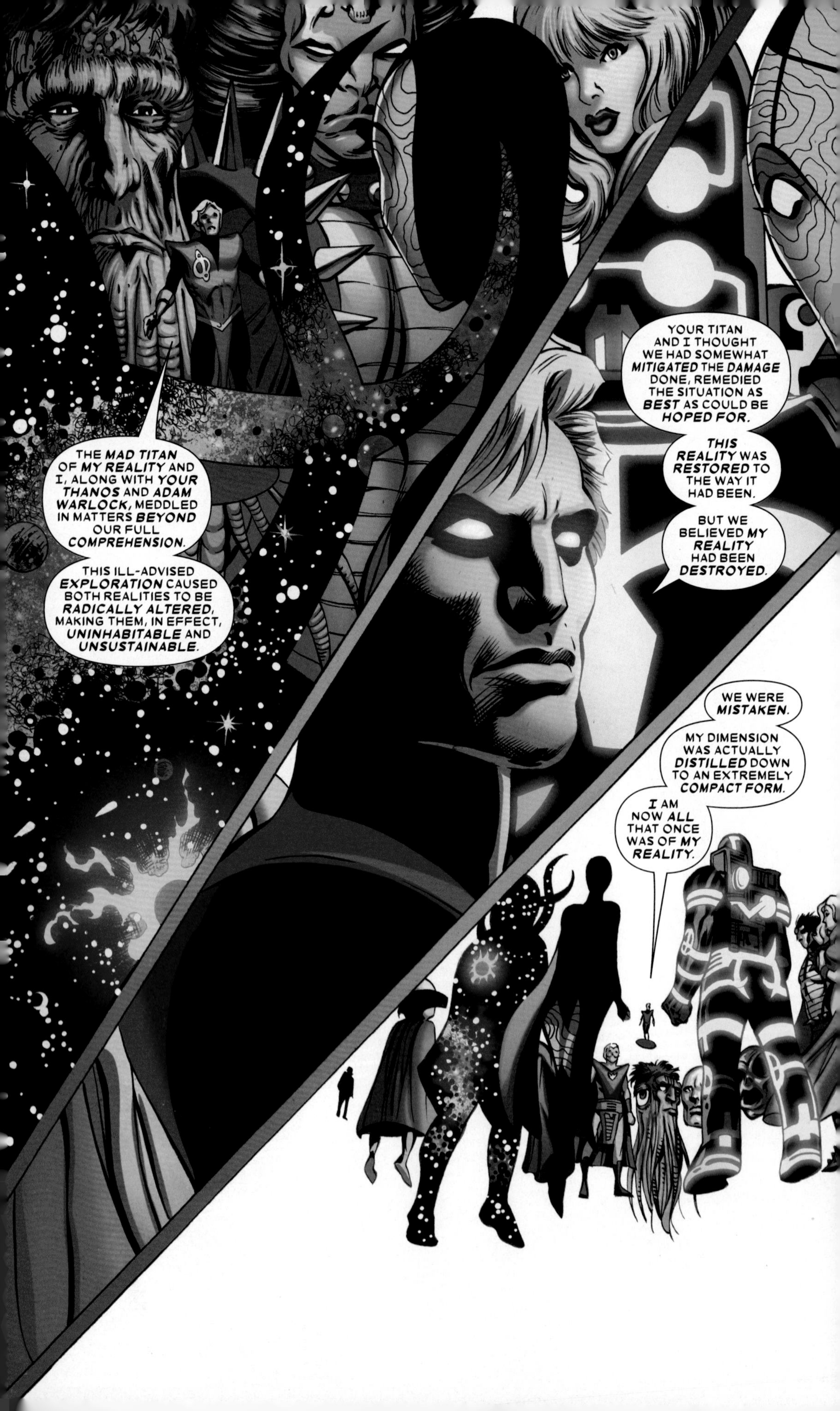
THE MAD TITAN OF MY REALITY AND I, ALONG WITH YOUR THANOS AND ADAM WARLOCK, MEDDLED IN MATTERS BEYOND OUR FULL COMPREHENSION.
THIS ILL-ADVISED EXPLORATION CAUSED BOTH REALITIES TO BE RADICALLY ALTERED, MAKING THEM, IN EFFECT, UNINHABITABLE AND UNSUSTAINABLE.
YOUR TITAN AND I THOUGHT WE HAD SOMEWHAT MITIGATED THE DAMAGE DONE, REMEDIED THE SITUATION AS BEST AS COULD BE HOPED FOR.
THIS REALITY WAS RESTORED TO THE WAY IT HAD BEEN.
BUT WE BELIEVED MY REALITY HAD BEEN DESTROYED.
WE WERE MISTAKEN.
MY DIMENSION WAS ACTUALLY DISTILLED DOWN TO AN EXTREMELY COMPACT FORM.
I AM NOW ALL THAT ONCE WAS OF MY REALITY.

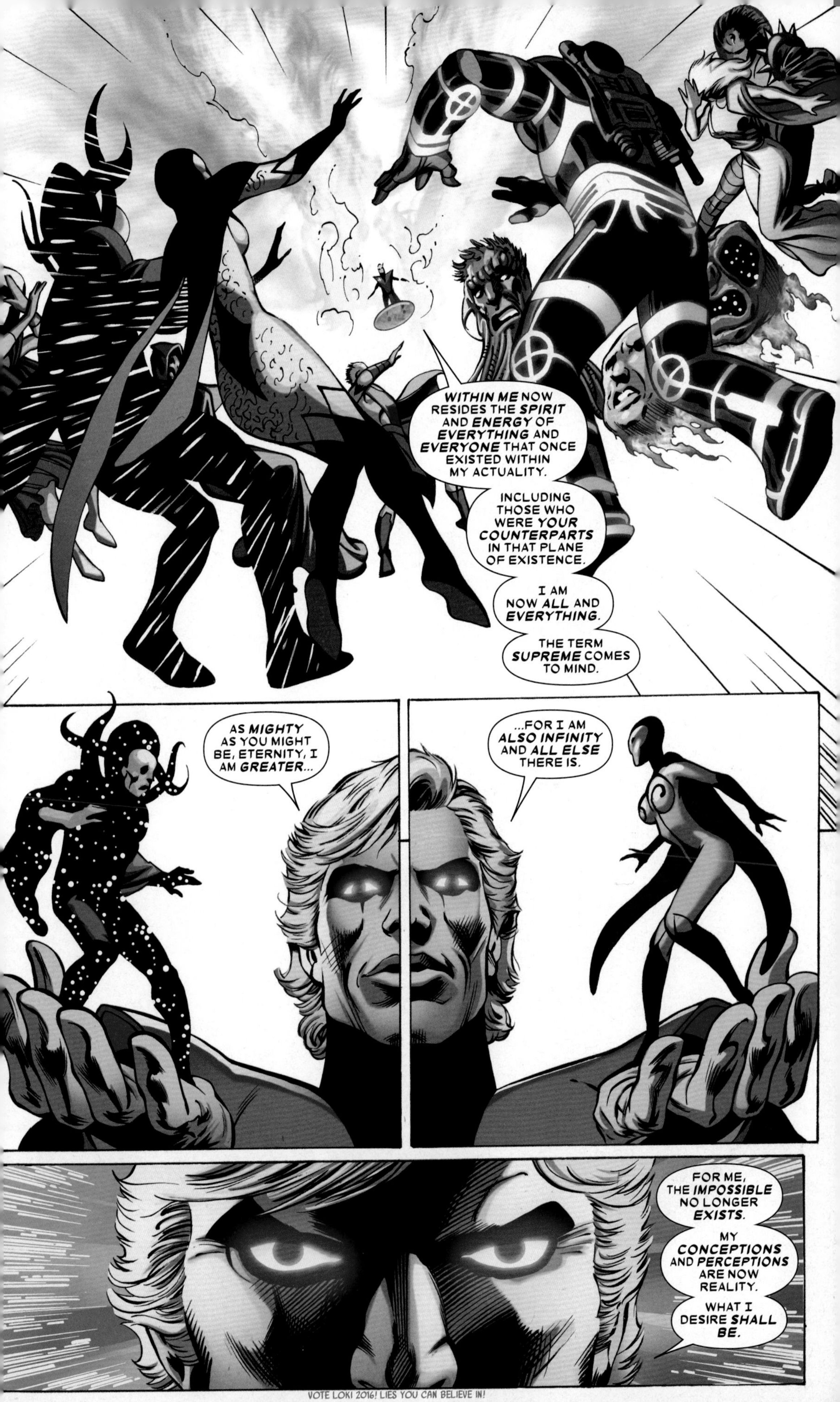
WITHIN ME NOW RESIDES THE SPIRIT AND ENERGY OF EVERYTHING AND EVERYONE THAT ONCE EXISTED WITHIN MY ACTUALITY.
INCLUDING THOSE WHO WERE YOUR COUNTERPARTS IN THAT PLANE OF EXISTENCE.
I AM NOW ALL AND EVERYTHING.
THE TERM SUPREME COMES TO MIND.
AS MIGHTY AS YOU MIGHT BE, ETERNITY, I AM GREATER...
...FOR I AM ALSO INFINITY AND ALL ELSE THERE IS.
FOR ME, THE IMPOSSIBLE NO LONGER EXISTS.
MY CONCEPTIONS AND PERCEPTIONS ARE NOW REALITY.
WHAT I DESIRE SHALL BE.

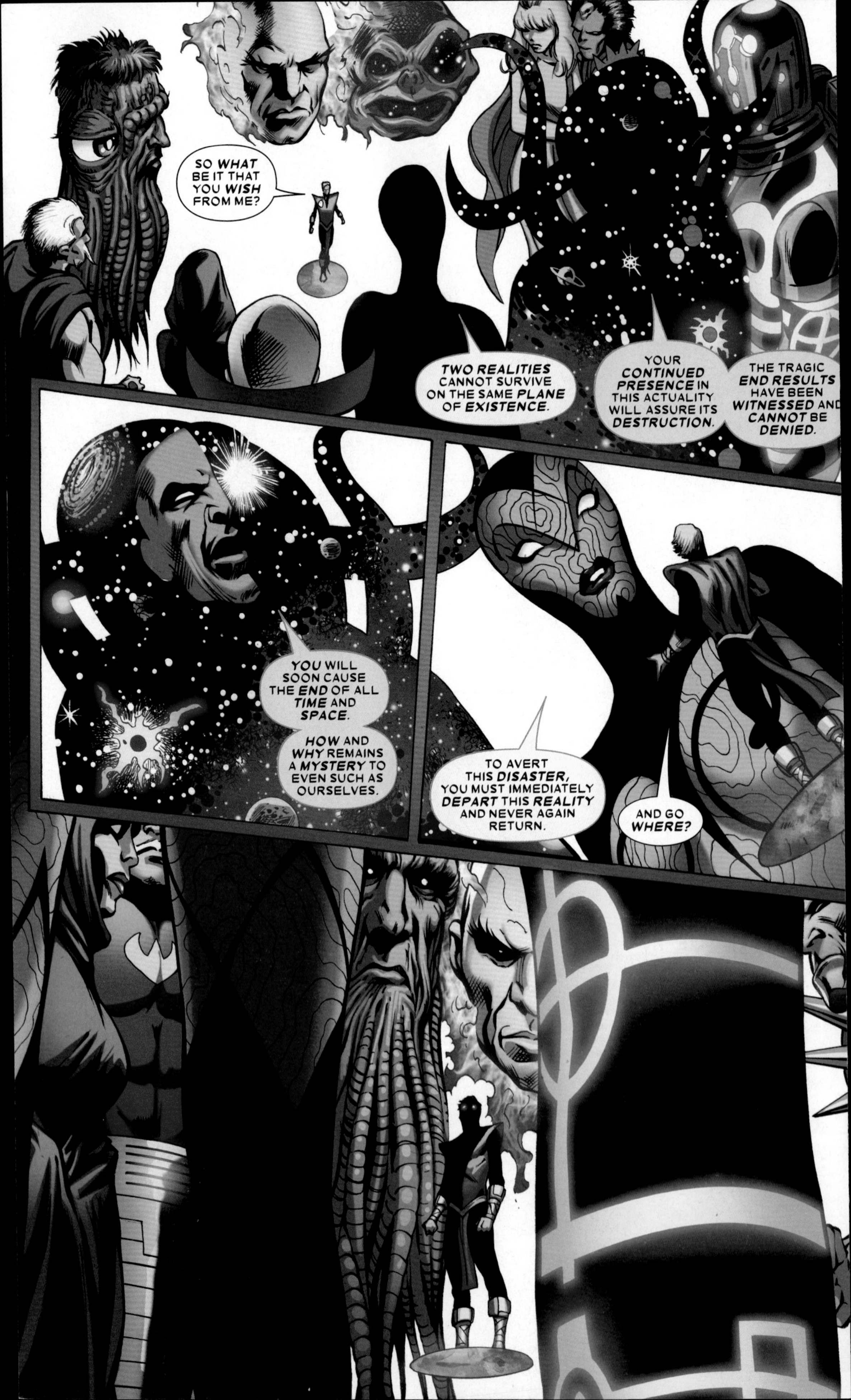
SO WHAT BE IT THAT YOU WISH FROM ME?
TWO REALITIES CANNOT SURVIVE ON THE SAME PLANE OF EXISTENCE.
YOUR CONTINUED PRESENCE IN THIS ACTUALITY WILL ASSURE ITS DESTRUCTION.
THE TRAGIC END RESULTS HAVE BEEN WITNESSED AND CANNOT BE DENIED.
YOU WILL SOON CAUSE THE END OF ALL TIME AND SPACE.
HOW AND WHY REMAINS A MYSTERY TO EVEN SUCH AS OURSELVES.
TO AVERT THIS DISASTER, YOU MUST IMMEDIATELY DEPART THIS REALITY AND NEVER AGAIN RETURN.
AND GO WHERE?

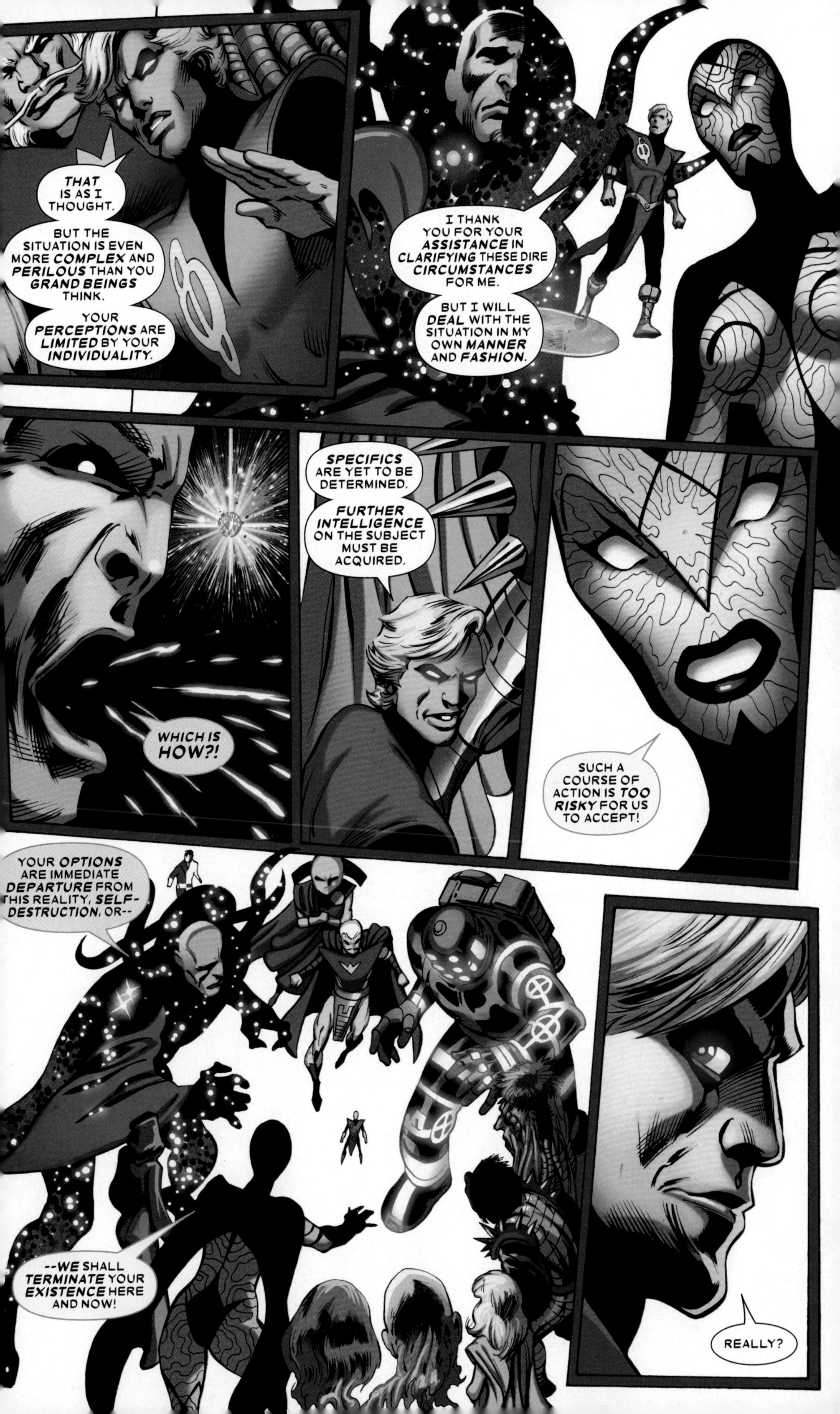
THAT IS AS I THOUGHT.
BUT THE SITUATION IS EVEN MORE COMPLEX AND PERILOUS THAN YOU GRAND BEINGS THINK.
YOUR PERCEPTIONS ARE LIMITED BY YOUR INDIVIDUALITY.
I THANK YOU FOR YOUR ASSISTANCE IN CLARIFYING THESE DIRE CIRCUMSTANCES FOR ME.
BUT I WILL DEAL WITH THE SITUATION IN MY OWN MANNER AND FASHION.
WHICH IS HOW?!
SPECIFICS ARE YET TO BE DETERMINED.
FURTHER INTELLIGENCE ON THE SUBJECT MUST BE ACQUIRED.
SUCH A COURSE OF ACTION IS TOO RISKY FOR US TO ACCEPT!
YOUR OPTIONS ARE IMMEDIATE DEPARTURE FROM THIS REALITY, SELF-DESTRUCTION, OR--
--WE SHALL TERMINATE YOUR EXISTENCE HERE AND NOW!
REALLY?

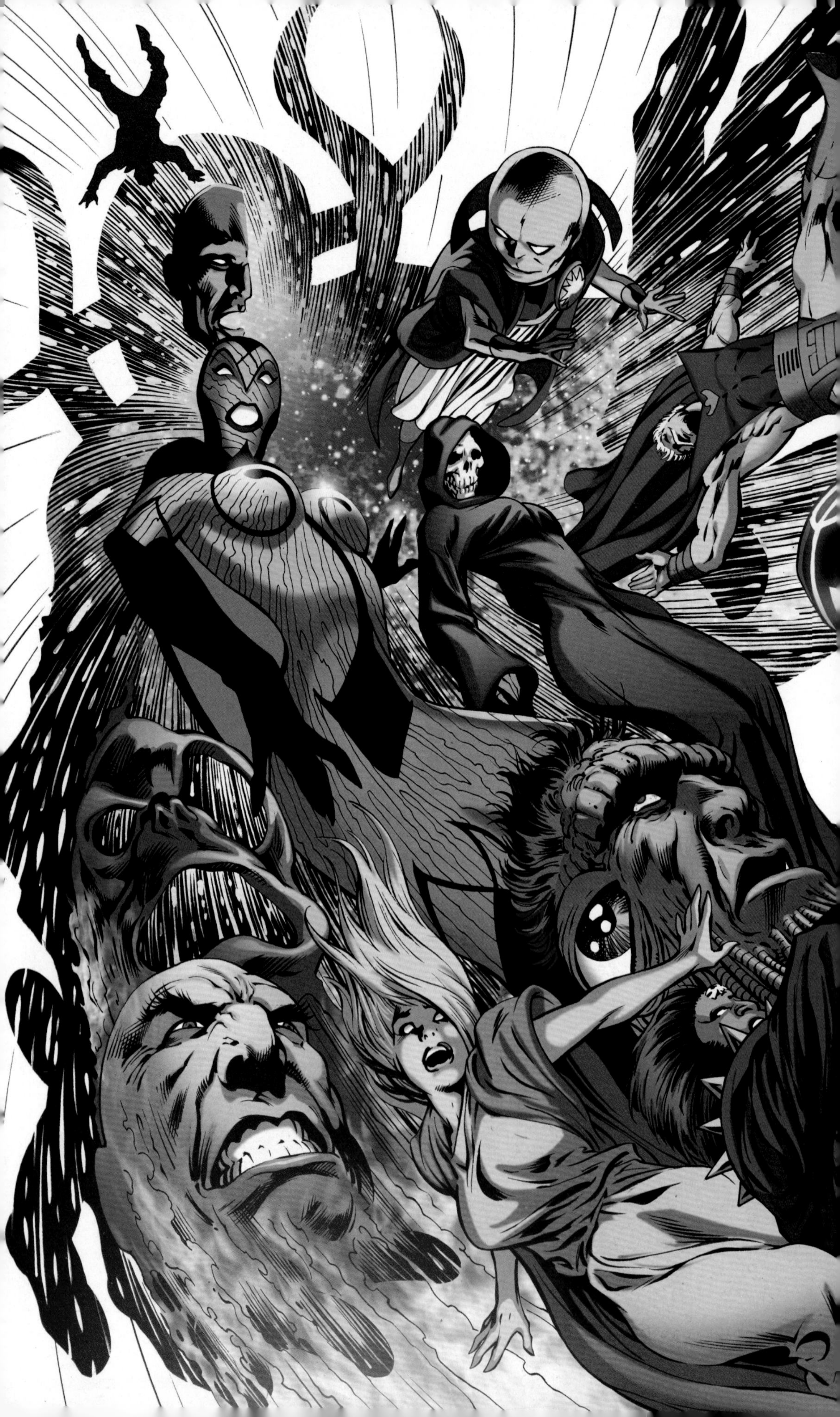

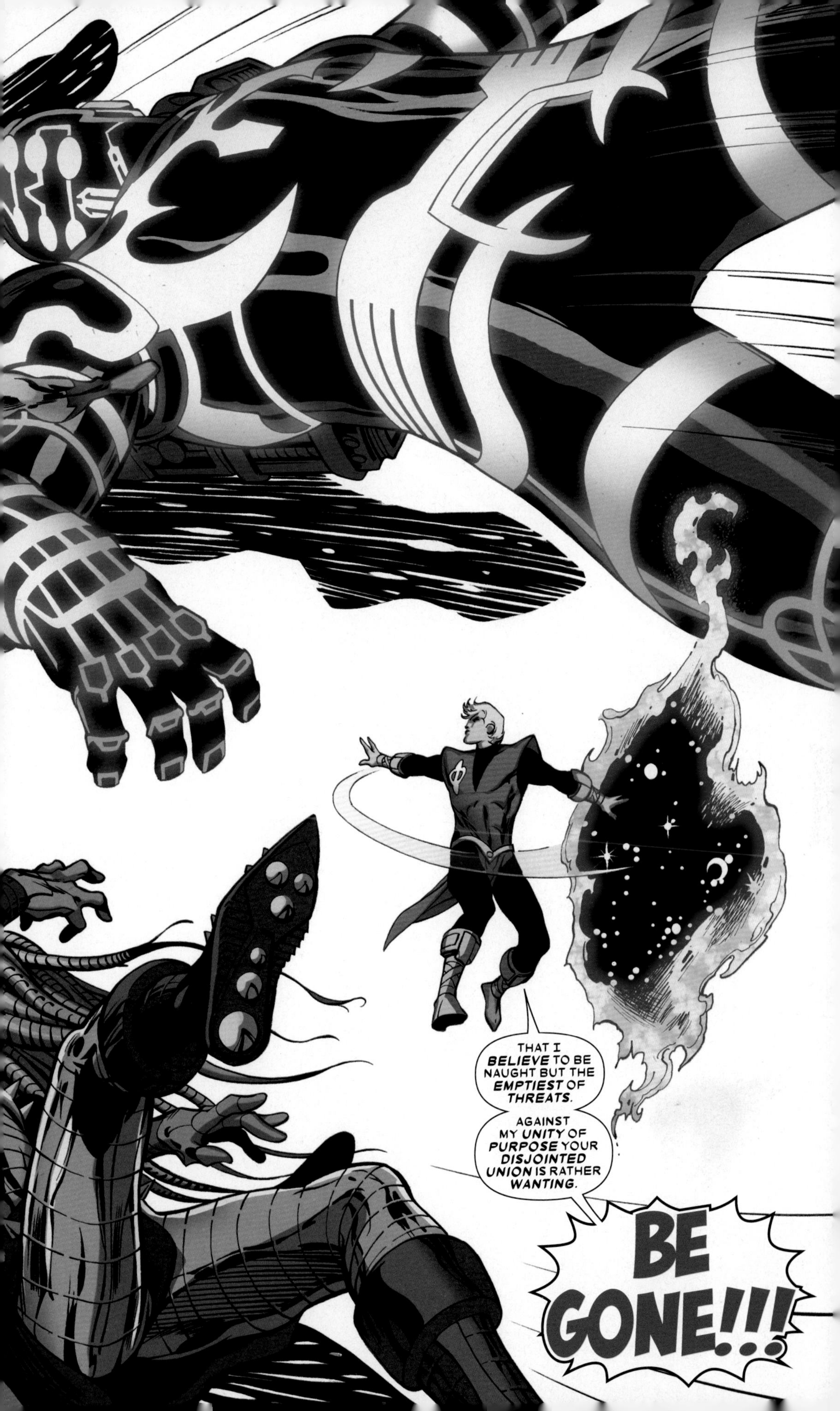
THAT I *BELIEVE* TO BE NAUGHT BUT THE *EMPTIEST* OF *THREATS*.
AGAINST MY *UNITY* OF *PURPOSE* YOUR *DISJOINTED UNION* IS RATHER *WANTING*.
BE GONE!!!

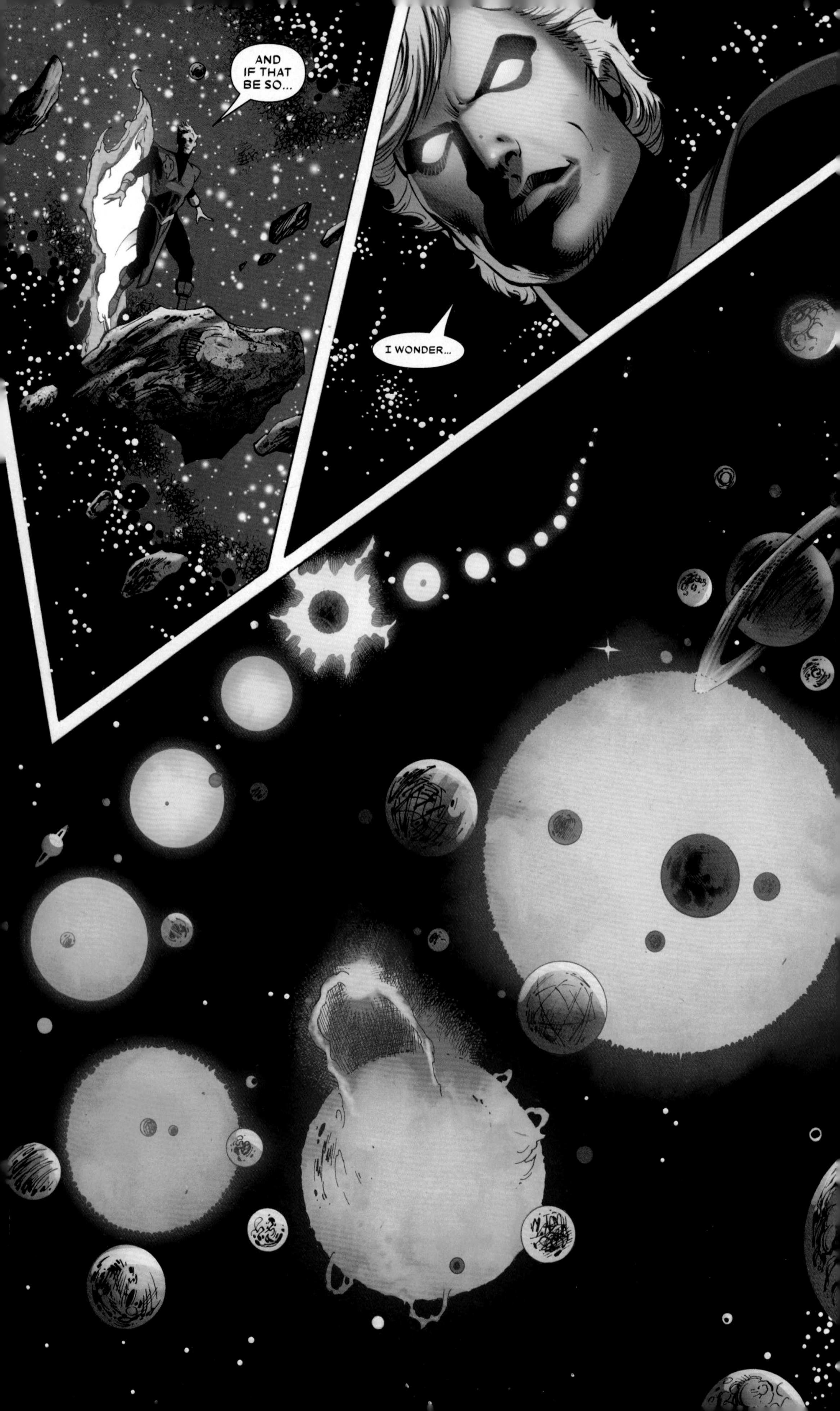
AND IF THAT BE SO...
I WONDER...

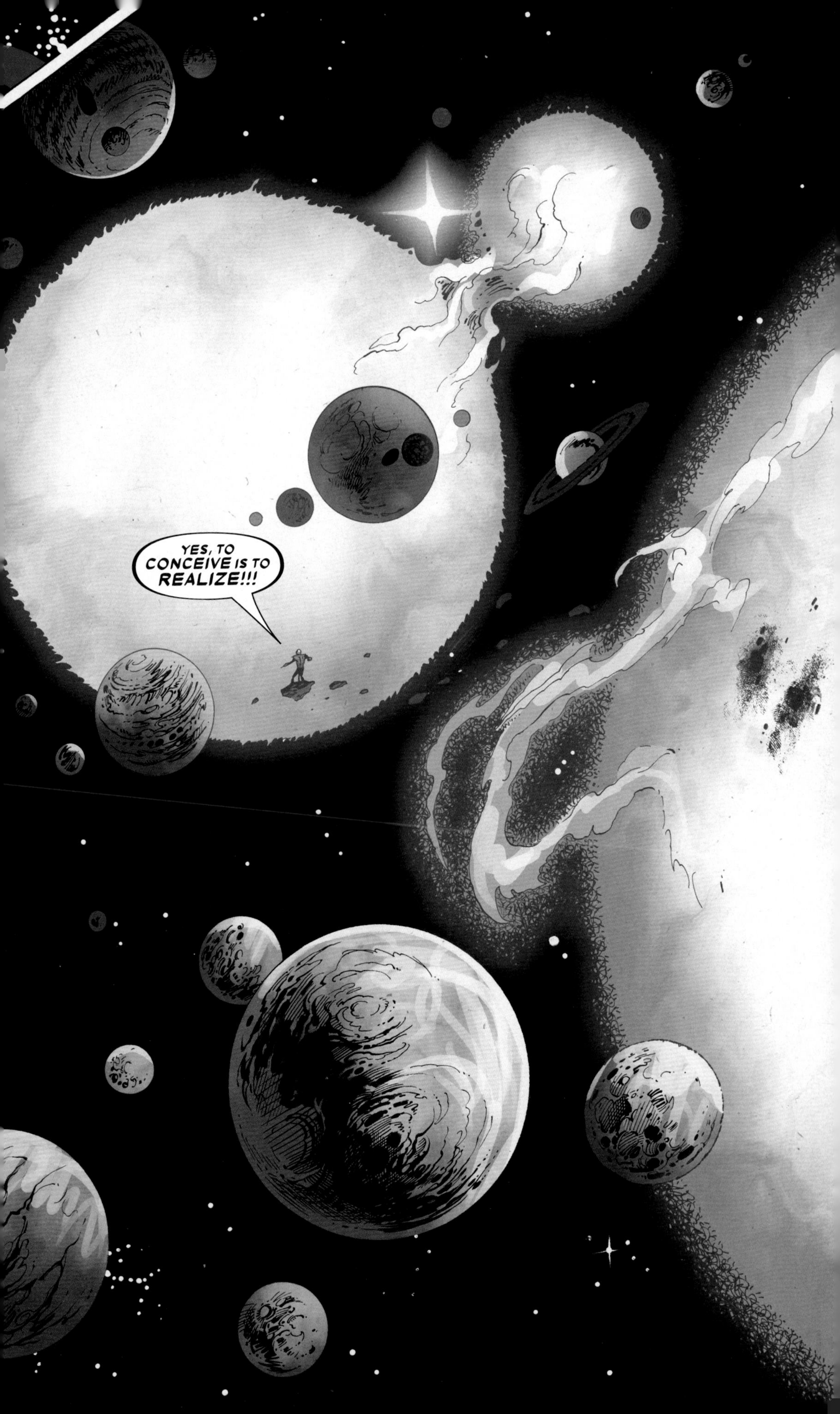
YES, TO CONCEIVE IS TO REALIZE!!!

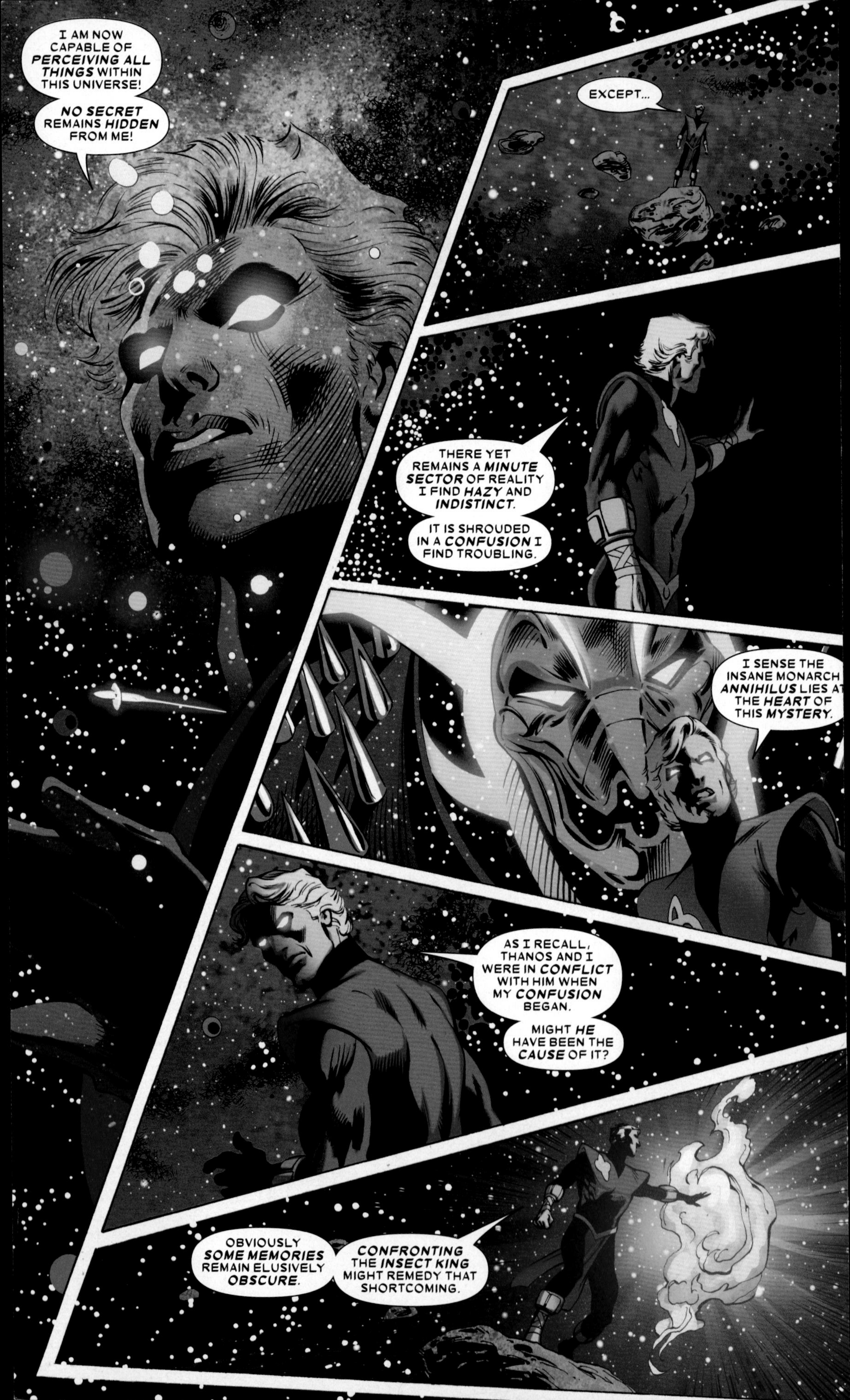
I AM NOW CAPABLE OF PERCEIVING ALL THINGS WITHIN THIS UNIVERSE!
NO SECRET REMAINS HIDDEN FROM ME!
EXCEPT...
THERE YET REMAINS A MINUTE SECTOR OF REALITY I FIND HAZY AND INDISTINCT.
IT IS SHROUDED IN A CONFUSION I FIND TROUBLING.
I SENSE THE INSANE MONARCH ANNIHILUS LIES AT THE HEART OF THIS MYSTERY.
AS I RECALL, THANOS AND I WERE IN CONFLICT WITH HIM WHEN MY CONFUSION BEGAN.
MIGHT HE HAVE BEEN THE CAUSE OF IT?
OBVIOUSLY SOME MEMORIES REMAIN ELUSIVELY OBSCURE.
CONFRONTING THE INSECT KING MIGHT REMEDY THAT SHORTCOMING.

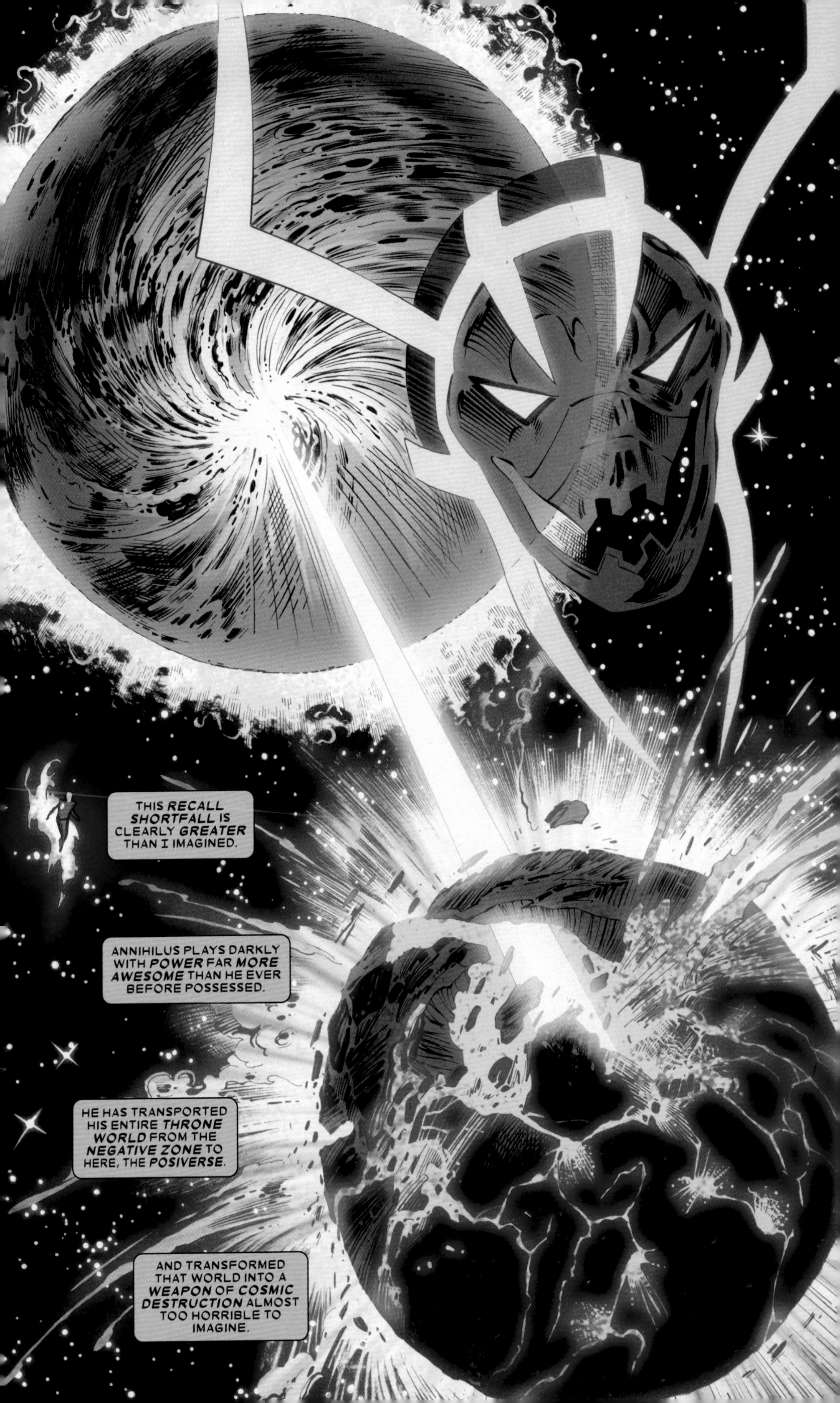
THIS RECALL SHORTFALL IS CLEARLY GREATER THAN I IMAGINED.
ANNIHILUS PLAYS DARKLY WITH POWER FAR MORE AWESOME THAN HE EVER BEFORE POSSESSED.
HE HAS TRANSPORTED HIS ENTIRE THRONE WORLD FROM THE NEGATIVE ZONE TO HERE, THE POSIVERSE.
AND TRANSFORMED THAT WORLD INTO A WEAPON OF COSMIC DESTRUCTION ALMOST TOO HORRIBLE TO IMAGINE.

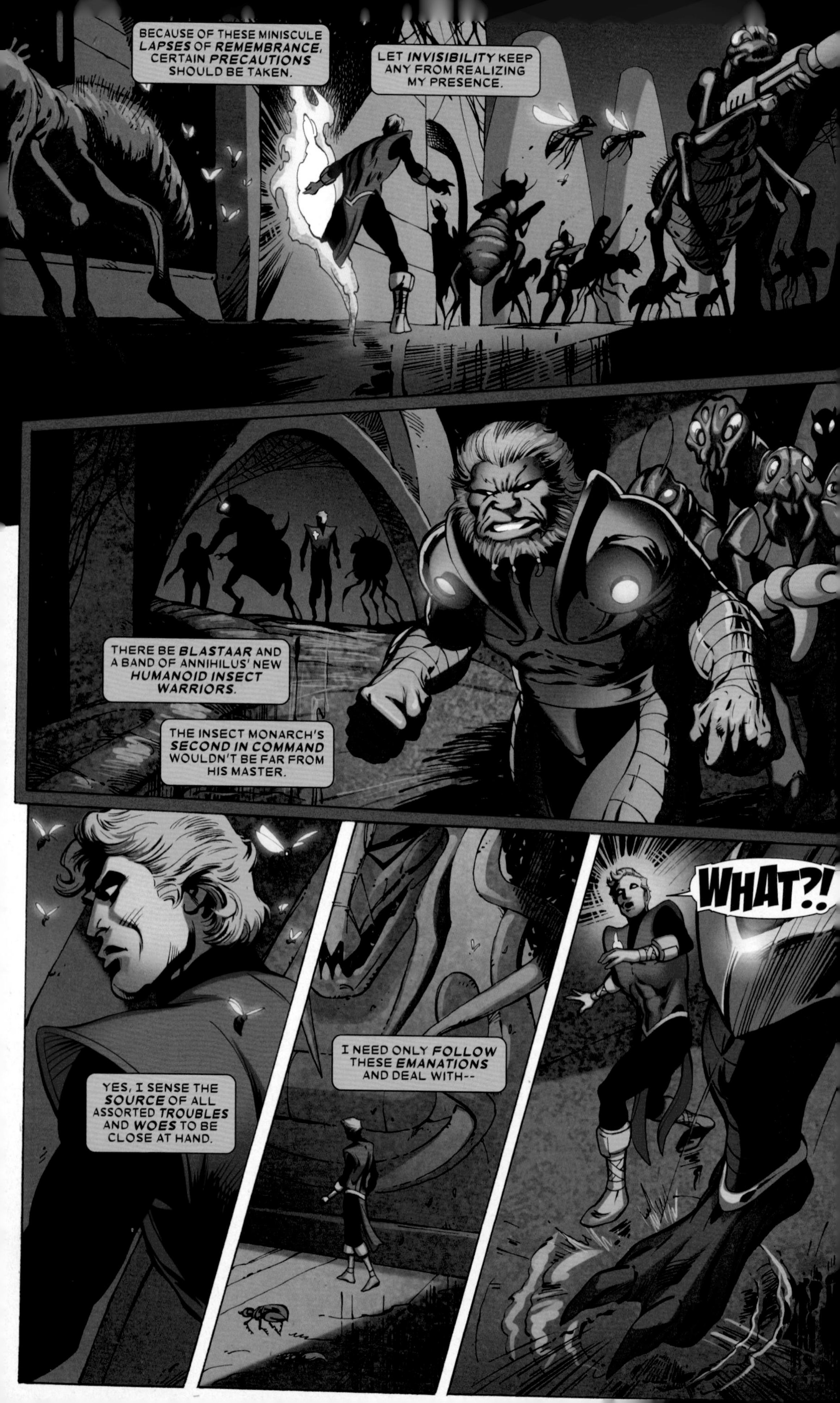
BECAUSE OF THESE MINISCULE LAPSES OF REMEMBRANCE, CERTAIN PRECAUTIONS SHOULD BE TAKEN.
LET INVISIBILITY KEEP ANY FROM REALIZING MY PRESENCE.
THERE BE BLASTAAR AND A BAND OF ANNIHILUS' NEW HUMANOID INSECT WARRIORS.
THE INSECT MONARCH'S SECOND IN COMMAND WOULDN'T BE FAR FROM HIS MASTER.
YES, I SENSE THE SOURCE OF ALL ASSORTED TROUBLES AND WOES TO BE CLOSE AT HAND.
I NEED ONLY FOLLOW THESE EMANATIONS AND DEAL WITH--
WHAT?!

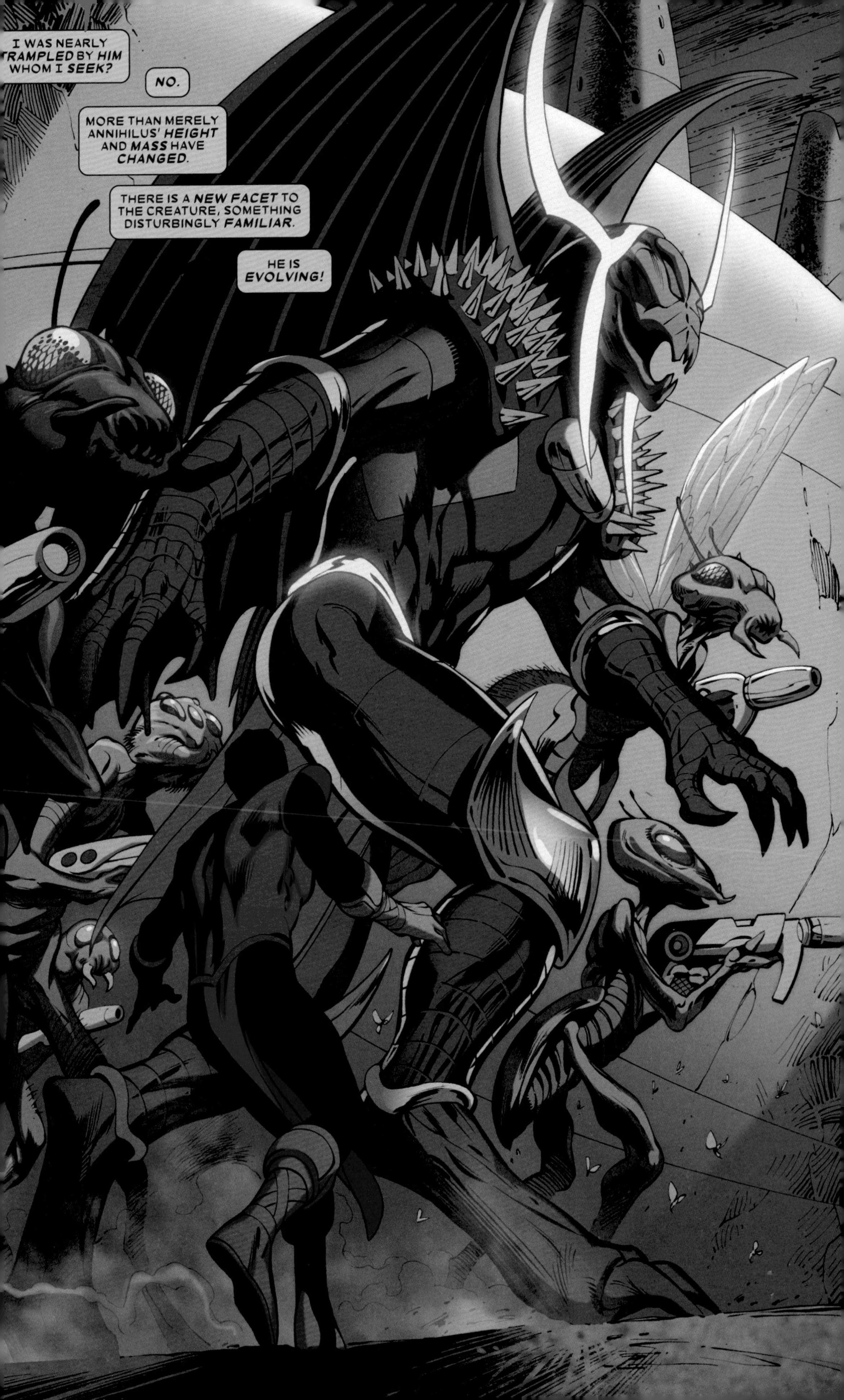
I WAS NEARLY TRAMPLED BY HIM WHOM I SEEK?
NO.
MORE THAN MERELY ANNIHILUS' HEIGHT AND MASS HAVE CHANGED.
THERE IS A NEW FACET TO THE CREATURE, SOMETHING DISTURBINGLY FAMILIAR.
HE IS EVOLVING!

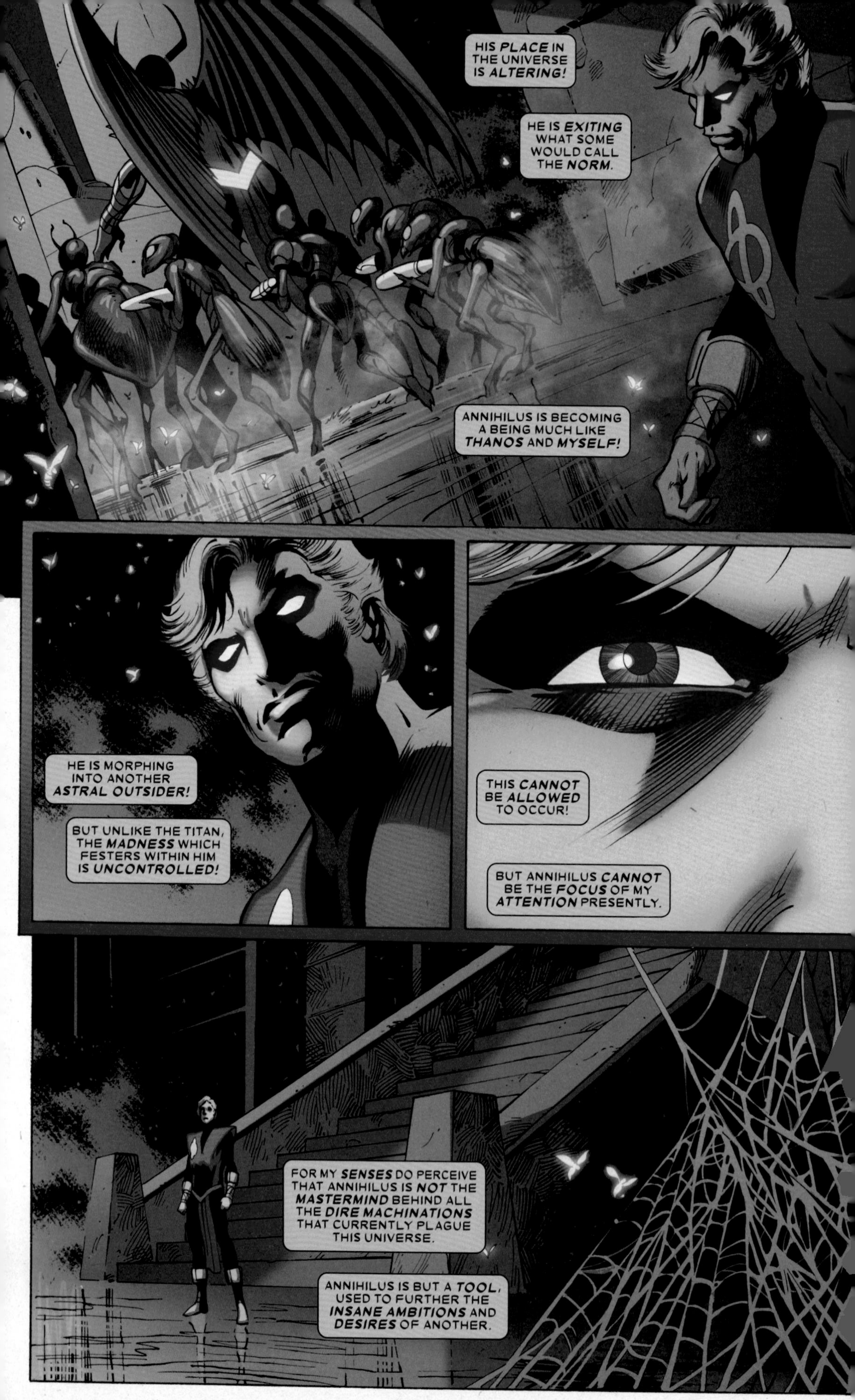

HIS *PLACE* IN THE UNIVERSE IS *ALTERING!*
HE IS *EXITING* WHAT SOME WOULD CALL THE *NORM*.
ANNIHILUS IS BECOMING A BEING MUCH LIKE *THANOS* AND *MYSELF!*
HE IS MORPHING INTO ANOTHER *ASTRAL OUTSIDER!*
BUT UNLIKE THE TITAN, THE *MADNESS* WHICH FESTERS WITHIN HIM IS *UNCONTROLLED!*
THIS *CANNOT* BE *ALLOWED* TO OCCUR!
BUT ANNIHILUS *CANNOT* BE THE *FOCUS* OF MY *ATTENTION* PRESENTLY.
FOR MY *SENSES* DO PERCEIVE THAT ANNIHILUS IS *NOT* THE *MASTERMIND* BEHIND ALL THE *DIRE MACHINATIONS* THAT CURRENTLY PLAGUE THIS UNIVERSE.
ANNIHILUS IS BUT A *TOOL*, USED TO FURTHER THE *INSANE AMBITIONS* AND *DESIRES* OF ANOTHER.

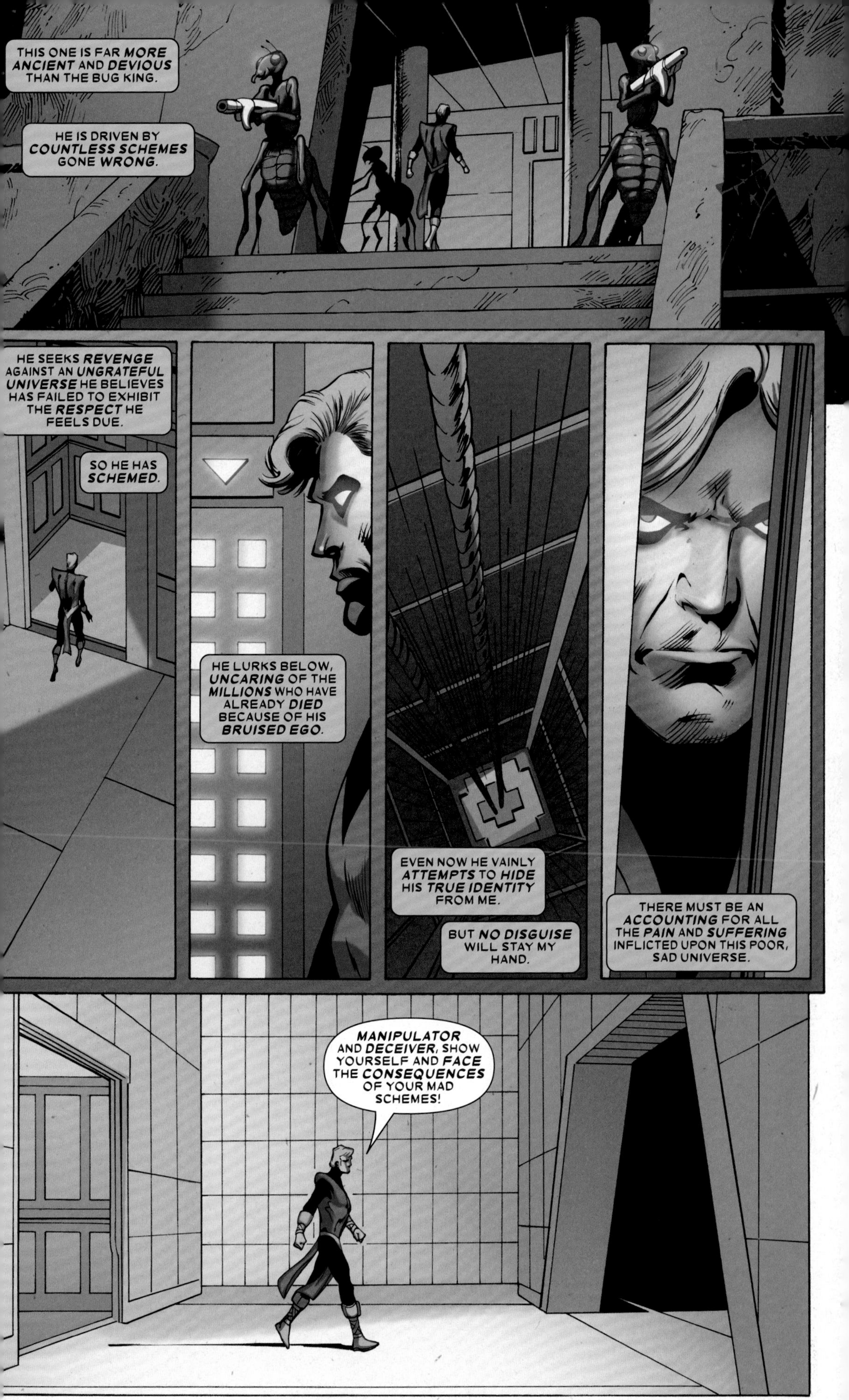

THIS ONE IS FAR MORE ANCIENT AND DEVIOUS THAN THE BUG KING.
HE IS DRIVEN BY COUNTLESS SCHEMES GONE WRONG.
HE SEEKS REVENGE AGAINST AN UNGRATEFUL UNIVERSE HE BELIEVES HAS FAILED TO EXHIBIT THE RESPECT HE FEELS DUE.
SO HE HAS SCHEMED.
HE LURKS BELOW, UNCARING OF THE MILLIONS WHO HAVE ALREADY DIED BECAUSE OF HIS BRUISED EGO.
EVEN NOW HE VAINLY ATTEMPTS TO HIDE HIS TRUE IDENTITY FROM ME.
BUT NO DISGUISE WILL STAY MY HAND.
THERE MUST BE AN ACCOUNTING FOR ALL THE PAIN AND SUFFERING INFLICTED UPON THIS POOR, SAD UNIVERSE.
MANIPULATOR AND DECEIVER, SHOW YOURSELF AND FACE THE CONSEQUENCES OF YOUR MAD SCHEMES!

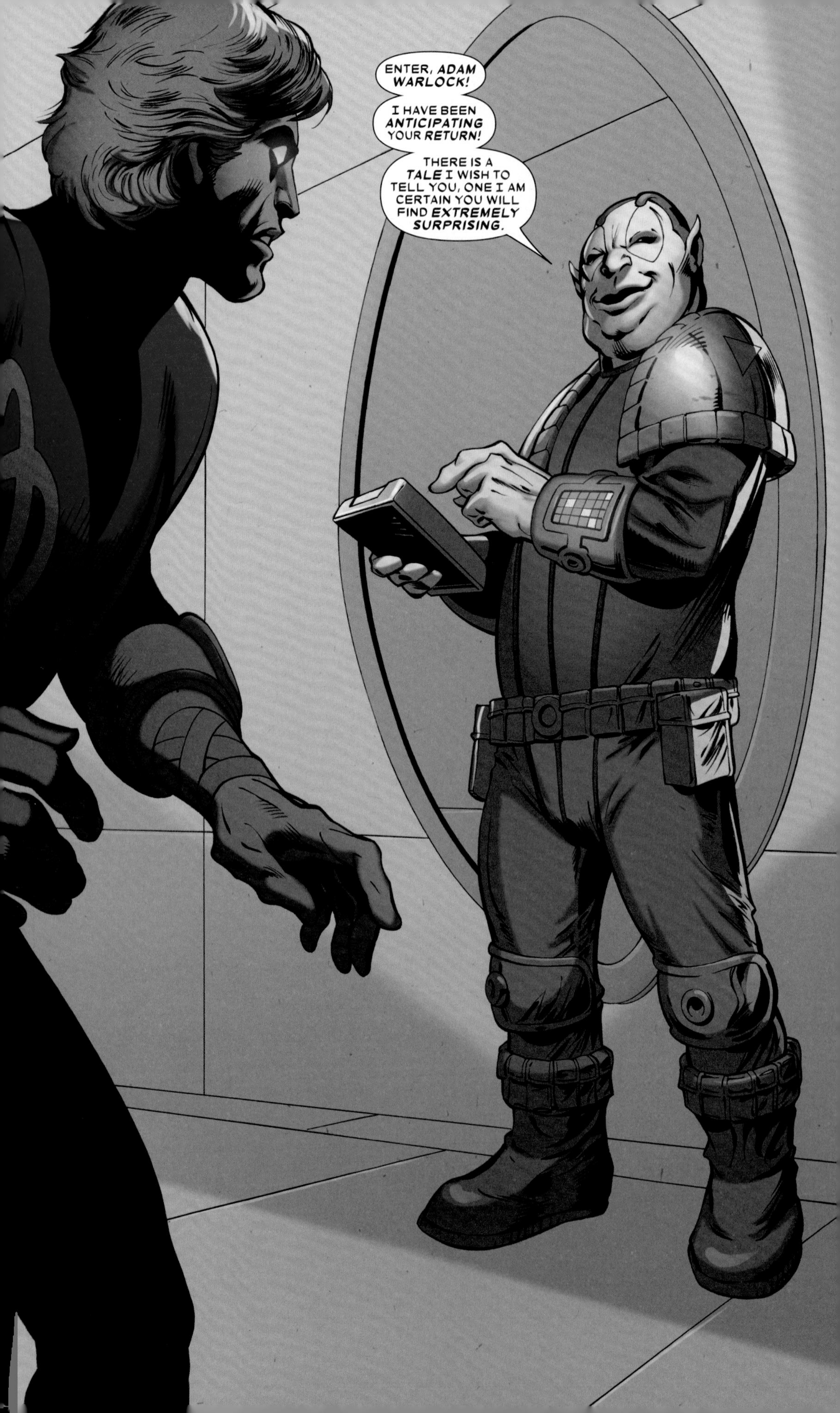
ENTER, ADAM WARLOCK!
I HAVE BEEN ANTICIPATING YOUR RETURN!
THERE IS A TALE I WISH TO TELL YOU, ONE I AM CERTAIN YOU WILL FIND EXTREMELY SURPRISING.

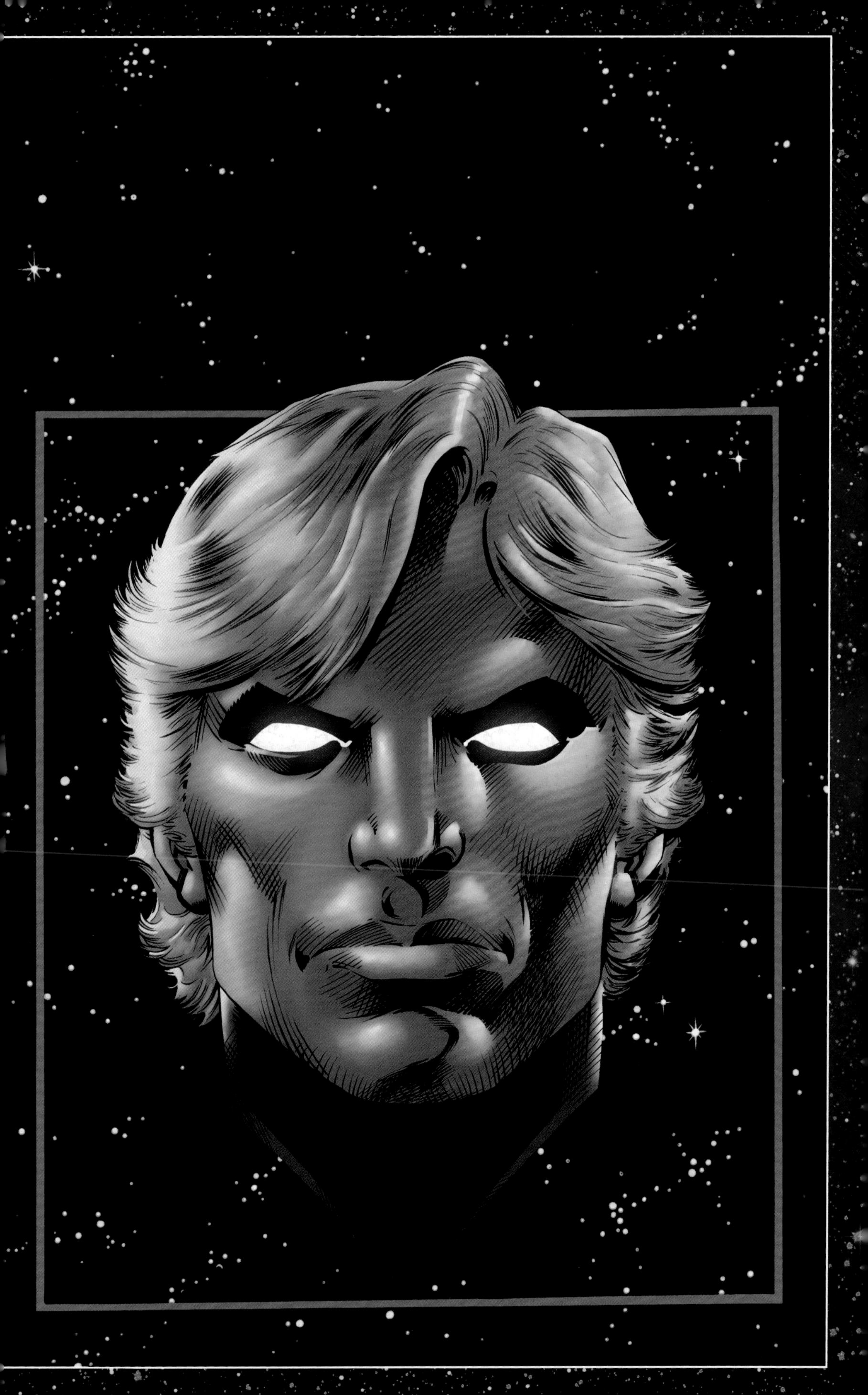

4: THE TRUTH

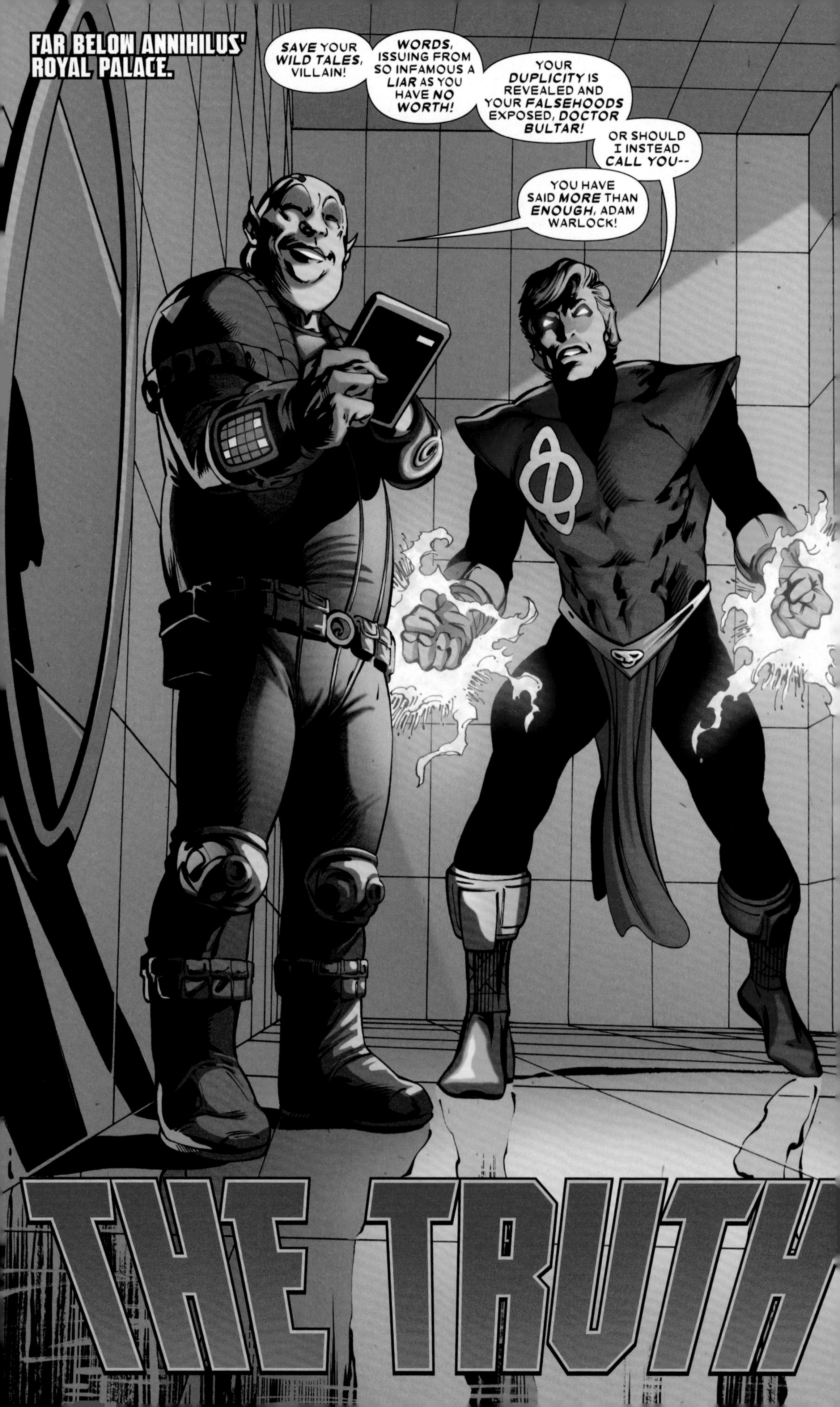
FAR BELOW ANNIHILUS' ROYAL PALACE.
SAVE YOUR WILD TALES, VILLAIN!
WORDS, ISSUING FROM SO INFAMOUS A LIAR AS YOU HAVE NO WORTH!
YOUR DUPLICITY IS REVEALED AND YOUR FALSEHOODS EXPOSED, DOCTOR BULTAR!
OR SHOULD I INSTEAD CALL YOU--
YOU HAVE SAID MORE THAN ENOUGH, ADAM WARLOCK!
THE TRUTH

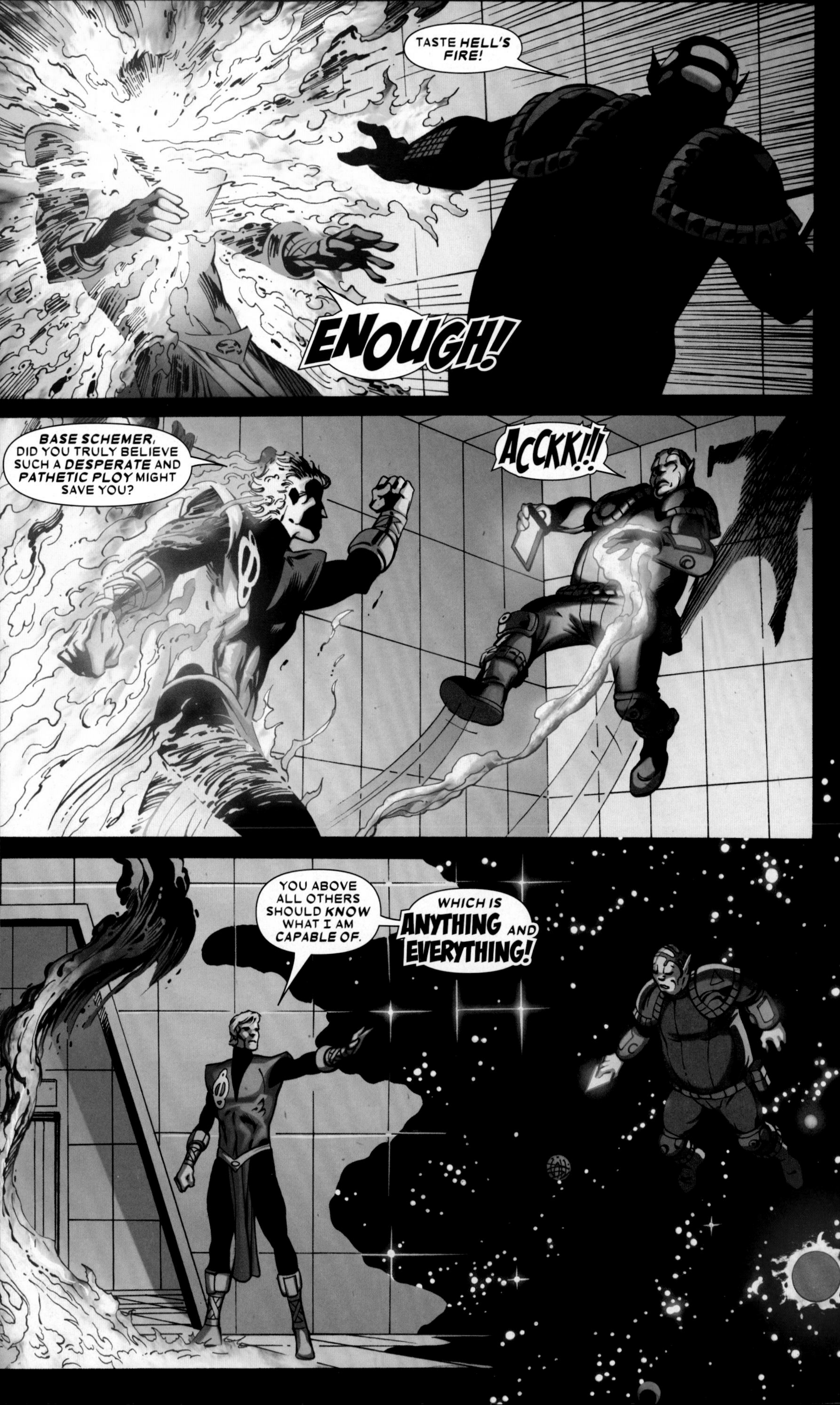
TASTE HELL'S FIRE!
ENOUGH!
BASE SCHEMER, DID YOU TRULY BELIEVE SUCH A DESPERATE AND PATHETIC PLOY MIGHT SAVE YOU?
ACCKK!!!
YOU ABOVE ALL OTHERS SHOULD KNOW WHAT I AM CAPABLE OF.
WHICH IS ANYTHING AND EVERYTHING!

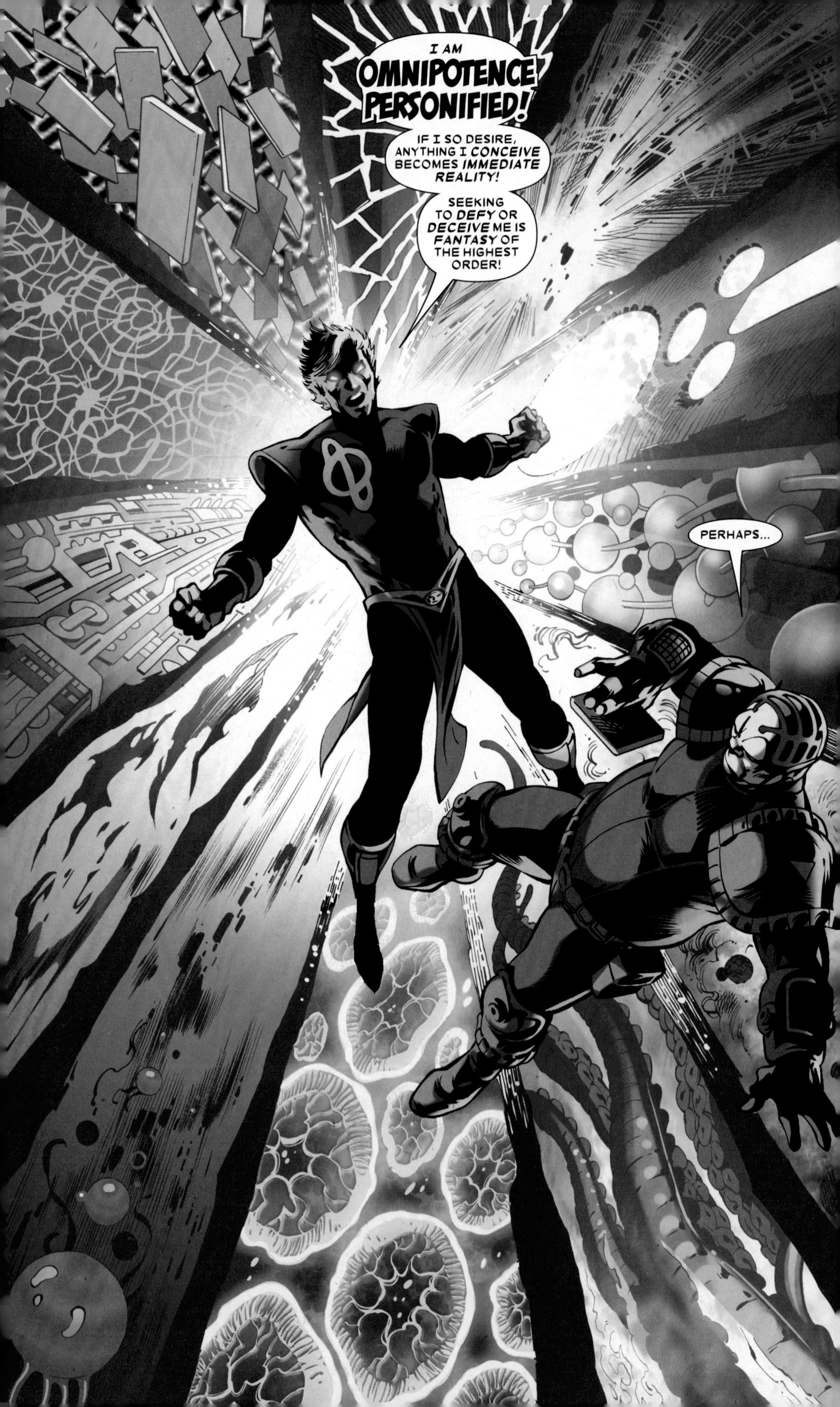
I AM OMNIPOTENCE PERSONIFIED!
IF I SO DESIRE, ANYTHING I CONCEIVE BECOMES IMMEDIATE REALITY!
SEEKING TO DEFY OR DECEIVE ME IS FANTASY OF THE HIGHEST ORDER!
PERHAPS...

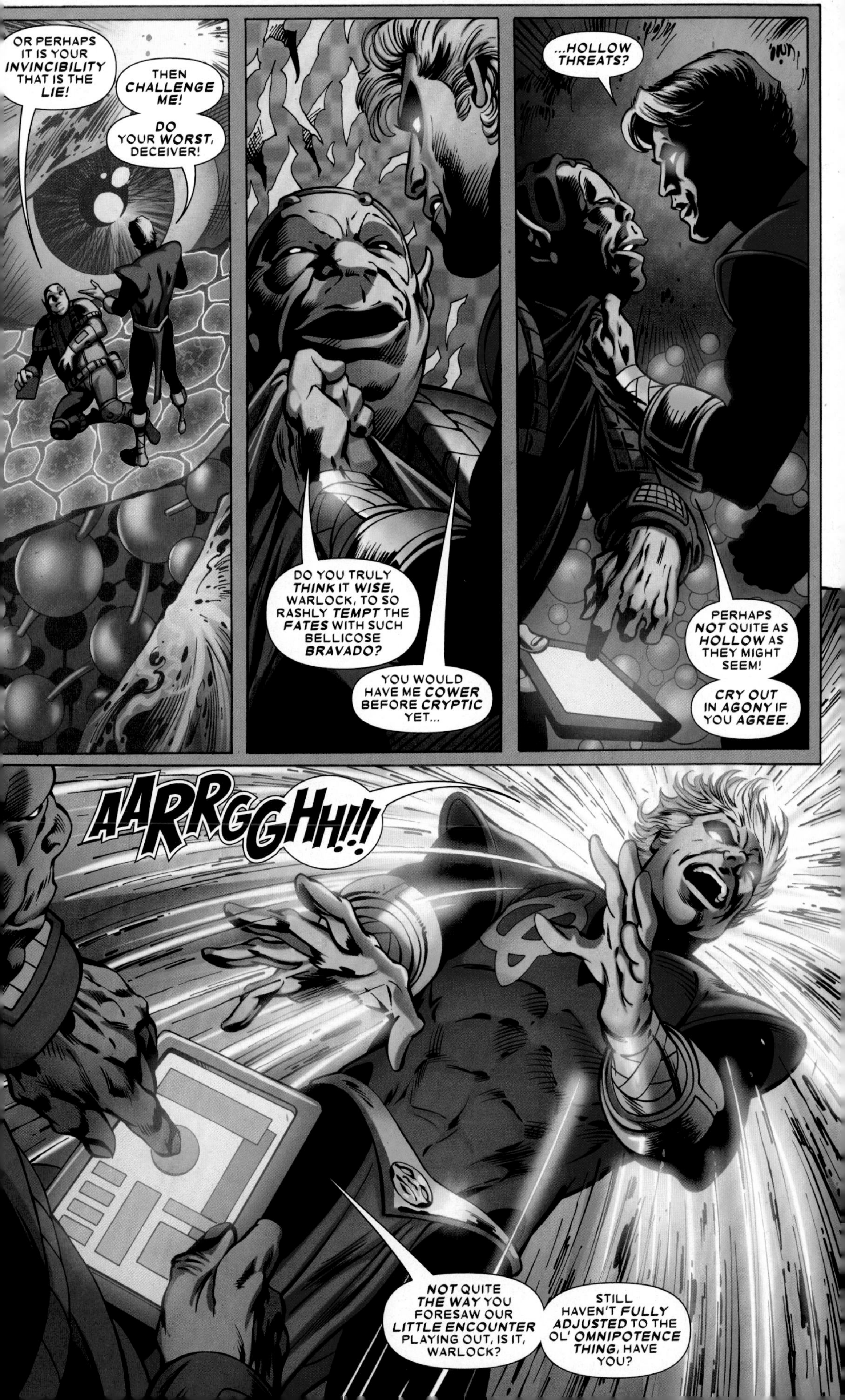
OR PERHAPS IT IS YOUR INVINCIBILITY THAT IS THE LIE!
THEN CHALLENGE ME!
DO YOUR WORST, DECEIVER!
DO YOU TRULY THINK IT WISE, WARLOCK, TO SO RASHLY TEMPT THE FATES WITH SUCH BELLICOSE BRAVADO?
YOU WOULD HAVE ME COWER BEFORE CRYPTIC YET...
...HOLLOW THREATS?
PERHAPS NOT QUITE AS HOLLOW AS THEY MIGHT SEEM!
CRY OUT IN AGONY IF YOU AGREE.
AARRGGHH!!!
NOT QUITE THE WAY YOU FORESAW OUR LITTLE ENCOUNTER PLAYING OUT, IS IT, WARLOCK?
STILL HAVEN'T FULLY ADJUSTED TO THE OL' OMNIPOTENCE THING, HAVE YOU?

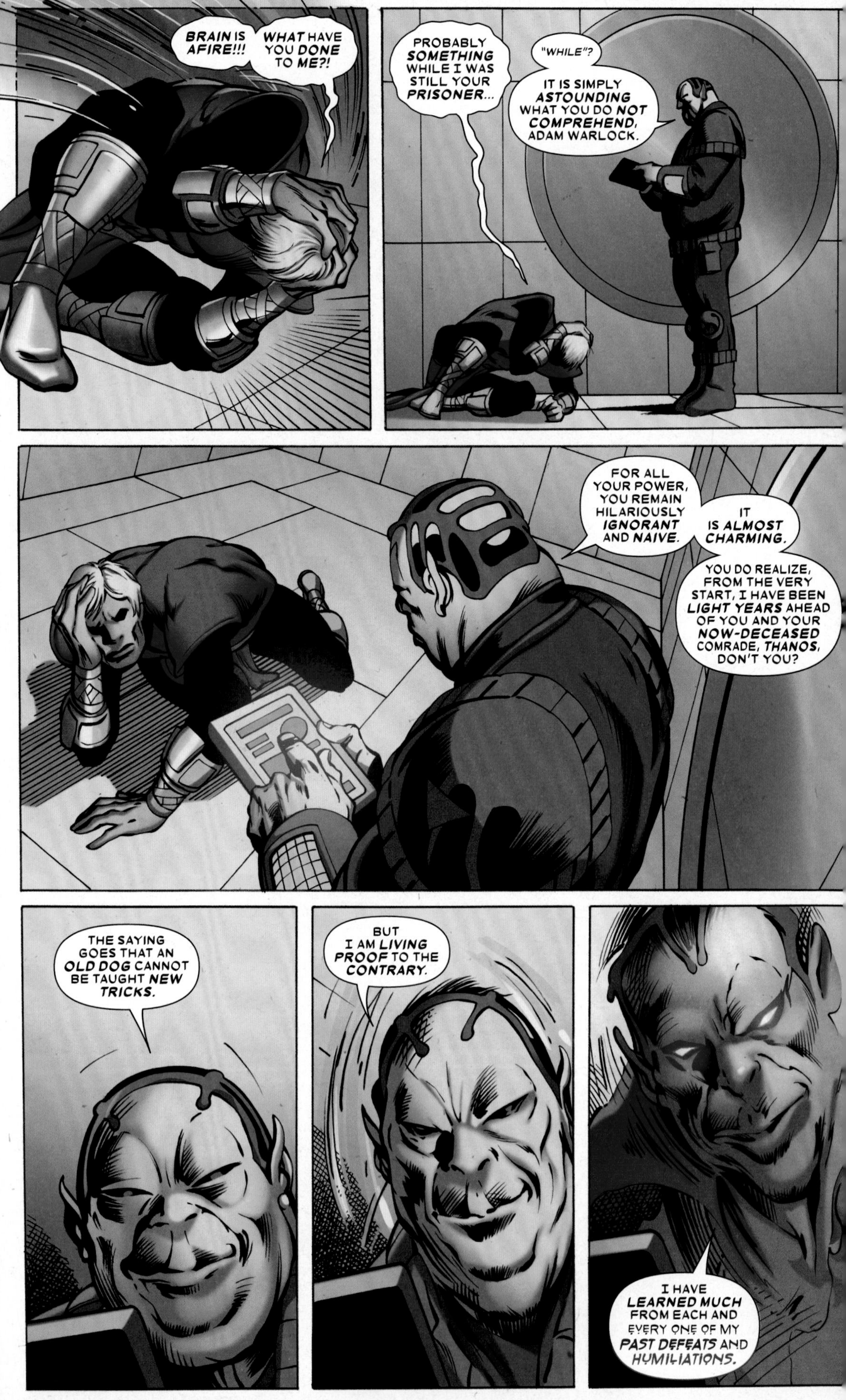
BRAIN IS AFIRE!!!
WHAT HAVE YOU DONE TO ME?!
PROBABLY SOMETHING WHILE I WAS STILL YOUR PRISONER...
"WHILE"?
IT IS SIMPLY ASTOUNDING WHAT YOU DO NOT COMPREHEND, ADAM WARLOCK.
FOR ALL YOUR POWER, YOU REMAIN HILARIOUSLY IGNORANT AND NAIVE.
IT IS ALMOST CHARMING.
YOU DO REALIZE, FROM THE VERY START, I HAVE BEEN LIGHT YEARS AHEAD OF YOU AND YOUR NOW-DECEASED COMRADE, THANOS, DON'T YOU?
THE SAYING GOES THAT AN OLD DOG CANNOT BE TAUGHT NEW TRICKS.
BUT I AM LIVING PROOF TO THE CONTRARY.
I HAVE LEARNED MUCH FROM EACH AND EVERY ONE OF MY PAST DEFEATS AND HUMILIATIONS.

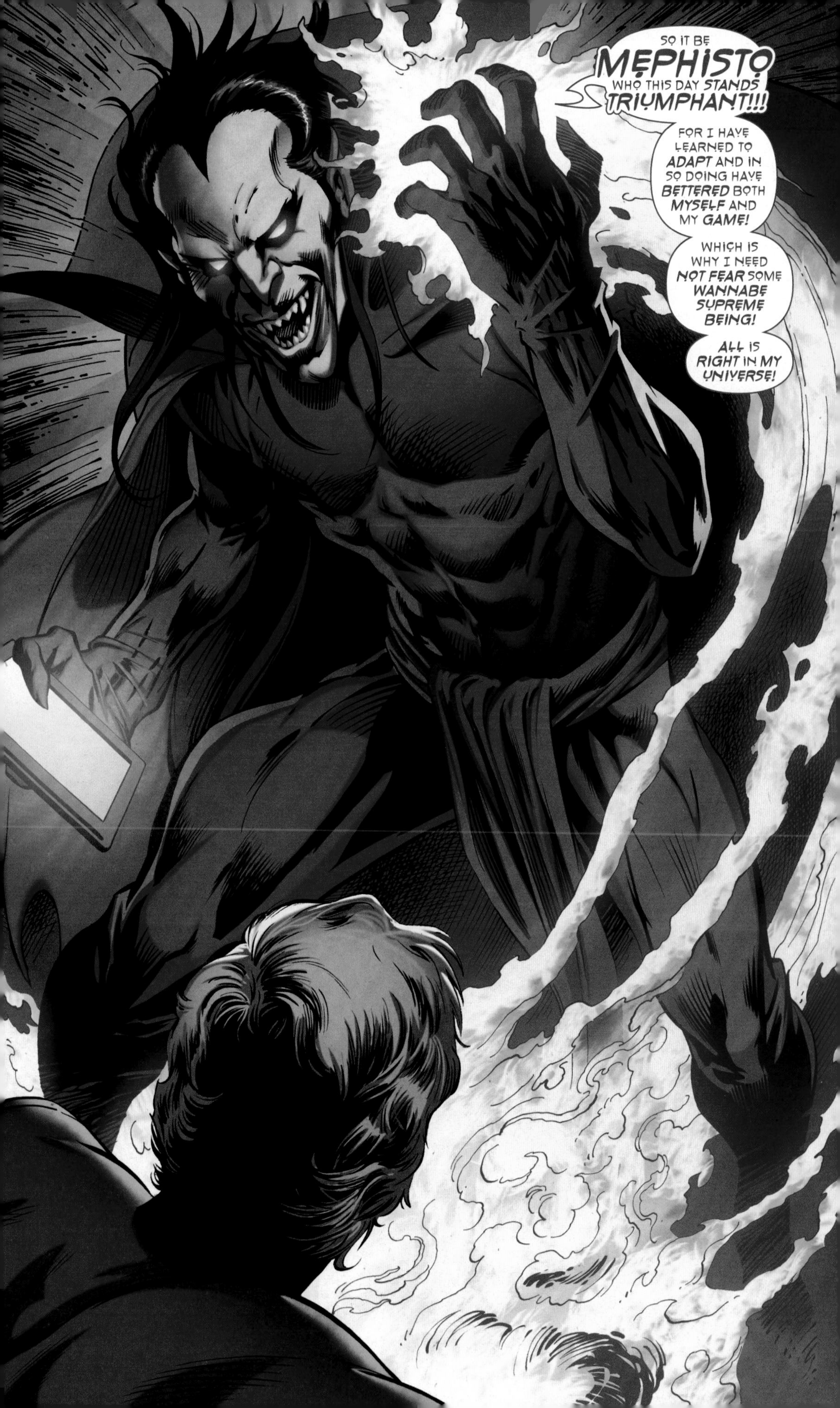
SO IT BE MEPHISTO WHO THIS DAY STANDS TRIUMPHANT!!!
FOR I HAVE LEARNED TO ADAPT AND IN SO DOING HAVE BETTERED BOTH MYSELF AND MY GAME!
WHICH IS WHY I NEED NOT FEAR SOME WANNABE SUPREME BEING!
ALL IS RIGHT IN MY UNIVERSE!

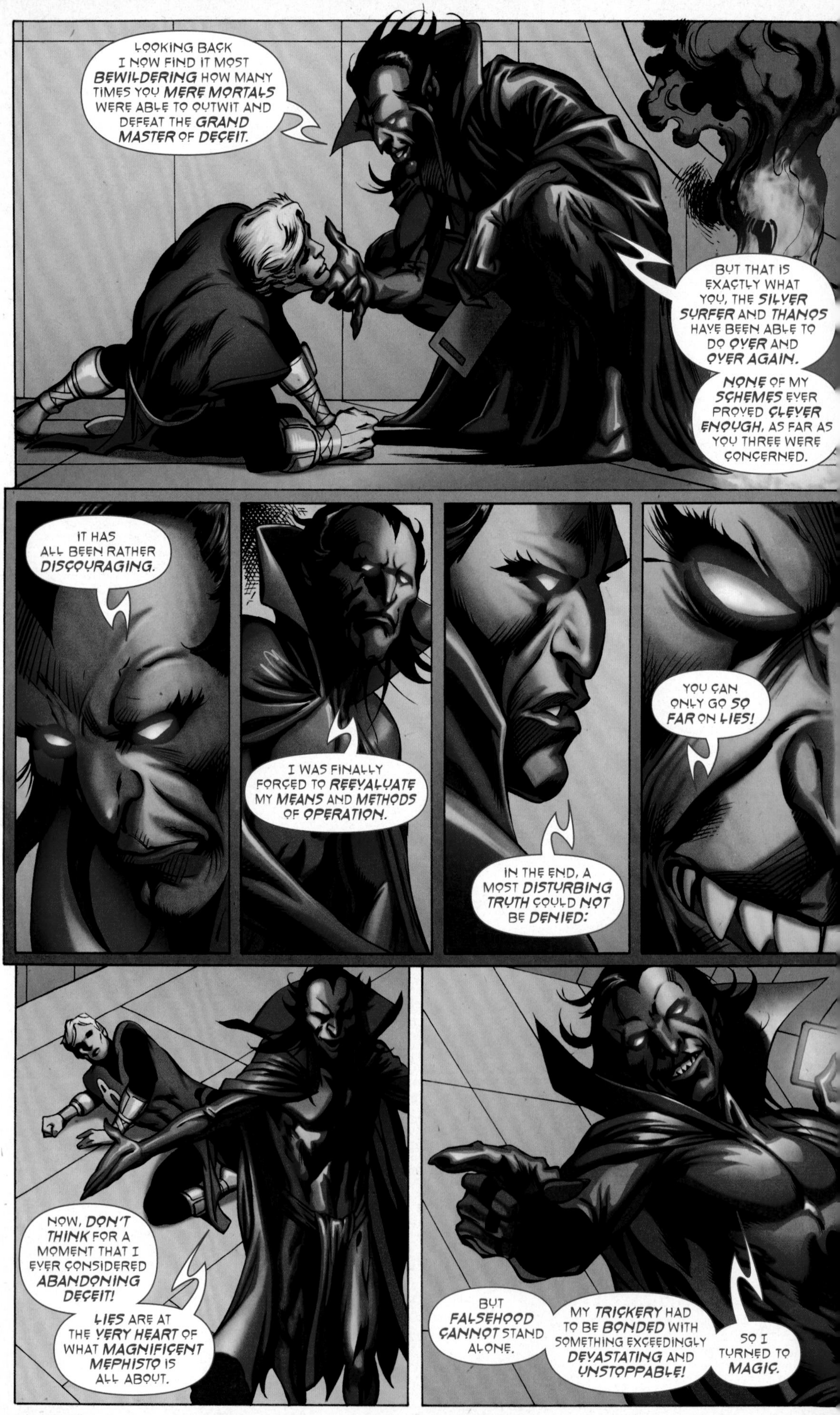
LOOKING BACK I NOW FIND IT MOST BEWILDERING HOW MANY TIMES YOU MERE MORTALS WERE ABLE TO OUTWIT AND DEFEAT THE GRAND MASTER OF DECEIT.
BUT THAT IS EXACTLY WHAT YOU, THE SILVER SURFER AND THANOS HAVE BEEN ABLE TO DO OVER AND OVER AGAIN.
NONE OF MY SCHEMES EVER PROVED CLEVER ENOUGH, AS FAR AS YOU THREE WERE CONCERNED.
IT HAS ALL BEEN RATHER DISCOURAGING.
I WAS FINALLY FORCED TO REEVALUATE MY MEANS AND METHODS OF OPERATION.
IN THE END, A MOST DISTURBING TRUTH COULD NOT BE DENIED:
YOU CAN ONLY GO SO FAR ON LIES!
NOW, DON'T THINK FOR A MOMENT THAT I EVER CONSIDERED ABANDONING DECEIT!
LIES ARE AT THE VERY HEART OF WHAT MAGNIFICENT MEPHISTO IS ALL ABOUT.
BUT FALSEHOOD CANNOT STAND ALONE.
MY TRICKERY HAD TO BE BONDED WITH SOMETHING EXCEEDINGLY DEVASTATING AND UNSTOPPABLE!
SO I TURNED TO MAGIC.

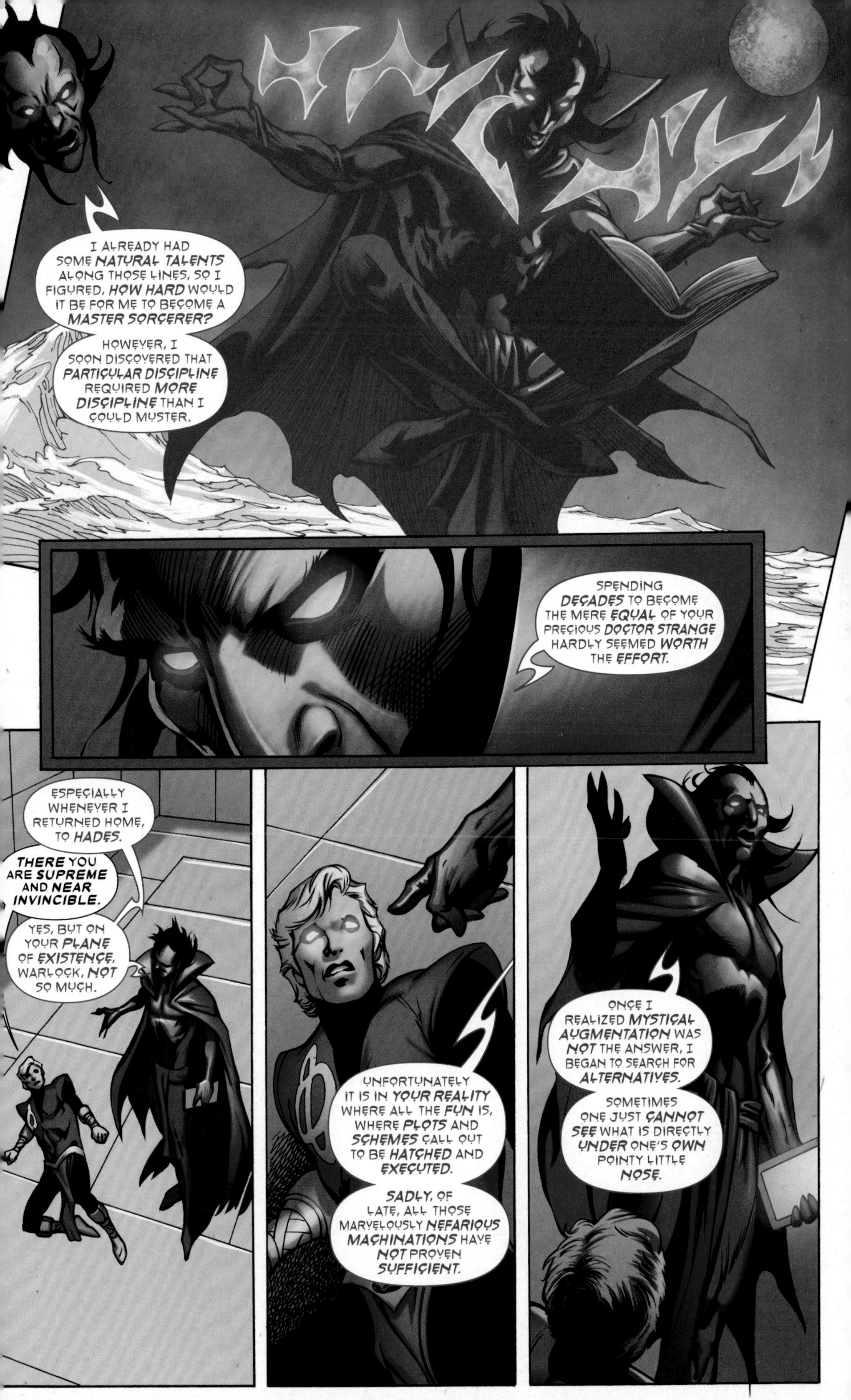
I ALREADY HAD SOME NATURAL TALENTS ALONG THOSE LINES, SO I FIGURED, HOW HARD WOULD IT BE FOR ME TO BECOME A MASTER SORCERER?
HOWEVER, I SOON DISCOVERED THAT PARTICULAR DISCIPLINE REQUIRED MORE DISCIPLINE THAN I COULD MUSTER.
SPENDING DECADES TO BECOME THE MERE EQUAL OF YOUR PRECIOUS DOCTOR STRANGE HARDLY SEEMED WORTH THE EFFORT.
ESPECIALLY WHENEVER I RETURNED HOME, TO HADES.
THERE YOU ARE SUPREME AND NEAR INVINCIBLE.
YES, BUT ON YOUR PLANE OF EXISTENCE, WARLOCK, NOT SO MUCH.
UNFORTUNATELY IT IS IN YOUR REALITY WHERE ALL THE FUN IS, WHERE PLOTS AND SCHEMES CALL OUT TO BE HATCHED AND EXECUTED.
SADLY, OF LATE, ALL THOSE MARVELOUSLY NEFARIOUS MACHINATIONS HAVE NOT PROVEN SUFFICIENT.
ONCE I REALIZED MYSTICAL AUGMENTATION WAS NOT THE ANSWER, I BEGAN TO SEARCH FOR ALTERNATIVES.
SOMETIMES ONE JUST CANNOT SEE WHAT IS DIRECTLY UNDER ONE'S OWN POINTY LITTLE NOSE.

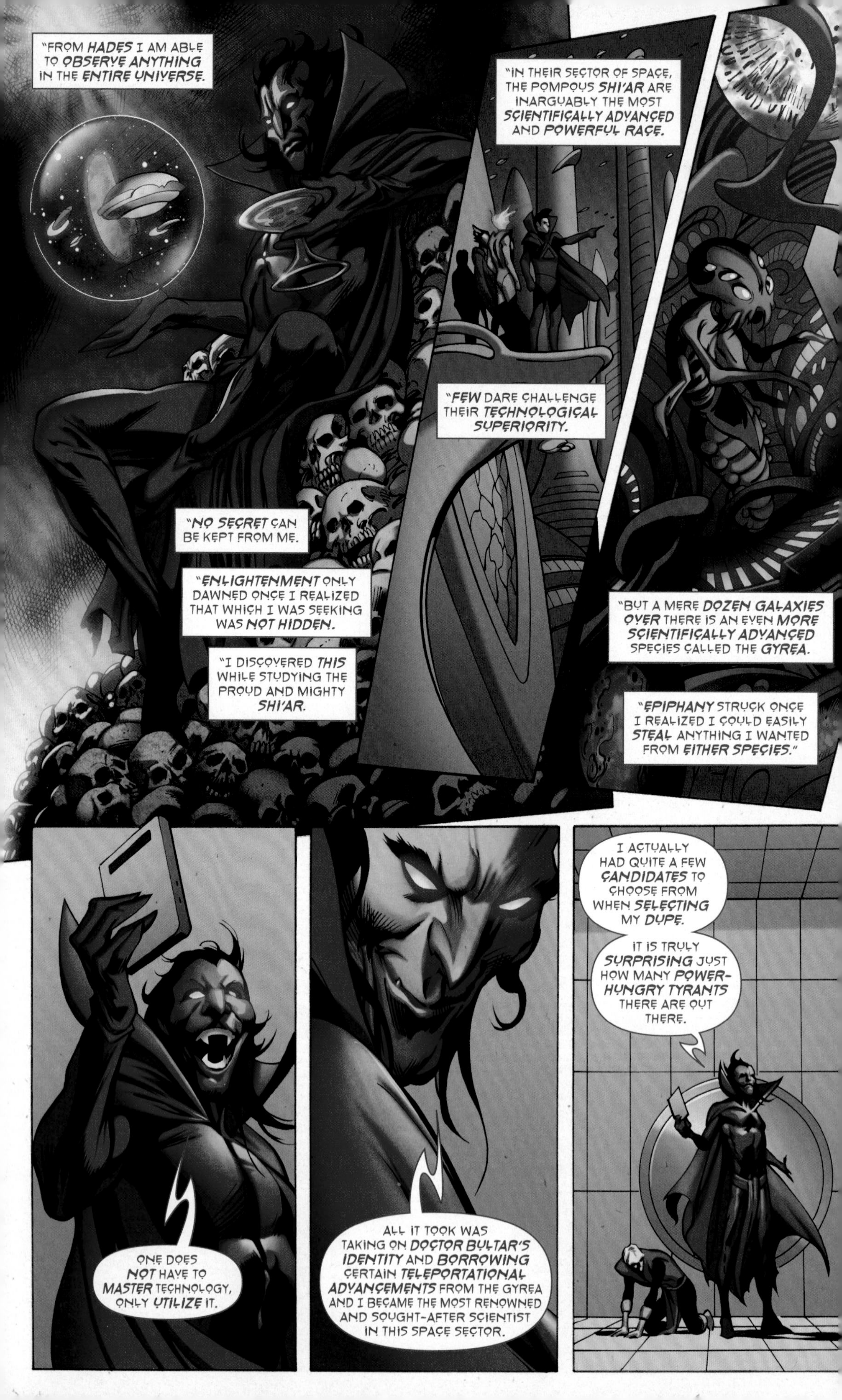
"FROM HADES I AM ABLE TO OBSERVE ANYTHING IN THE ENTIRE UNIVERSE.
"NO SECRET CAN BE KEPT FROM ME.
"ENLIGHTENMENT ONLY DAWNED ONCE I REALIZED THAT WHICH I WAS SEEKING WAS NOT HIDDEN.
"I DISCOVERED THIS WHILE STUDYING THE PROUD AND MIGHTY SHI'AR.
"IN THEIR SECTOR OF SPACE, THE POMPOUS SHI'AR ARE INARGUABLY THE MOST SCIENTIFICALLY ADVANCED AND POWERFUL RACE.
"FEW DARE CHALLENGE THEIR TECHNOLOGICAL SUPERIORITY.
"BUT A MERE DOZEN GALAXIES OVER THERE IS AN EVEN MORE SCIENTIFICALLY ADVANCED SPECIES CALLED THE GYREA.
"EPIPHANY STRUCK ONCE I REALIZED I COULD EASILY STEAL ANYTHING I WANTED FROM EITHER SPECIES."
ONE DOES NOT HAVE TO MASTER TECHNOLOGY, ONLY UTILIZE IT.
ALL IT TOOK WAS TAKING ON DOCTOR BULTAR'S IDENTITY AND BORROWING CERTAIN TELEPORTATIONAL ADVANCEMENTS FROM THE GYREA AND I BECAME THE MOST RENOWNED AND SOUGHT-AFTER SCIENTIST IN THIS SPACE SECTOR.
I ACTUALLY HAD QUITE A FEW CANDIDATES TO CHOOSE FROM WHEN SELECTING MY DUPE.
IT IS TRULY SURPRISING JUST HOW MANY POWER-HUNGRY TYRANTS THERE ARE OUT THERE.

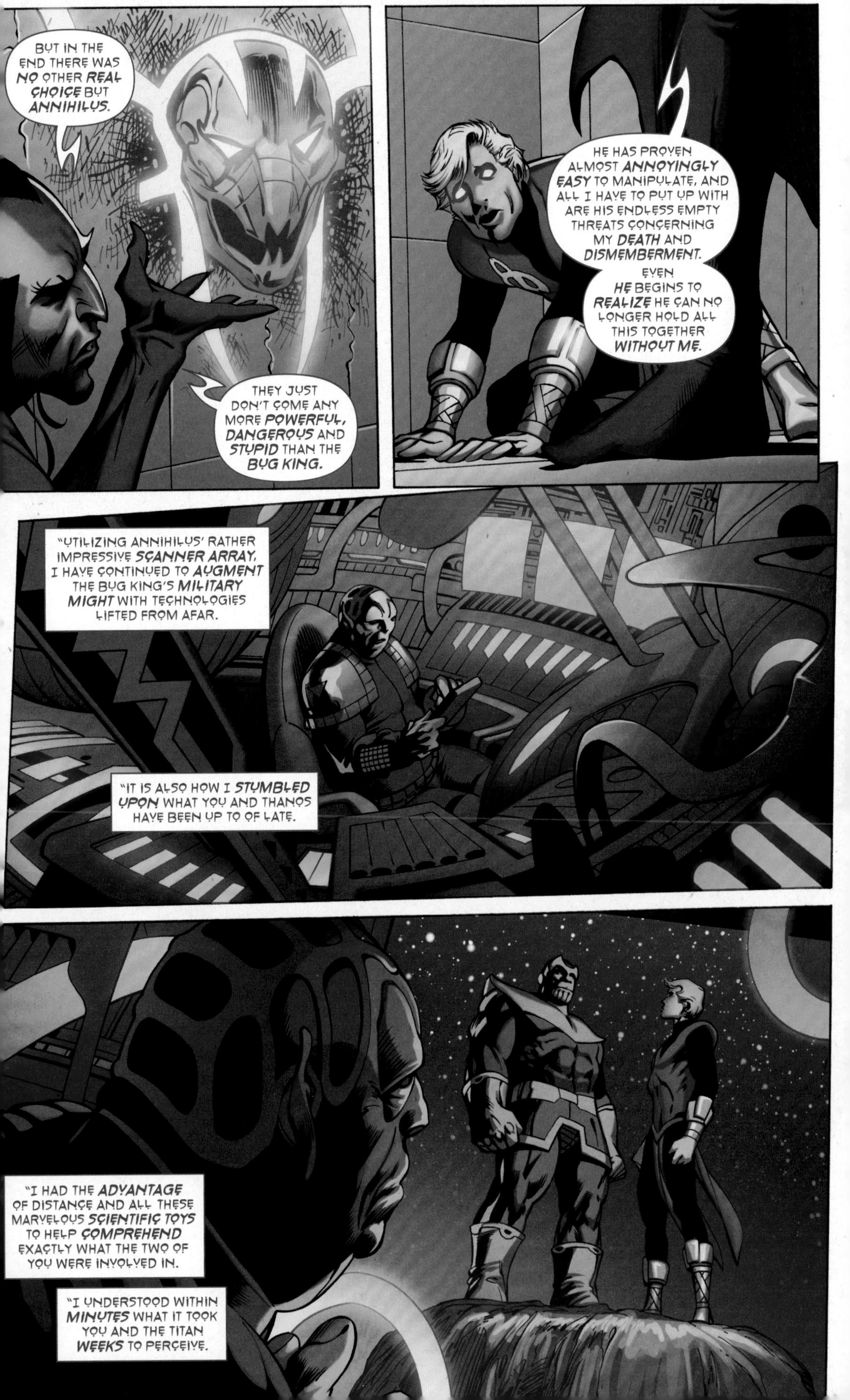
BUT IN THE END THERE WAS NO OTHER REAL CHOICE BUT ANNIHILUS.
THEY JUST DON'T COME ANY MORE POWERFUL, DANGEROUS AND STUPID THAN THE BUG KING.
HE HAS PROVEN ALMOST ANNOYINGLY EASY TO MANIPULATE, AND ALL I HAVE TO PUT UP WITH ARE HIS ENDLESS EMPTY THREATS CONCERNING MY DEATH AND DISMEMBERMENT.
EVEN HE BEGINS TO REALIZE HE CAN NO LONGER HOLD ALL THIS TOGETHER WITHOUT ME.
"UTILIZING ANNIHILUS' RATHER IMPRESSIVE SCANNER ARRAY, I HAVE CONTINUED TO AUGMENT THE BUG KING'S MILITARY MIGHT WITH TECHNOLOGIES LIFTED FROM AFAR.
"IT IS ALSO HOW I STUMBLED UPON WHAT YOU AND THANOS HAVE BEEN UP TO OF LATE.
"I HAD THE ADVANTAGE OF DISTANCE AND ALL THESE MARVELOUS SCIENTIFIC TOYS TO HELP COMPREHEND EXACTLY WHAT THE TWO OF YOU WERE INVOLVED IN.
"I UNDERSTOOD WITHIN MINUTES WHAT IT TOOK YOU AND THE TITAN WEEKS TO PERCEIVE.

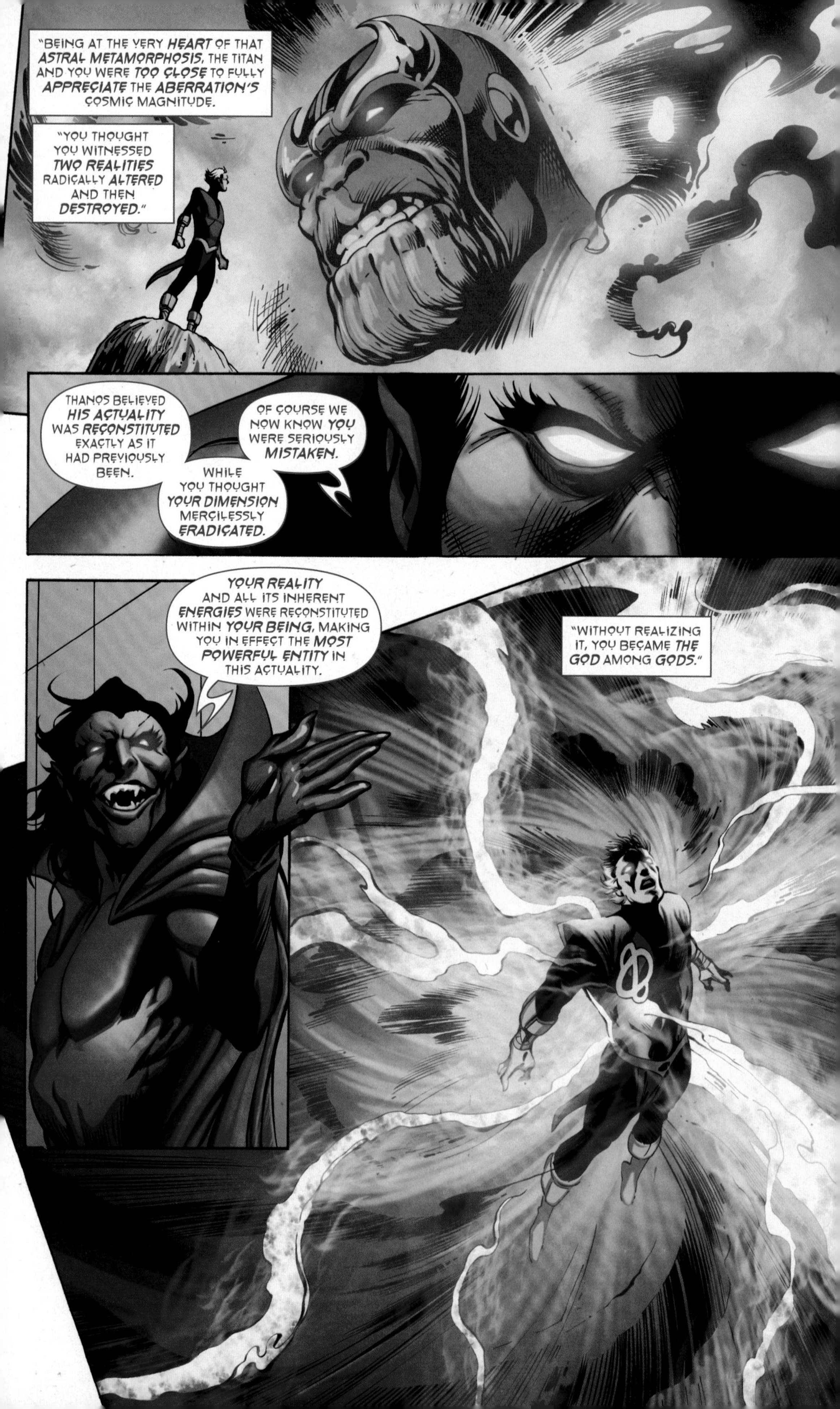
"BEING AT THE VERY HEART OF THAT ASTRAL METAMORPHOSIS, THE TITAN AND YOU WERE TOO CLOSE TO FULLY APPRECIATE THE ABERRATION'S COSMIC MAGNITUDE.
"YOU THOUGHT YOU WITNESSED TWO REALITIES RADICALLY ALTERED AND THEN DESTROYED."
THANOS BELIEVED HIS ACTUALITY WAS RECONSTITUTED EXACTLY AS IT HAD PREVIOUSLY BEEN.
WHILE YOU THOUGHT YOUR DIMENSION MERCILESSLY ERADICATED.
OF COURSE WE NOW KNOW YOU WERE SERIOUSLY MISTAKEN.
YOUR REALITY AND ALL ITS INHERENT ENERGIES WERE RECONSTITUTED WITHIN YOUR BEING, MAKING YOU IN EFFECT THE MOST POWERFUL ENTITY IN THIS ACTUALITY.
"WITHOUT REALIZING IT, YOU BECAME THE GOD AMONG GODS."

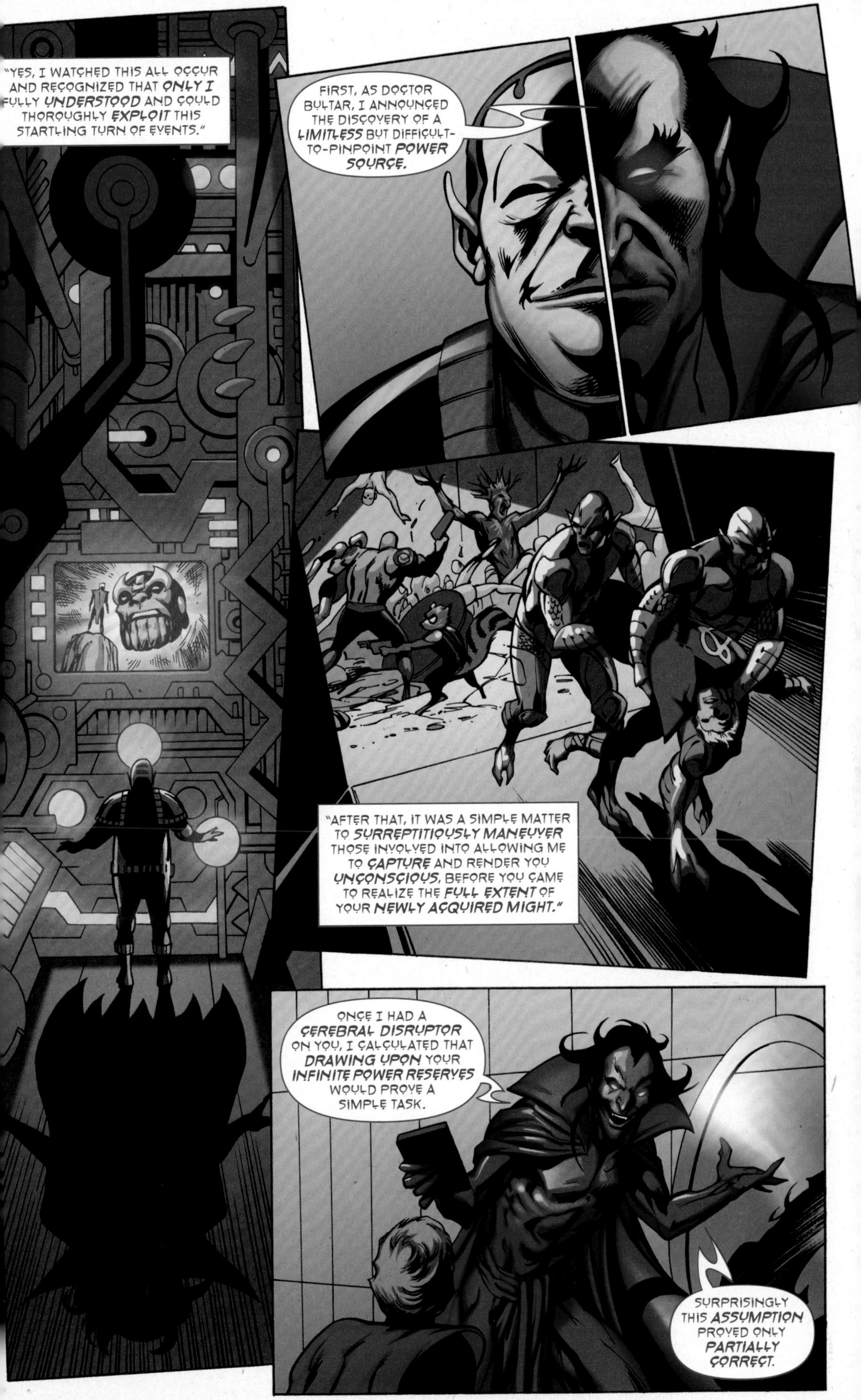
"YES, I WATCHED THIS ALL OCCUR AND RECOGNIZED THAT ONLY I FULLY UNDERSTOOD AND COULD THOROUGHLY EXPLOIT THIS STARTLING TURN OF EVENTS."
FIRST, AS DOCTOR BULTAR, I ANNOUNCED THE DISCOVERY OF A LIMITLESS BUT DIFFICULT-TO-PINPOINT POWER SOURCE.
"AFTER THAT, IT WAS A SIMPLE MATTER TO SURREPTITIOUSLY MANEUVER THOSE INVOLVED INTO ALLOWING ME TO CAPTURE AND RENDER YOU UNCONSCIOUS, BEFORE YOU CAME TO REALIZE THE FULL EXTENT OF YOUR NEWLY ACQUIRED MIGHT."
ONCE I HAD A CEREBRAL DISRUPTOR ON YOU, I CALCULATED THAT DRAWING UPON YOUR INFINITE POWER RESERVES WOULD PROVE A SIMPLE TASK.
SURPRISINGLY THIS ASSUMPTION PROVED ONLY PARTIALLY CORRECT.

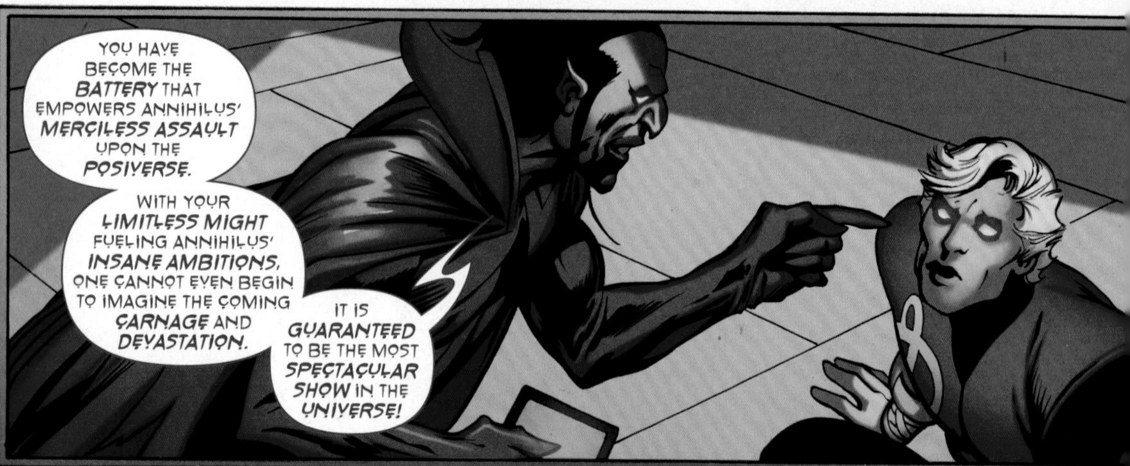
YOU HAVE BECOME THE BATTERY THAT EMPOWERS ANNIHILUS' MERCILESS ASSAULT UPON THE POSIVERSE.
WITH YOUR LIMITLESS MIGHT FUELING ANNIHILUS' INSANE AMBITIONS, ONE CANNOT EVEN BEGIN TO IMAGINE THE COMING CARNAGE AND DEVASTATION.
IT IS GUARANTEED TO BE THE MOST SPECTACULAR SHOW IN THE UNIVERSE!

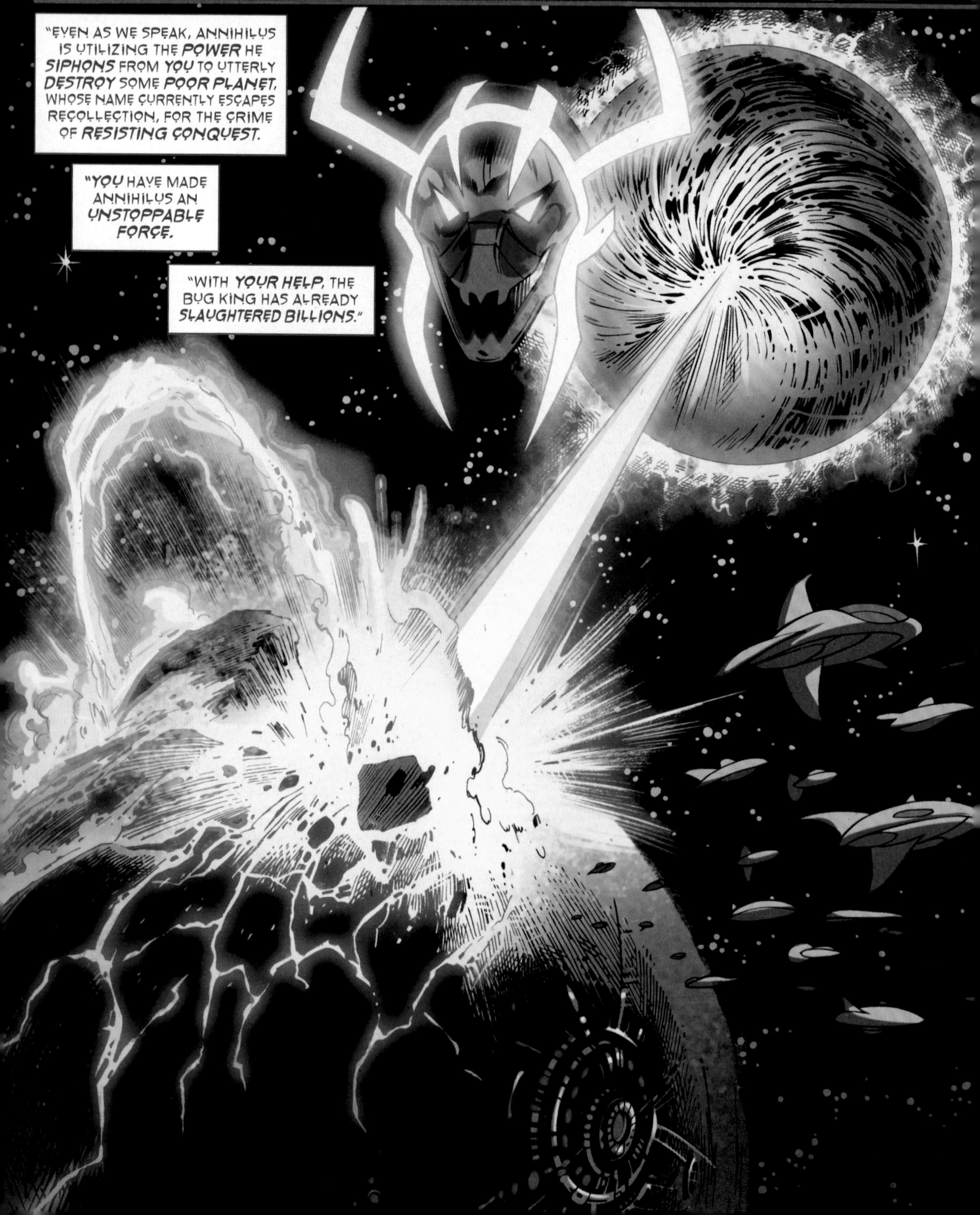
"EVEN AS WE SPEAK, ANNIHILUS IS UTILIZING THE POWER HE SIPHONS FROM YOU TO UTTERLY DESTROY SOME POOR PLANET, WHOSE NAME CURRENTLY ESCAPES RECOLLECTION, FOR THE CRIME OF RESISTING CONQUEST.
"YOU HAVE MADE ANNIHILUS AN UNSTOPPABLE FORCE.
"WITH YOUR HELP, THE BUG KING HAS ALREADY SLAUGHTERED BILLIONS."

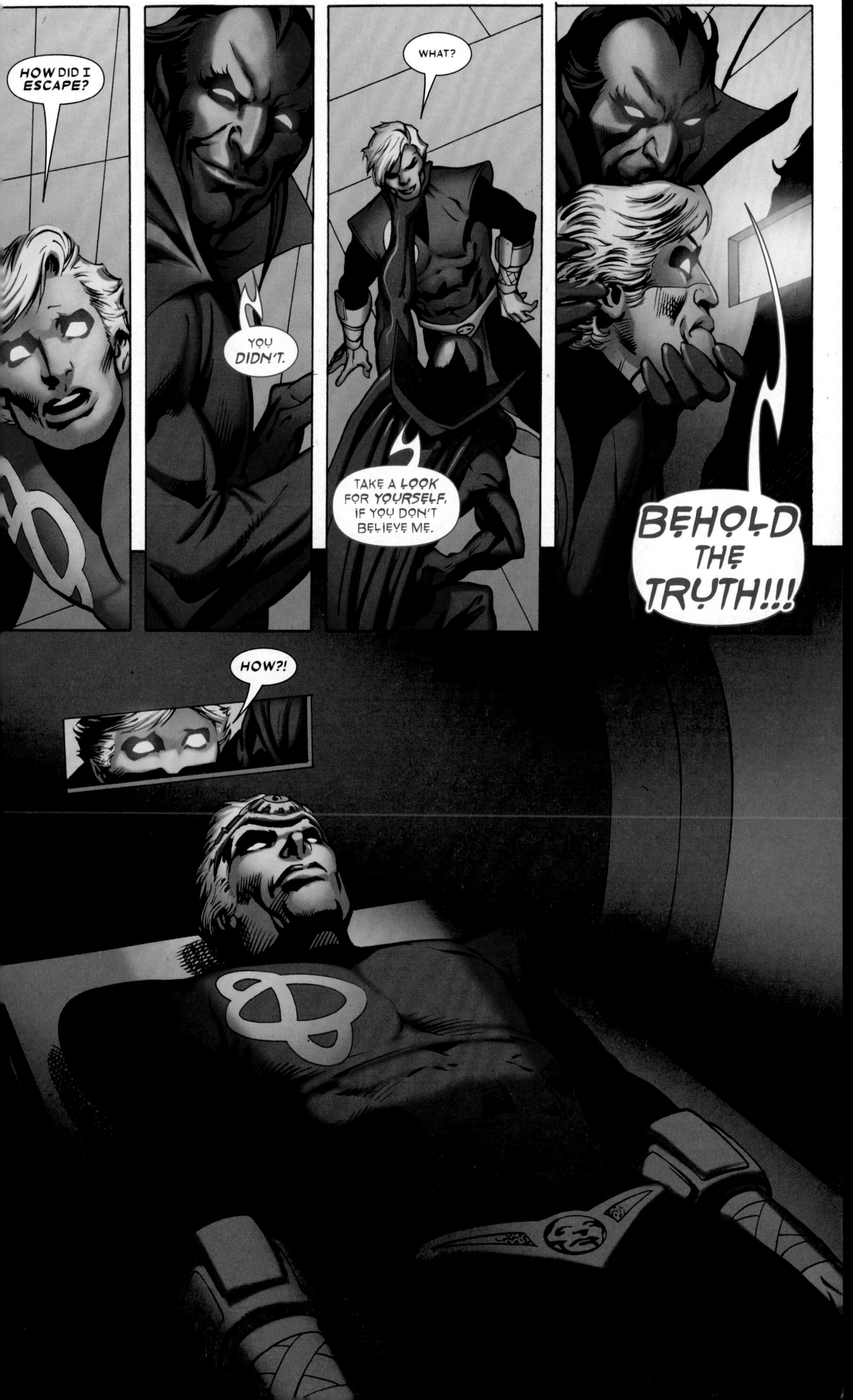
HOW DID I ESCAPE?
YOU DIDN'T.
WHAT?
TAKE A LOOK FOR YOURSELF, IF YOU DON'T BELIEVE ME.
BEHOLD THE TRUTH!!!
HOW?!

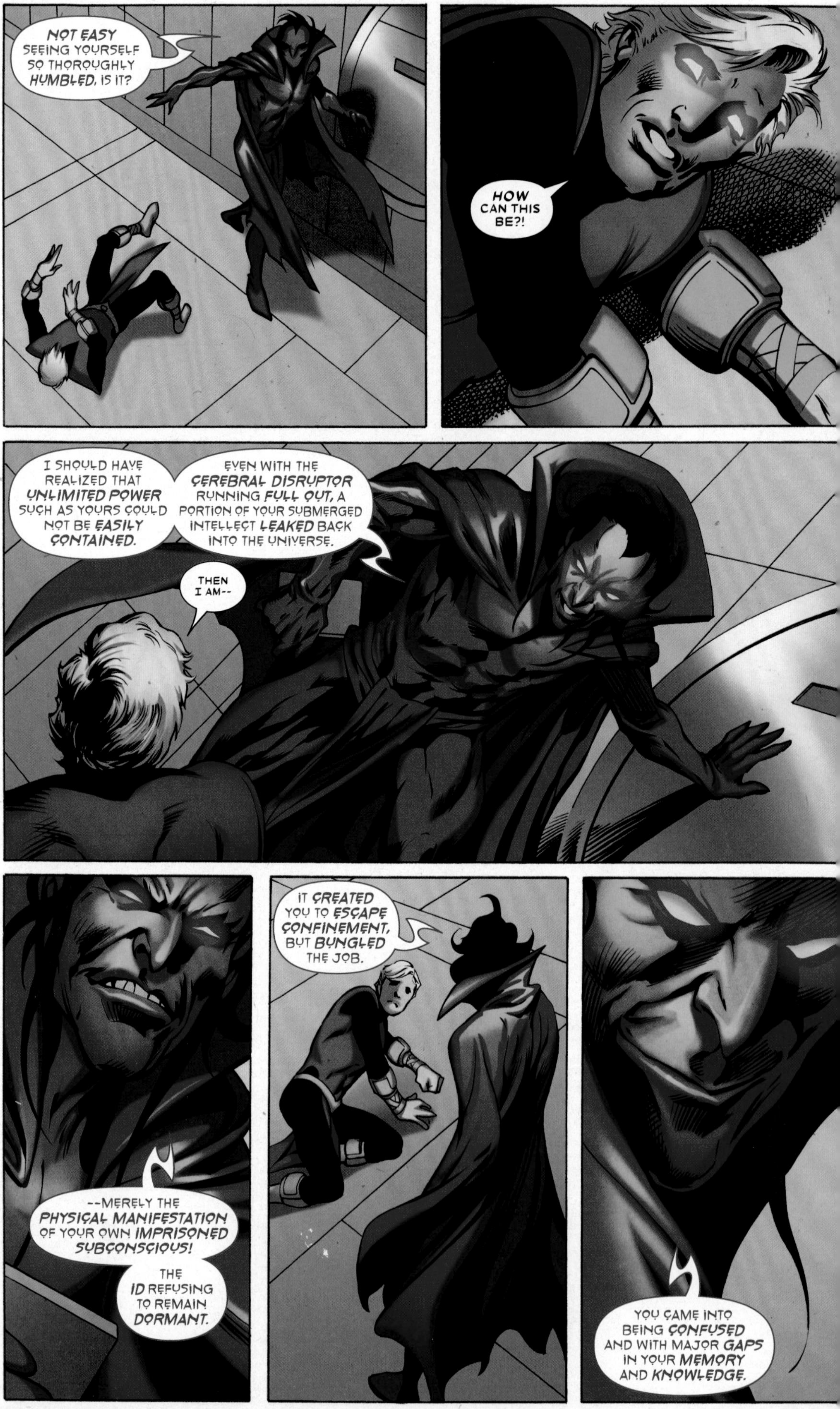
NOT EASY SEEING YOURSELF SO THOROUGHLY HUMBLED, IS IT?
HOW CAN THIS BE?!
I SHOULD HAVE REALIZED THAT UNLIMITED POWER SUCH AS YOURS COULD NOT BE EASILY CONTAINED.
EVEN WITH THE CEREBRAL DISRUPTOR RUNNING FULL OUT, A PORTION OF YOUR SUBMERGED INTELLECT LEAKED BACK INTO THE UNIVERSE.
THEN I AM--
--MERELY THE PHYSICAL MANIFESTATION OF YOUR OWN IMPRISONED SUBCONSCIOUS!
THE ID REFUSING TO REMAIN DORMANT.
IT CREATED YOU TO ESCAPE CONFINEMENT, BUT BUNGLED THE JOB.
YOU CAME INTO BEING CONFUSED AND WITH MAJOR GAPS IN YOUR MEMORY AND KNOWLEDGE.

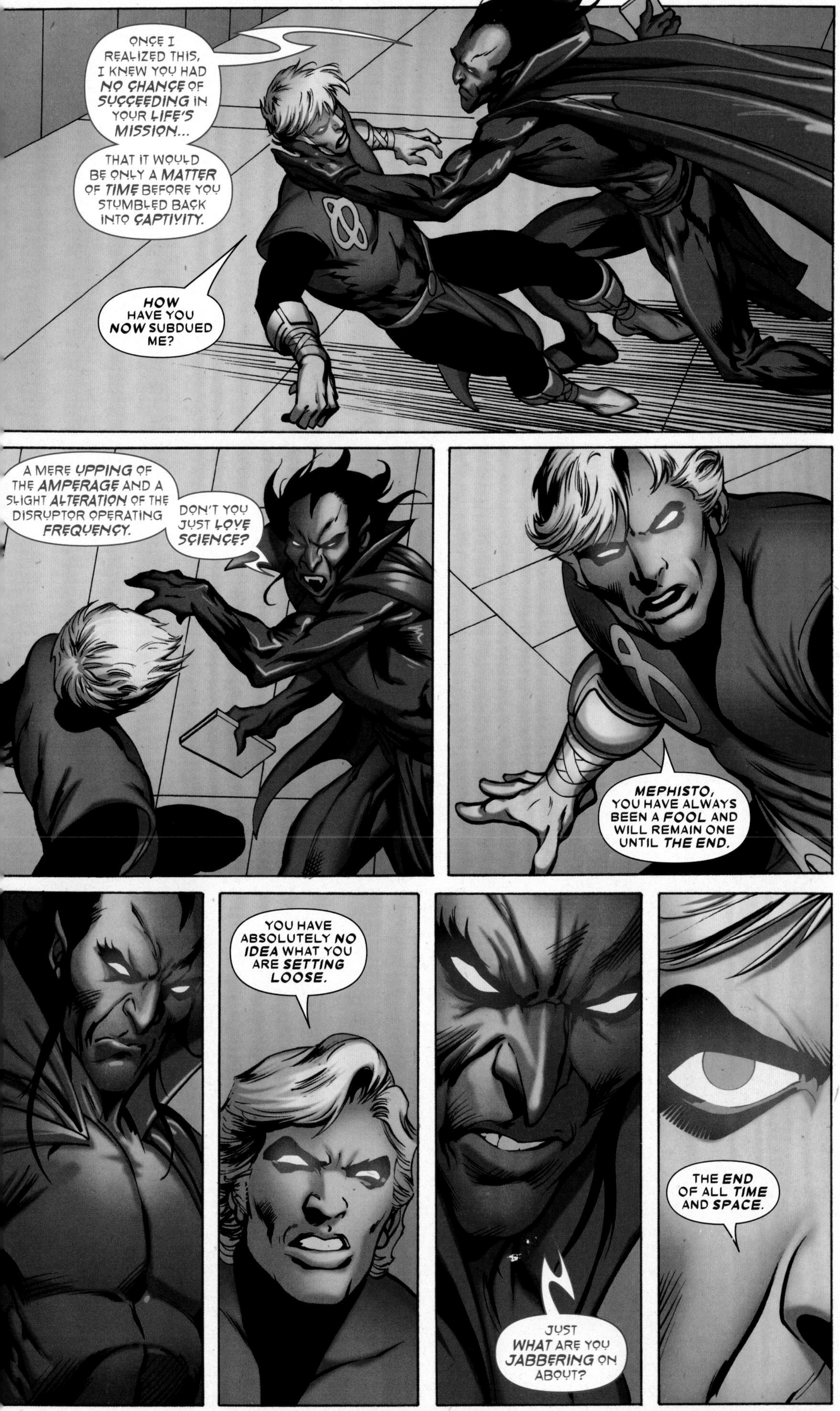
ONCE I REALIZED THIS, I KNEW YOU HAD NO CHANCE OF SUCCEEDING IN YOUR LIFE'S MISSION...
THAT IT WOULD BE ONLY A MATTER OF TIME BEFORE YOU STUMBLED BACK INTO CAPTIVITY.
HOW HAVE YOU NOW SUBDUED ME?
A MERE UPPING OF THE AMPERAGE AND A SLIGHT ALTERATION OF THE DISRUPTOR OPERATING FREQUENCY.
DON'T YOU JUST LOVE SCIENCE?
MEPHISTO, YOU HAVE ALWAYS BEEN A FOOL AND WILL REMAIN ONE UNTIL THE END.
YOU HAVE ABSOLUTELY NO IDEA WHAT YOU ARE SETTING LOOSE.
JUST WHAT ARE YOU JABBERING ON ABOUT?
THE END OF ALL TIME AND SPACE.

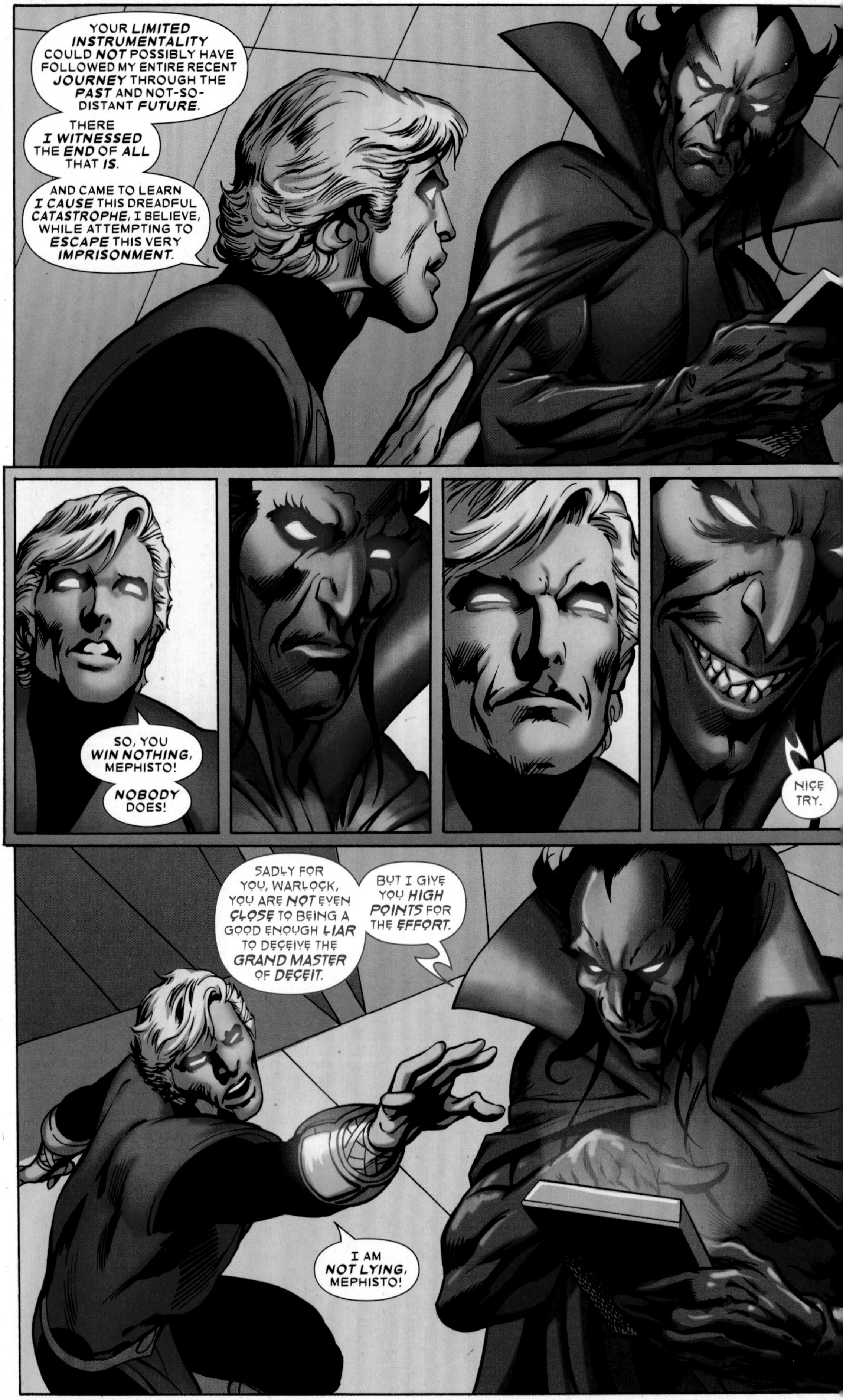

YOUR LIMITED INSTRUMENTALITY COULD NOT POSSIBLY HAVE FOLLOWED MY ENTIRE RECENT JOURNEY THROUGH THE PAST AND NOT-SO-DISTANT FUTURE.
THERE I WITNESSED THE END OF ALL THAT IS.
AND CAME TO LEARN I CAUSE THIS DREADFUL CATASTROPHE, I BELIEVE, WHILE ATTEMPTING TO ESCAPE THIS VERY IMPRISONMENT.
SO, YOU WIN NOTHING, MEPHISTO!
NOBODY DOES!
NICE TRY.
SADLY FOR YOU, WARLOCK, YOU ARE NOT EVEN CLOSE TO BEING A GOOD ENOUGH LIAR TO DECEIVE THE GRAND MASTER OF DECEIT.
BUT I GIVE YOU HIGH POINTS FOR THE EFFORT.
I AM NOT LYING, MEPHISTO!

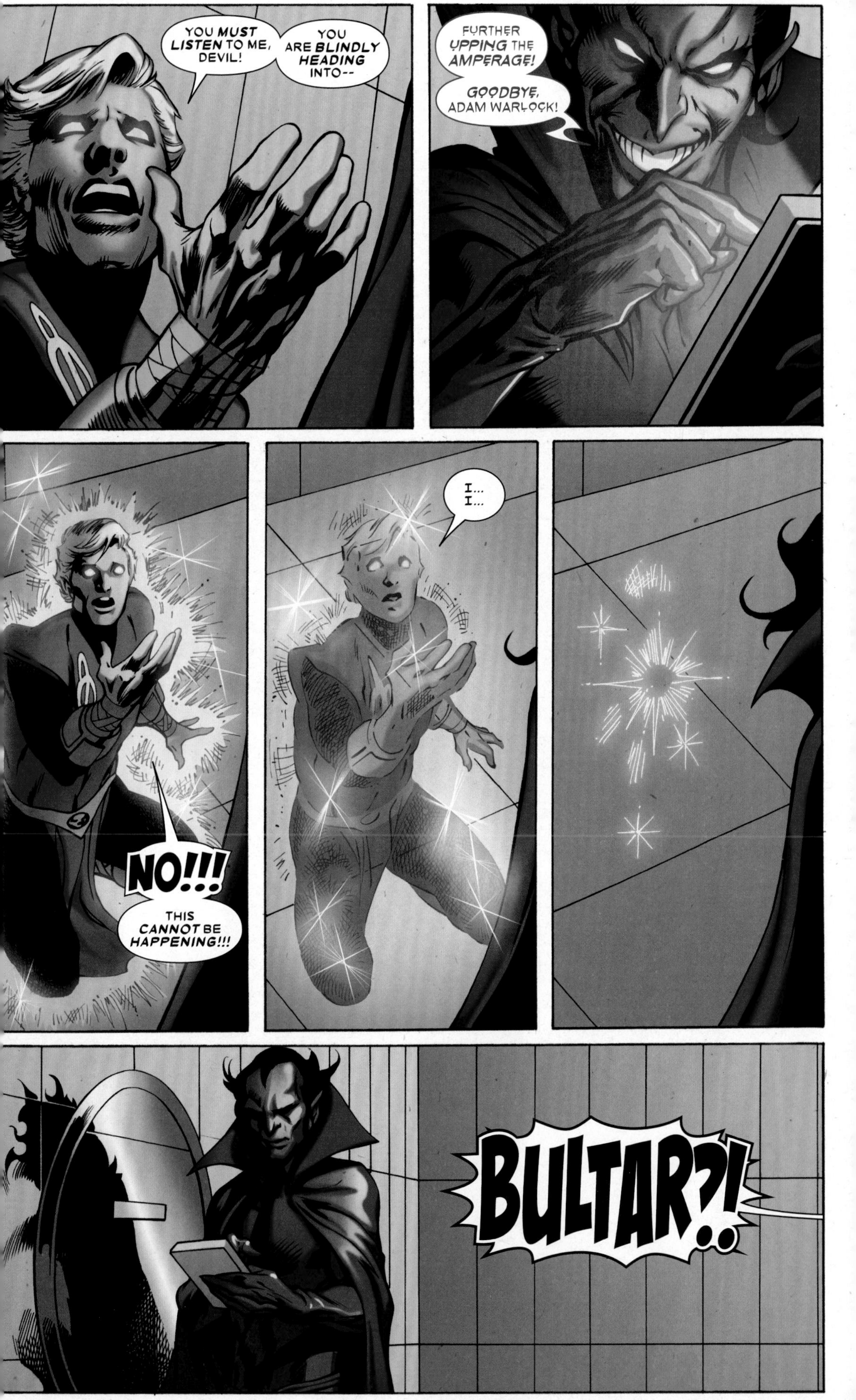
YOU MUST LISTEN TO ME, DEVIL!
YOU ARE BLINDLY HEADING INTO--
FURTHER UPPING THE AMPERAGE!
GOODBYE, ADAM WARLOCK!
NO!!!
THIS CANNOT BE HAPPENING!!!
I... I...
BULTAR?!

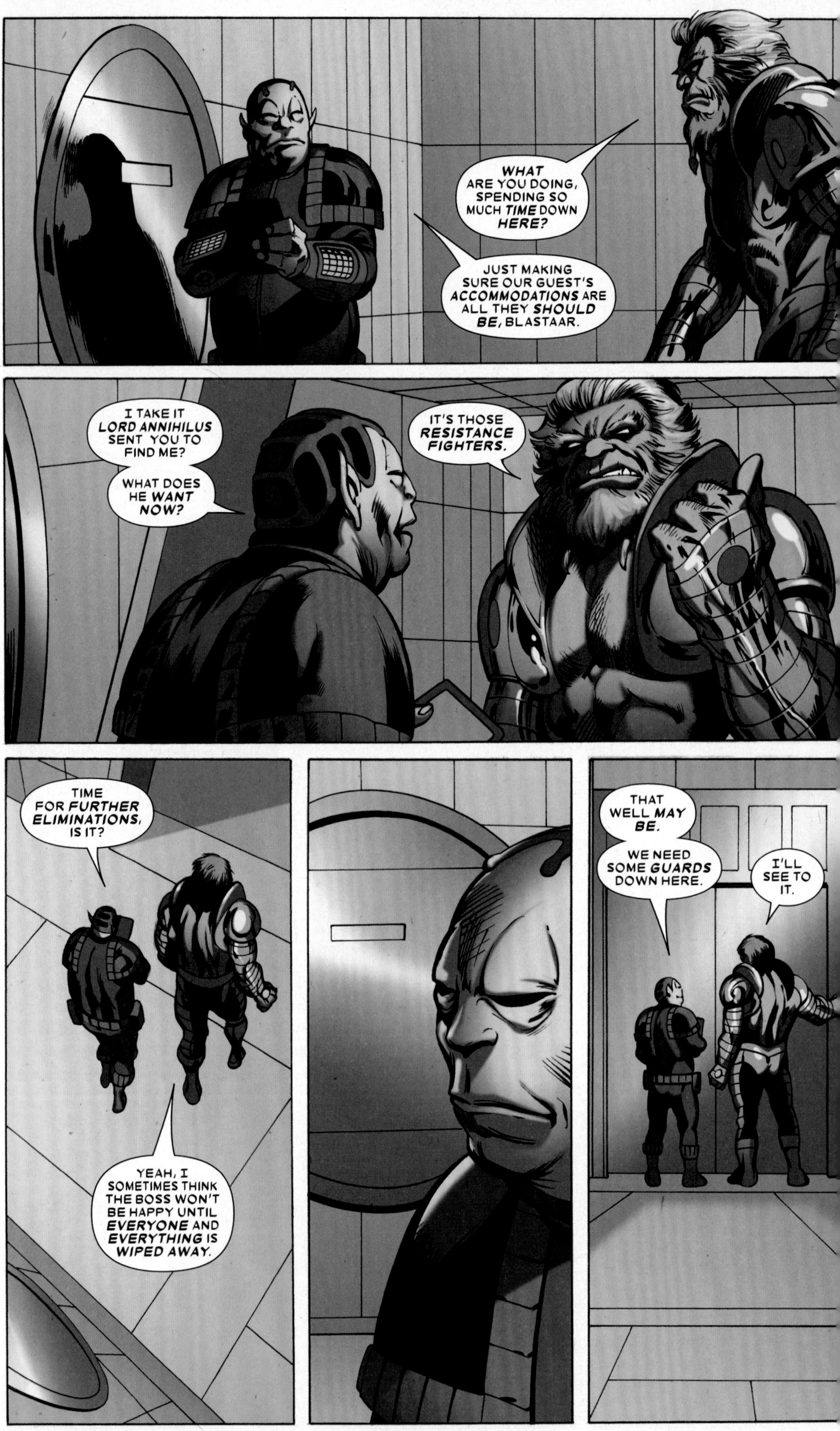

WHAT ARE YOU DOING, SPENDING SO MUCH TIME DOWN HERE?
JUST MAKING SURE OUR GUEST'S ACCOMMODATIONS ARE ALL THEY SHOULD BE, BLASTAAR.
I TAKE IT LORD ANNIHILUS SENT YOU TO FIND ME?
WHAT DOES HE WANT NOW?
IT'S THOSE RESISTANCE FIGHTERS.
TIME FOR FURTHER ELIMINATIONS, IS IT?
YEAH, I SOMETIMES THINK THE BOSS WON'T BE HAPPY UNTIL EVERYONE AND EVERYTHING IS WIPED AWAY.
THAT WELL MAY BE.
WE NEED SOME GUARDS DOWN HERE.
I'LL SEE TO IT.

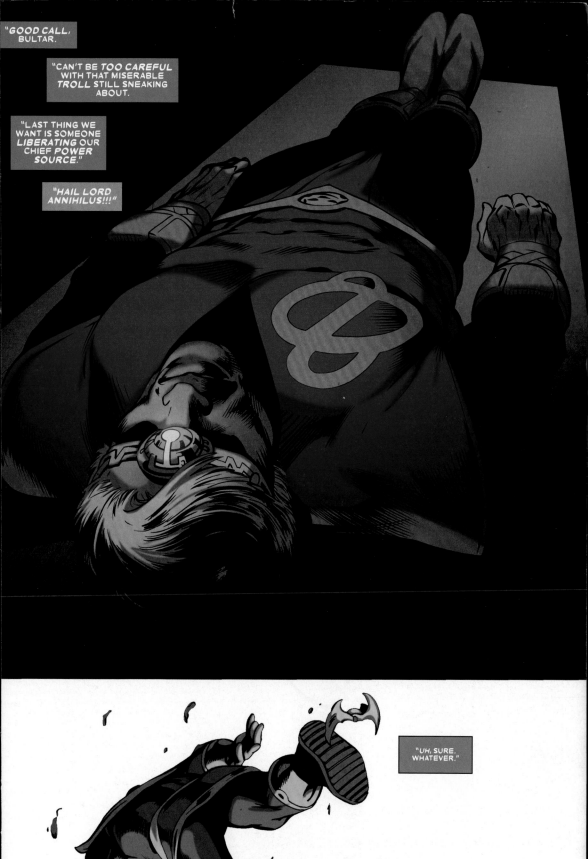

"*GOOD CALL,*
BULTAR.

"*CAN'T BE TOO CAREFUL*
WITH THAT *MISERABLE*
TROLL STILL SNEAKING
ABOUT.

"*LAST THING WE*
WANT IS SOMEONE
LIBERATING OUR
CHIEF *POWER*
SOURCE.

"*HAIL LORD*
ANNIHILUS!!!"

"*UH, SURE.*
WHATEVER."

THE STORY CONCLUDES IN...

THANOS

THE INFINITY FINALE

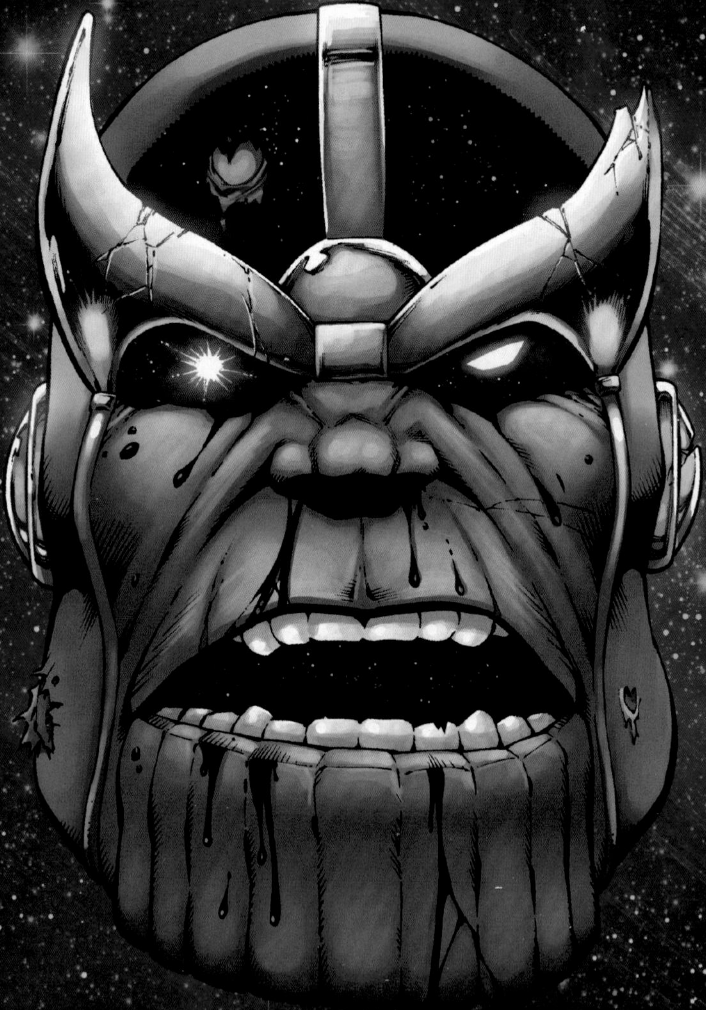

JIM STARLIN • RON LIM

ANDY SMITH • GURU-eFX

MARVEL OGN